I0795228

ANTI-BLACK VIOLENCE IN TWENTIETH-CENTURY TEXAS

ANTI-BLACK VIOLENCE IN TWENTIETH-CENTURY TEXAS

EDITED BY BRUCE A. GLASRUD

FOREWORD BY W. MARVIN DULANEY

Texas A&M University Press
College Station, Texas

First edition

This paper meets the requirements of ANSI/NISO Z39.48–1992 (Permanence of Paper).
Binding materials have been chosen for durability.
Manufactured in the United States of America

LIBRARY OF CONGRESS CATALOGING-IN-PUBLICATION DATA

Anti-Black violence in twentieth-century Texas / edited by Bruce A. Glasrud; foreword by W. Marvin Dulaney. — First edition.
pages cm
All contributions (except the Afterword) have been previously published in books or as articles.
Includes bibliographical references and index.
ISBN 978-1-62349-333-2 (pbk. : alk. paper) —
ISBN 978-1-62349-334-9 (e-book)
1. African Americans—Violence against—Texas. 2. African Americans—Crimes against—Texas. 3. Hate crimes—Texas. 4. Texas—Race relations—History—20th century. I. Glasrud, Bruce A., editor.
E185.93.T4A58 2015
305.896'07307640904—dc23
2015014228

Contents

Foreword

Wanton anti-black violence by whites has always been a part of the African American experience. Stemming from the days of slavery, when slave-owners used violence to impose a forced labor system and to keep enslaved African Americans in fear, violence against African Americans became, to paraphrase the words of Rap Brown, "as American as apple pie." Yet, one reads in contemporary social media and in recent polls the constant contention that whites are actually the long-suffering victims of black violence. Indeed, many of the recent killings of unarmed African American men by law enforcement officers, as well as by white citizens, have been justified as a legitimate response to perceived and imagined black violence against whites. The same sources have even attributed the disproportionate number of incarcerated young African American men to the ongoing notion of black violence against whites. In short, since African Americans commit so many violent acts against innocent white victims, any violent acts against them (even those who are innocent) by law enforcement officers and random white citizens are more than justified.

Bruce Glasrud's volume of essays tells a different story. It rebuts the ongoing lie that black violence against whites caused and has continued to cause the taking of black lives. These essays document patterns of anti-black violence that have become endemic not only in the state of Texas, but also throughout the nation. These essays are a much-needed corrective to a historic and contemporary narrative and discourse that African American citizens have been and continue to be a threat to whites.

In reality, these essays about anti-black violence in Texas only scratch the surface of an ongoing history of abuse, racial intimidation, and violence. For example, none of them address the history of anti-black violence that occurred in the city of Dallas. In Dallas, incidents of anti-black violence occurred with such frequency that recounting them would form more than a substantial part of the current volume. Here are some examples. In 1910, Allen Brooks, a black man accused of raping a white child, was mobbed by whites, thrown out of the window of the Little Red Court House in downtown Dallas with a noose around his neck, and lynched in the middle of downtown on Elk's Arch. In 1921, members of the Ku Klux Klan kidnapped Anthony Johnson, a bellhop at the Adolphus Hotel who had bragged about his sexual relations with white women guests at the hotel, and carved the letters "KKK" on his forehead. In 1938, three white men assaulted George Porter, a teacher at Booker T. Washington High School and the secretary of the Dallas Branch of the NAACP, by throwing him down the concrete steps of the Little Red Court House, because he tried to serve on a jury. In 1940 and 1941, white citizens bombed the homes of several African Americans who had moved into an area near a new black high school, but too close to a white neighborhood. Ten years later, white vigilantes bombed ten more homes owned by African Americans in an effort to force them out of a neighborhood that was transitioning from white to black in South Dallas. Unlike the other instances of anti-black violence where the city's police had failed to act and arrest anyone, in this case the Texas Rangers investigated the incidents and arrested two white men for the bombings. But both men were later found not guilty.

As the essays in this volume illustrate, white violence against African Americans in Dallas declined, as it did in other parts of the state. But similarly, the city's criminal justice system replaced the physical anti-black violence with false arrests and race-based convictions by all-white juries. Two cases in Dallas County—those of Joyce Ann Brown and Lenell Jeter—mirror the case of Clarence Brandley, one of the prominent wrongful conviction cases featured in this volume. Moreover, when residents elected Dallas County's first African American district attorney in 2007, he worked with the Innocence Project and used DNA testing to exonerate thirty people who had been wrongfully convicted by previous district attorneys. All but five of the wrongfully convicted were African Americans.

Given the seriousness of anti-black violence in Texas and in the nation in general, this volume of essays deserves a wide readership. The cases that it documents in the state's sordid racial past have largely been forgotten. Thus, many of the state's current politicians and citizens advocating "law and order," maximum penalties for crimes, and the death penalty for people who may or may not have committed crimes continue to perpetuate the myth that it is citizens of color who should bear the brunt of such harsh penalties. Reading about such cases as the "Waco Horror" and the Sherman Riot should at least make them aware that much of today's crime and violence pale in comparison to the history of anti-black violence by whites.

—W. MARVIN DULANEY
Department of History
University of Texas at Arlington

Acknowledgments

Publishing a book takes considerable help and support; *Anti-Black Violence in Twentieth-Century Texas* was no exception. The book began as the presidential address for the East Texas Historical Association and shortly thereafter became an article published in the *East Texas Historical Journal.* In the above process I spoke to M. Scott Sosebee, executive director of the East Texas Historical Association and to Mary Lenn Dixon, then editor-in-chief at Texas A&M University Press. Both encouraged my thoughts about a book; Dixon also suggested goals to work toward in preparing the study. I should add that reading the book's introduction and afterword is a little like listening to Mary Lenn; my best thanks to her. After completing the volume, I asked Jay Dew, the newly appointed senior editor at Texas A&M University Press, whether he would be interested in publishing the manuscript. He was; thanks for the help and support, Jay. Patricia Clabaugh, associate editor, skillfully produced this book from a less than perfect manuscript. Thanks Patricia.

I also want to thank a number of other individuals. Without the hard work and ability of the authors, of course, the book would not have been feasible. I thank the twelve authors whose studies are featured in this book, and I thank the publishers of their works, who allowed use of the essays. One journal, the *East Texas Historical Journal*, allowed the use of four articles; two additional articles were originally published in *Texas Monthly.* University of Texas at Arlington historian W. Marvin Dulaney graciously agreed to write the foreword; thanks, Marvin. Two readers asked pertinent questions, made suggestions, and supported publication. Kristine Robb, in addition to taking classes and working at the East Foundation, scanned and edited the articles. Pearlene Vestal Glasrud, as always, read, edited, and polished my work. Any errors or omissions, however, I realize are my own for which I remain responsible.

—Bruce A. Glasrud

ANTI-BLACK VIOLENCE IN TWENTIETH-CENTURY TEXAS

Introduction

Racism's Ugly Past—White Texas' Twentieth-Century Actions

Bruce A. Glasrud

In August 1919, John R. Shillady, the white executive secretary of the militant (to Texas whites, anyway) National Association for the Advancement of Colored People (NAACP) arrived in Austin to meet with Texas state political leaders about the state's harassment of NAACP local branches, especially the one headquartered in Austin. Shillady had a short, unproductive meeting with W. A. Keeling, the interim attorney general, and subsequently was subpoenaed to appear before a special court of inquiry, where he was verbally abused with irrelevant and racist questions. The next day, while walking, he was attacked and brutally beaten by a small mob of white men, some of whom were local politicians, such as County Judge Dave Pickle and Constable Charles Hamby. Nevertheless, Governor W. P. Hobby blamed Shillady for the attack, and suggested that he and the NAACP leave the state. As a result of the vicious beating, Shillady's declining mental and physical health forced him to resign as the NAACP's executive secretary.[1]

Beginning the introduction with this violent attack on a white northern supporter of black rights and humanity was purposeful, not to downplay the excessive anti-black violence prevalent in Texas society, but to indicate the extreme antagonism directed by white Texans toward anyone who would befriend blacks, whether white and from a prominent national organization, or those black residents of Texas who dared confront the white Texas racial system. The antipathy exhibited by Texas political and legal authorities in the Shillady attack demonstrated a fear of black citizenry and their supporters organizing, as well as a continuing determination to maintain the white supremacy that was a part of the Texas social culture. The Shillady assault was also a measure of the importance of the NAACP, a newly established civil rights organization.

Originally published as "Anti-Black Violence in 20th Century East Texas," *East Texas Historical Journal* 52.1 (2014): 87–99. Revised and reprinted with permission of the East Texas Historical Association.

By the late summer of 1919, there were thirty-five local NAACP branches in the Lone Star State with a total membership nearing 8,000. The San Antonio chapter boasted over one thousand members. This formidable black organization threatened those Texans bent on preserving "white supremacy." Shillady, too, as a white man from the North, was anathema to white Texans—he represented the "Yankee" North, and he espoused a belief in equality for black Texans. By late 1919 the NAACP had chastised white Texas behavior in reports on violent incidents in Waco, Houston, and Longview, among others. In fact, part of the rapid increase in NAACP membership in the state and nation likely arose due to the eight-page special "Waco Horror" supplement published in July 1916 by the NAACP's *The Crisis* magazine.[2] The Shillady episode was representative of the overall white supremacist, anti-black views—blacks were inferior and must be kept in a subordinate place by any means necessary—that continued through the remainder of the twentieth and even into the twenty-first century.

Texas was not the only southern state with such vehement anti-black behavior patterns, as students and scholars have investigated. Among the vast number of such studies, a few stand out. Allen D. Grimshaw's two books, an edited collection, *Racial Violence in the United States*, and the other, *A Social History of Racial Violence*, are good starting places. Prominent historians have considered lynching and its numerous ramifications; W. Fitzhugh Brundage's important anthology, *Under Sentence of Death: Lynching in the South*, as well as his *Lynching in the New South: Georgia and Virginia, 1880–1930*, ask and answer vital questions about white violence in the South. William D. Carrigan published *Lynching Reconsidered: New Perspectives in the Study of Mob Violence*, and with Christopher Waldrep, *Swift to Wrath: Lynching in Global Perspective*. Christopher Waldrep is not to be outdone; his other works on lynching include *Lynching in America: A History in Documents*; *African Americans Confront Lynching: Strategies of Resistance from the Civil War to the Civil Rights Era*; and *The Many Faces of Judge Lynch*. Walter Howard focused on a short period in Florida in his *Lynchings: Extra-Legal Violence in Florida during the 1930s*.[3]

Race riots are also an important part of anti-black violence. Sheila Smith McKoy, in her thoughtful work, *When Whites Riot: Writing Race and Violence in American and South African Cultures*, compares white violence in the two societies. Ann V. Collins limited her investigation to approximately thirty years of violent confrontations, but enabled us to better grasp the regional and national ramifications of race riots in *All Hell Broke Loose: American Race Riots from the Progressive Era through World War II*. Gail Williams O'Brien's thorough investigation, *The Color of the Law: Race, Violence, and Justice in the Post-World War II South*, ought to be replicated for other eras of southern history. Gregory Mixon clearly demonstrated an ability to depict white and black attitudes and behavior in his study, *The Atlanta Riot: Race, Class, and Violence in a New South City*, chronicling events of 1906. Elizabeth Wheaton also focused on a specific time and place in her critical investigation, *Codename Greenkill: The 1979 Greensboro Killings*.[4] These books represent a handful of the superb studies that have been published on southern anti-black relations, but none cover the entire twentieth century.

Other researchers examined the underpinnings for the vital question: Why did white Texans harbor anti-black sentiments? Their racism was often rooted in fear: fear of armed blacks, fear of black male/white female relationships, fear of an educated black citizenry, and fear of economic competition. White supremacy also served both an economic and a social objective, as a means to retain blacks in menial labor positions as well as to assure whites that they were indeed superior to blacks. Neil Foley, in *The White Scourge*, and William Carrigan, in *The Making of a Lynching Culture*, emphasize the changes transpiring in modern, twentieth-century Texas—changes such as an increase in black resistance that frightened white Texans. As Carrigan noted, these factors included "changing immigration patterns, demographic shifts, technological changes, formalization of disfranchisement, implementation of rigid residential segregation, and the rise of a new consumer culture."[5] At the turn of the century, in 1900–01, as noted by Cynthia Skove Nevels in *Lynching to Belong*, five blacks in Brazos County were lynched in incidents fomented in part by recent European immigrants bent on proving their whiteness.[6]

Lynching and mob violence, including riots and pogroms, were the principal means of enforcing white supremacy. In addition to Foley, Carrigan, and Nevels, there are a number of other informative studies on this issue, including four master's theses. A general summation of lynching in the *Handbook of Texas History Online* by John R. Ross is a first-rate starting point. The theses are significant studies that point to the overall extent of lynching and its use in Texas. They include David L. Chapman, "Lynching in Texas;" Mary Elizabeth Estes, "An Historical Survey of Lynchings in Oklahoma and Texas;" David W. Livingston, "The Lynching of Negroes in Texas, 1900–1925;" and James Lee Findley Jr., "Lynching and the Texas Anti-Lynch Law of 1897."[7] Two articles by Bruce A. Glasrud, "Enforcing White Supremacy in Texas" and "Child or Beast? White Texas' View of Blacks, 1900–1910," described the methods used by whites to enforce white supremacy and explored white attitudes toward African Americans in the Lone Star State. A valuable book depicting anti-lynching efforts in Texas is Jacqueline Dowd Hall, *Revolt Against Chivalry*.[8]

With all of the previously published, solid studies, the question emerges, why this book? Reasons for publishing *Anti-Black Violence in Twentieth-Century Texas* have been touched upon above, but a more systematic answer can be made. First, we need to better understand and recognize our history, both its positive and negative elements. Writers and researchers have provided us with first-rate studies on race violence in Texas, including books, articles, theses, and dissertations. Much has been done, for example, about Reconstruction anti-black violence in the Lone Star State; as a useful starting point, see Kenneth W. Howell's anthology, *Still the Arena of the Civil War: Violence and Turmoil in Reconstruction Texas, 1865–1874*.[9]

In spite of the extensive and well-researched investigations of disturbing, yet little known, anti-black violence in twentieth-century Texas that have been produced, the output too often escaped attention from the general public. This book showcases a significant number of these studies, each of which adds to our understanding of the modern era. In addition, no work to this point investigates the entirety of anti-black violence in twentieth-century Texas, or in any other southern state for that matter. On the remainder of the South, a comparable book by Marvin Dunn, *The Beast in Florida: A History of Anti-Black Violence*, was published in 2013, but no copies appear available. Of course, George C. Wright's path-breaking works on Kentucky are important and available, but they pertain little to the second half of the century.[10] *Time Longer Than Rope*, an anthology edited by Charles M. Payne and Adam Green, includes anti-black violence, but its focus is on African American activism in the years from 1850 to 1950. The authors' emphasis in *Time Longer Than Rope* on the importance of memory is well worth acknowledging; our memories reflect our history, our race, and our knowledge. As one author put it, "The power of remembering depends on what we remember."[11] We need to be sure that our history is complete, open, and accessible, thus, *Anti-Black Violence in Twentieth-Century Texas*.

Throughout the twentieth century, and even before, Texas was one of the most violently anti-black states; it generally ranked third in the number and brutality of lynching events. Since the modern civil rights revolution, and particularly over the past three decades, Texas likely has witnessed the greatest extent of anti-black violence in the South. We must realize too, that in spite of an overall reduction in violence between 1900 and 2000, as we learn from contributors to this book, acts of racial violence continue to appear in the state. To look further at the topic of anti-black violence, this book focuses on a few of the hundreds of violent anti-black episodes in the Lone Star State that occurred in the twentieth century.

Paris, Texas Violence—1890–1920

Twentieth-century anti-black racial violence in Texas had its roots in nineteenth-century anti-black behavior, as does twenty-first-century behavior reflect twentieth-century behavior. As Brandon Jett pointed out so clearly in his thirty-year study of racial violence in Paris, Texas, at the turn of the twentieth century, the situation did not appear to change much with time, if at all. Vicious anti-black violence existed, spread, and continued through those years. At least nine African Americans were lynched in Paris, some in spectacular events and happenings. Whites in the community defended such behavior by blaming blacks and accusing blacks of being monsters and brutes. A Paris businessman, John M. Early, even published a book entitled *An Eye for an Eye* in which he explained why blacks must be lynched. However, by 1920, when another spectacular and brutal lynching occurred, local white leaders finally spoke out against the anti-black violence.[12] Not enough, probably; even a century later, blacks in and around Paris are killed in likely race-related actions (see the afterword).

Waco Horror—1916

Even though nearly five hundred lynchings took place in Texas from the late nineteenth century to 1930, and one hundred African Americans in Texas alone were lynched in the first decade of the twentieth century, it was the troubling 1916 lynching at Waco that brought national attention to Texas and led to the growth of the NAACP in the state and nation. The heinous incident became known as "The Waco Horror." Jesse Washington, an illiterate black teenager, was accused and found guilty of murdering and raping a local white woman. Although no evidence or proof of guilt existed (he was physically forced to plead guilty), he was taken from the court house by a crazed white mob, his extremities cut off, chained to a tree, hanged, and burned. After all that, and while photos were taken, his body was dragged through town and parts sold for souvenirs. Despite photographic evidence of the perpetrators' identities, no one was arrested or tried for this horrendous murder. Even *The Crisis'* dramatic and important supplement produced photos to no avail.[13] This cruel incident has been mentioned by many scholars and authors; the most thorough explanation and study is Patricia Bernstein's book, *The First Waco Horror: The Lynching of Jesse Washington and the Rise of the NAACP*. Two other works, Rogers Melton Smith, "The Waco Lynching of 1916: Perspective and Analysis" and James M. SoRelle, "The 'Waco Horror': The Lynching of Jesse Washington," also examine the sordid event.[14]

Black Soldiers in Houston—1917

The white Texas fear of armed blacks can be discerned in a variety of ways but especially in the distrust of black soldiers of the US Army. Race incidents in the early twentieth century between local men and black soldiers at El Paso, Del Rio, Waco, and especially Brownsville have been studied and discussed by Garna L. Christian, *Black Soldiers in Jim Crow Texas*, and by James N. Leiker, *Racial Borders: Black Soldiers along the Rio Grande*. The 1906

Brownsville incident specifically has been investigated by Ann J. Lane, *The Brownsville Affair* and John D. Weaver, *The Brownsville Raid*.[15] But it was a 1917 event known as the "Houston Riot or Mutiny" that represented the attitudes of whites most distinctly.

On August 23, 1917, some recently stationed black soldiers of the Twenty-fourth Infantry fought with white police and citizens of Houston. Twenty people, white and black, were killed. Although Secretary of War Newton D. Baker told President Woodrow Wilson that the basic causes of the trouble were "the so-called Jim Crow laws" of Houston, that view did not prevail in Houston or even in the military. Ultimately 110 black soldiers were sentenced to death or life imprisonment by military courts-martial, even though each claimed innocence. Thirteen were secretly killed before any other military or civilian review could be accomplished.[16]

Scholars who studied the Houston episode, in general, agreed that black soldiers were involved, but two distinct approaches developed with respect to causation. Robert V. Haynes, in *A Night of Violence: The Houston Riot of 1917*, depicts the role in the riot played by African American soldiers, although he also conceptualizes those actions within the racist environment that the soldiers confronted in Houston and within the military. The courts-martial focused principal blame on the soldiers. Calvin Smith, in two well-constructed articles, argues persuasively that it was the white citizens of Houston who were to blame. From the first entrance of the black soldiers, in Houston, the white citizens, and especially the police, had vigorously enforced Jim Crow laws and disdainfully treated the black soldiers not as men of the US Army but as interlopers. Smith's general interpretation agreed with that of Secretary of War Newton Baker.[17] In his recent work *Two Texas Race Riots*, Fred L. McGhee argued that the white officers of the Twenty-fourth along with the War Department were to blame for the riot. Other studies of the riot or mutiny included the NAACP investigation, two master's theses, two articles, and a refreshing analysis by Arthur E. Barbeau and Florette Henri in their broader history of World War I, *The Unknown Soldiers: African American Troops in World War I*. For a readable, succinct summation of this event, check Garna L. Christian, "All Hell Broke Loose," in his *Black Soldiers in Jim Crow Texas*.[18]

Longview Race Riot—1919

By the summer of 1919 the First World War was over, and black and white soldiers returned to their homes in the Lone Star State. Black soldiers, back from "making the world safe for democracy," were determined that they too would benefit from democracy. That objective was still remote in Texas. On June 17, in Longview, Texas, the sheriff turned over to a Longview mob Lemuel Walters, a black man accused of being in love with a white woman, who may have returned the feeling. The black man was lynched. After an article appeared in the *Chicago Defender* describing the lynching and its causes, Samuel L. Jones, a black teacher accused of writing the article, was severely beaten by a group of whites, and when even more—a mob—arrived at his house to attack the man, the white mob was greeted by armed resistance from friends and supporters of the black man. Whites set fire to two homes, including that of the teacher, as well as a dance hall. Texas Rangers and the state National Guardsmen who were sent to Longview to prevent further violence arrested 17 whites and 21 blacks, but no one was criminally charged in the incident.[19]

At Longview, blacks sent notice that they would and could defend themselves. Among the friends of the black teacher Samuel Jones was Longview's black medical doctor, Calvin P. Davis. A relative of the doctor, Sarah Davis Elias, has added to our understanding of this violence with two works, her master's thesis at Morgan State University and an informative account, *Recalling Longview: An Account of the Longview, Texas Riot, July 11, 1919*. Any future investigation cannot overlook her studies.[20] The riot has also been well documented by other sources, including W. E. B. Du Bois' *Crisis* article. Later efforts of particular help are articles by Kenneth Durham, George Ohler, William Tuttle, and Jared Wheeler. Tuttle's article is carried as chapter four in this book. Annette Moye included Longview in her master's thesis, "Major Race Riots in the Red Summer of 1919;" Arthur Waskow's *From Race Riot to Sit-In* and Harry Krenek's *The Power Vested: The Use of Martial Law and the National Guard in Texas Domestic Crisis* both mentioned the Longview Riot in chapters in their respective books. Lawrence Olson's Southwest Texas State University thesis, "Black Texans in the 'Red Summer' of 1919," covered the topic also.[21]

Kirven, Texas—1922

As is apparent in the aforementioned confrontations, Texas' urban centers such as Austin, Waco, Houston, and Longview frequently occupied center stage in racial atrocities in the Lone Star State. The largest number of such anti-black incidents, however, took place in rural East Texas. In 1910, for example, whites in Anderson County began killing blacks in their communities apparently without cause or provocation. The episode is commonly referred to as the "Slocum Massacre." Ultimately, in this racial pogrom eighteen to twenty-three black Texas citizens were killed. Two interesting depictions of this killing spree and its background can be found in as yet unpublished papers written by Norris White Jr., a Stephen F. Austin State University student, "Bad Saturday: Revisiting the 1910 Slocum Massacre," and Linda Sue Stuard, a University of Texas-Tyler student, "Racial Disorder in East Texas: The 1910 Slocum Incident." The most complete account of the Slocum racial strife is E. R. Bills' recent book, *The 1910 Slocum Massacre: An Act of Genocide in East Texas*. Bills persuasively argued that the earlier figures were inadequate to explain the extent of the anti-black violence, as he reported, "The consensus among descendants of the Slocum Massacre victims is that hundreds died in the bloodshed, and this estimate is not unreasonable. In fact, the evidence plainly suggests it." All were black victims.[22]

Twelve years later (1922), in rural Freestone County another violent anti-black episode occurred. Monte Akers recounts the violence in his book, *Flames After Midnight: Murder, Vengeance, and the Desolation of a Texas Community*. In the small, thriving community of Kirven, a young white woman was brutally murdered. Even though evidence pointed toward certain white men in the community as the killer or killers, vigilantes (including the likely murderers) in the community proclaimed blacks guilty. Three innocent black men were burned alive (they were tied to a plow to keep them upright and alive longer), three others were soon lynched, and a month-long reign of terror ensued. Once more blacks were killed with impunity; the estimated number of black deaths ranged from eleven to twenty-three. Eventually Kirven and other Freestone County whites arrived at Simsboro and killed two more African American citizens. After the murders, Simsboro blacks armed themselves, joined together, and convinced the white marauders that neither side wanted to die. The Kirven-Simsboro episode ended. No whites were convicted. The murderers of the woman went free. Blacks immediately left Kirven, whites soon after, and the town virtually disappeared.[23]

The events in Kirven prompted an increase in anti-lynching discussions across the nation, as well as in editorials from Texas newspapers. On the other hand, the actual specifics of the violence were not determined until Akers' thorough and convincing research. A few scholars mentioned the incident in earlier studies, but little else has been produced. Carrigan, however, clearly summarized the incident: "In Freestone County on the edge of central Texas, a brutal act of racial violence occurred in May 1922. A mob in Kirven burned three black men alive, then went on a month long binge of racial intimidation and terrorism. Meanwhile local authorities concealed the identity of the probable white murderers."[24]

Sherman Riot—1930

By 1930, economic problems fostered by the onset of the Depression led to increased tension between black and white tenant farmers; the city of Sherman also experienced monetary difficulties that fed anti-black attitudes. The Sherman Riot of 1930 stemmed from the arrest of a black man who allegedly assaulted a white woman; Texas Rangers were called to protect the prisoner and did so for a time. After the suspect was placed in a vault for his supposed protection, a white mob set fire to the courthouse and burned the victim alive. (There is a growing body of evidence that indicates that he did not die in the fire, specifics being recorded in the state police reports.) Next the mob acquired the black man's body, hooked it to a car, dragged it through the streets, and then tied it up and burned it. Surprisingly, after the vicious lynching the Rangers left. The rioters immediately looted and burned the black section of town and virtually seized control of Sherman. When troops of the Texas National Guard arrived, they were attacked by the mob, and before martial law restored order, more homes and businesses in the African American section of town were destroyed. Prominent western historian Robert M. Utley in his Texas Ranger study referred to the Sherman racial uprising as "one of the most brutish and shameful episodes in the history of Texas."[25]

The black section of town, alive with thriving businesses prior to the riot, never recovered, and numerous black leaders and workers left the area. For information on this aspect of the riot, see Donna J. Kumler's dissertation, "'They have gone from Sherman': The Courthouse Riot of 1930 and its Imprint on the Black Professional Class." Numerous other historians have also explored the 1930 Sherman Riot. Mike Cox and Robert Utley related the riot to Texas Ranger history, and Harry Krenek to that of the Texas National Guard. The best single article on the riot is that of Edward Hake Phillips, originally published in the *East Texas Historical Journal*. Other accounts have included Durward Pruden, whose sociological thesis did not mention names or the city, and a 1931 thesis by Thomas Michael Murphy, written almost immediately after its culmination. Additional information can be located in Arthur Franklin Raper's 1933 classic book *The Tragedy of Lynching* and Nolan Thompson's piece for *The Handbook of Texas Online*. For a fictionalized short story account by a prominent black female author, read Njoki McElroy's tale, "The Ninth Day of May."[26]

Beaumont Race Riot—1943

Changes precipitated by World War II set off a violent race riot in Beaumont, Texas. In 1943 employment in the shipyards was opened to blacks and, as a result, competitive tensions between white and black workers increased. Early in June a black man allegedly raped a white Beaumont telephone operator; police eventually shot and killed the man as he likely resisted arrest. Ten days later, violence flared when on June 15 and 16: whites and blacks clashed after white Beaumont shipyard workers learned that a white woman had accused a black man of raping her. On the evening of June 15, more than two thousand angry and alarmed workers started walking downtown. As they moved toward City Hall the size of the mob grew, ultimately reaching four thousand members. Even though the woman could not identify the suspect (a few reports indicate she fabricated the event), the white workers and other mob partisans began breaking into stores in the black section of downtown Beaumont. They proceeded to terrorize black neighborhoods in central and north Beaumont. Blacks were assaulted, several restaurants and stores were pillaged, a number of buildings were burned, and more than one hundred African American homes were ransacked. The Texas State Guard and Texas Rangers were called in to halt the devastation, though too late for the black structures. Eventually more than two hundred people were arrested, fifty were injured, and two were killed. No one was convicted. With martial law established, an interesting and ironic twist emerged: black workers were not allowed to go to work, while white laborers returned to work.[27]

The Beaumont Race Riot could stand some new study; however, two good articles that concern this affair have been published, one by James A. Burran and one by James S. Olson and Sharon Phair. Olson subsequently wrote an essay on the "Beaumont Riot of 1943" for the *Handbook of Texas Online*; he referenced the two articles and depicted the rioters as terrorizing neighborhoods, assaulting blacks, and pillaging stores, and noted the reemergence of the Ku Klux Klan in wartime Beaumont.[28]

Racial violence against blacks was a consistent and overwhelming threat and presence to black Texans during the first half of the twentieth century. It continued but in less frequent occurrences as the century progressed. As many scholars have noted, race violence persisted during the civil rights era in the Lone Star State despite political, economic, and social pressures to both overlook the violence and to try to prevent its occurrence. With an unfortunate similarity to the earlier attacks on NAACP Executive Secretary Shillady, and in a single effort to stifle black organization and protest, Texas segregationist governor Alan Shivers and his attorney general, John Ben Shepperd, raided the offices of the NAACP in 1956 and sued the organization as being subversive. The court, meeting in Tyler, granted an injunction against the Texas NAACP that disallowed the civil rights organization from operating in the state, except on a very limited basis. That same year, violence broke out near Fort Worth at Mansfield High School when black students, pursuing a court order, attempted to integrate the Texas school. Then, as historian Alwyn Barr phrased it, "Governor Shivers used Texas Rangers, not to disperse the mob, but to remove the students." Mansfield was not integrated for an additional two years. During the 1960–61 sit-ins to desegregate public accommodations, little violence transpired in cities such as Houston, Marshall, and San Antonio.[29]

Texas Southern University Riot—1967

In May 1967 a riot took place at Texas Southern University. The police blamed black youths for the episode, while the black community blamed the police. Following days of demonstrations and the arrest on campus of a student, a few students began throwing rocks and bottles. Police arrived, surrounded the student dorms, and in the early evening a shot was fired that police believed came from a dorm; the police fired back. Overnight shooting continued; forty to sixty shots came from the dorms; the police responded with approximately two thousand rounds. One officer was killed (perhaps from a police ricochet bullet) and two more were injured. Two students were wounded and 488 were arrested, their dorm rooms torn apart and virtually destroyed, causing upwards of $30,000 in damages. There has been little study of this episode, and it is one that needs further investigation. Presently, however, Bernard Friedberg's "Houston and the TSU Riot" stands as the best (and only) examination of this event. Friedberg referred to the event as "a major racial incident" and "mostly a police affair," but as noted above, it has not been studied by anyone else.[30] Perhaps this episode does not reflect vicious anti-black violence as much as pogroms or lynchings, but it does, in the overwhelming response of police fire, once more illustrate the systemic anti-black feelings prevalent in at least some white Texans. Other violent occasions occurred in Texas, including several in the 1980s and after.

Conroe, Texas—1980

Early in the twentieth century, as we have noted, white suspicions that a black man assaulted a white woman fueled violence, lynching, and occasionally riots as a white response. Whether due to public pressure, new laws, or more robust police and legal scrutiny, the response of the white community to such black suspects began to change. An incident in Conroe, Texas, illustrated this changing dynamic. In August 1980, the nude body of a dead young white female student was discovered in the Conroe high school. Soon, a black man, Clarence Brandley, the school janitor, was arrested (with no apparent reason or evidence other than that he was a black man) for the murder. His arrest did not spark a violent anti-black outbreak. Nick Davies has examined this whole episode in a book entitled *White Lies: Rape, Murder, and Justice Texas Style*. White lies, from the district attorney, a racist Texas Ranger, other local officials and, in a way, the white people of Conroe led to Brandley's conviction by an all-white jury. As opposed to the early-twentieth-century methods, anti-black feelings in this instance collaborated with the modern judicial system. A legal judgment and likely death was in progress. After nine years of incarceration, and life on death row, however, Clarence Brandley won his freedom. He never returned to Conroe.[31]

Loyal Garner Case (Hemphill)—1987

During an eight-month period between late 1987 and early 1988, black Texans Troy Lee Starling, Loyal Garner Jr., and Kenneth "Hambone" Simpson died within one hundred miles of each other in a triangular part of the East Texas pine thickets. Each met death at the hands of white lawmen; the last faces they saw were white law officers. Starling was shot through the back of the neck by a .357 magnum issued by the Texas Department of Public Safety. Simpson's body was tied down in a small jail cell; eleven officers had been in the room with him. His body was horribly beaten. Only the death of Garner, who was beaten severely with a blackjack, was challenged via the court system. Garner's beating while in custody was not unique; during the course of the ensuing trials, considerable evidence indicated that in Hemphill beatings of prisoners in the jail were common. We know about this case due to the energy and ability of a tireless writer, Texas native Howard Swindle whose book, *Deliberate Indifference: A Story of Racial Injustice and Murder*, compellingly takes us through this episode of Texas racial violence. A song has also been written about the case, "The Ballad of Loyal Garner, Jr."[32]

Jasper—1998

Eleven years after the Loyal Garner murder, in another small town in East Texas, Jasper, a forty-nine-year-old black man, James Byrd Jr., walked home from a party. Three white men in a pick-up truck offered Byrd a ride home, and he willingly accepted. Soon the men, with Byrd along, turned away from the road to Byrd's home and drove to a secluded, wooded patch. At some point, Byrd was tortured, chained to the back of the pick-up, and dragged to his death. Portions of his body lay in various parts of the road. His unchained body was dropped off near a church. This crime of hate received national attention. Ultimately the three men were convicted: one man received life in prison and two of them received death sentences. The latter two men had previously served time in prison together and joined white supremacist groups. One had a tattoo of a black man hanging. Three authors have written books about the episode; though well-written, none includes a bibliography. As their titles suggest, the three authors developed their stories from differing perspectives—Joyce King, *Hate Crime: The Story of a Dragging in Jasper, Texas*; Dina Temple-Raston, *Death in Texas: A Story of Race, Murder, and a Small Town's Struggle for Redemption*; and Ricardo C. Ainslie, *Long Dark Road: Bill King and Murder in Jasper, Texas*. King, as her title suggests, saw this as an anti-black happening, as a hate crime. Ainslie focused on the convicted white leader and seemed to empathize with him. Temple-Raston viewed the event from the perspective of the local community.[33]

Tulia Injustice—1999

A less physically violent, but nonetheless revolting, anti-black occurrence took place in the West Texas community of Tulia, Texas. During 1999, in a series of highly corrupt and dishonorable arrests, a dishonest investigator accused black Texans in Tulia of drug peddling and smuggling. Subsequently the courts convicted the defendants and sentenced them to considerable time in prison. When rumors of perverted justice came to light, the government sought to release the long-suffering prisoners and return them to their homes. Nate Blakeslee, in *Tulia: Race, Cocaine, and Corruption in a Small Texas Town,* described well the sorry episode. Blakeslee also published articles about the Tulia arrests in *The Texas Observer* and *Texas Monthly.* Ultimately, 46 black citizens were arrested in 1999; not until 2003 did Governor Rick Perry pardon them.[34] This "pipeline to prisons" phenomenon seems to be a common story in modern Texas. Not only are African Americans physically punished and murdered, they comprise an overwhelming presence in the Texas prison system.

Conclusion

In the year 2015 we cannot say that anti-black racism has been extinguished in Texas. Conditions for blacks have improved. We do not have a yearly listing of lynchings anymore, and even separate violent race incidents are more likely to have a few years' hiatus before the next one takes place. The pattern of behavior that resulted in twentieth-century racial violence—and stemmed from a conviction of white superiority—seemingly has abated in twenty-first-century Texas, but the spirit of that conviction endures as Texas white political leadership seeks to limit voting rights and freedom of choice for those not favored. There are numerous citizens of Texas who remain comfortable with discrimination as a way of life, and it may be, unfortunately, that legal impediments to the exercise of citizenship again offer a means to keep them comfortable. Black Texans and their white and brown friends and neighbors must be watchful. We shall see what transpires.

Notes

1. NAACP, *Mobbing of John R. Shillady, Secretary of the National Association for the Advancement of Colored People* (New York: NAACP, October 1919), 1–11; Mark Robert Schneider, *"We Return Fighting": The Civil Rights Movement in the Jazz Age* (Boston: Northeastern University Press, 2002), 29–32.

2. Michael L. Gillette, "The NAACP in Texas, 1937–1957" (Ph.D. diss., University of Texas at Austin, 1984); Michael L. Gillette, "National Association for the Advancement of Colored People," *The Handbook of Texas Online* (http:www.tshaonline.org/handbook); Bruce A. Glasrud, "Anti-Black Violence in 20th Century East Texas," *East Texas Historical Journal* 52.1 (2014), 87–99; "The Waco Horror," *The Crisis* 3 (July 1916), supplement, 1–8.

3. Allen D. Grimshaw, ed., *Racial Violence in the United States* (Piscataway, NJ: Aldine, 1969); Allen D. Grimshaw, ed., *A Social History of Racial Violence* (Piscataway, NJ: Aldine Transaction, 2009); W. Fitzhugh Brundage, ed., *Under Sentence of Death: Lynching in the South* (Chapel Hill: University of North Carolina Press, 1997); W. Fitzhugh Brundage, ed., *Lynching in the New South: Georgia and Virginia, 1880–1930* (Urbana: University of Illinois Press, 1993); William D. Carrigan published *Lynching Reconsidered: New Perspectives in the Study of Mob Violence*, and with Christopher Waldrep, *Swift to Wrath: Lynching in Global Perspective.* Christopher Waldrep, ed., *Lynchings in America: A History in*

Documents (New York: New York University Press, 2006); Christopher Waldrep, *African Americans Confront Lynching: Strategies of Resistance from the Civil War to the Civil Rights Era* (Lanham, MD: Rowman and Littlefield, 2009); Christopher Waldrep, *The Many Faces of Judge Lynch* (New York: Palgrave Macmillan, 2004); Walter T. Howard, *Lynchings: Extra-Legal Violence in Florida during the 1930s* (Lincoln, NE: Authors Choice Press, 2005). On lynchings as spectacles, see Amy Louise Wood, *Lynching and Spectacle: Witnessing Racial Violence in America, 1890–1940* (Chapel Hill: University of North Carolina Press, 2009).

4. Sheila Smith McKoy, *When Whites Riot: Writing Race and Violence in American and South African Cultures* (Madison: University of Wisconsin Press, 2001); Ann V. Collins, *All Hell Broke Loose: American Race Riots from the Progressive Era through World War II* (New York: Praeger Publisher, 2012); Gail Williams O'Brien, *The Color of the Law: Race, Violence, and Justice in the Post-World War II South* (Chapel Hill: University of North Carolina Press, 1999); Gregory Mixon, *The Atlanta Riot: Race, Class, and Violence in a New South City* (Gainesville: University Press of Florida, 2008); Elizabeth Wheaton, *Codename Greenkill: The 1979 Greensboro Killings* (Athens: University of Georgia Press, 1987).

5. Neil Foley, *The White Scourge: Mexicans, Blacks, and Poor Whites in Texas Cotton Culture* (Berkeley: University of California Press, 1997); William D. Carrigan, *The Making of a Lynching Culture: Violence and Vigilantism in Central Texas, 1836–1916* (Urbana: University of Illinois Press, 2004), quote on page 184.

6. Cynthia Skove Nevels, *Lynching to Belong: Claiming Whiteness through Racial Violence* (College Station: Texas A&M University Press, 2007).

7. John R. Ross, "Lynching," *Handbook of Texas Online* (http://www.tshaonline.org/handbook); David L. Chapman, "Lynching in Texas" (Master's thesis, Texas Tech University, 1973); Mary Elizabeth Estes, "An Historical Survey of Lynchings in Oklahoma and Texas" (Master's thesis, University of Oklahoma, 1942); David W. Livingston, "The Lynching of Negroes in Texas, 1900–1925" (Master's thesis, East Texas State University, 1972); James Lee Findley, Jr., "Lynching and the Texas Anti-Lynch Law of 1897" (Master's thesis, Baylor University, 1974).

8. Bruce A. Glasrud, "Enforcing White Supremacy in Texas," *Red River Valley Historical Review* 4.4 (1979), 65–74; Bruce A. Glasrud, "Child or Beast? White Texas' View of Blacks, 1900–1910," *East Texas Historical Journal* 15.2 (1977), 38–44; Jacqueline Dowd Hall, *The Revolt against Chivalry: Jessie Daniel Ames and the Women's Campaign Against Lynching* (New York: Columbia University Press, 1979).

9. Kenneth W. Howell, ed., *Still the Arena of the Civil War: Violence and Turmoil in Reconstruction Texas, 1865–1874* (Denton: University of North Texas Press, 2012). On anti-black violence in Reconstruction Texas see also James M. Smallwood, Barry A. Crouch, and Larry Peacock, *Murder and Mayhem: The War of Reconstruction in Texas* (Lufkin: Best of East Texas Publishers, 2007).

10. Marvin Dunn, *The Beast in Florida: A History of Anti-Black Violence* (Gainesville: University Press of Florida, 2013); George C. Wright, *Racial Violence in Kentucky, 1865–1940: Lynchings, Mob Rule, and "Legal Lynchings"* (Baton Rouge: Louisiana State University Press, 1996); George C. Wright, *Life Behind the Veil: Blacks in Louisville, Kentucky* (Baton Rouge: Louisiana State University Press, 1985).

11. Charles M. Payne and Adam Green, eds., *Time Longer Than Hope: A Century of African American Activism, 1850–1950* (New York: New York University Press, 2003). The short citation is from Michael Honey, "The Power of Remembering," p. 329.

12. Brandon Jett, "Paris is Burning: Lynching and Racial Violence in Lamar County, 1890–1920," *East Texas Historical Journal* 51.2 (2013), 40–64.

13. "The Waco Horror," *The Crisis* 3 (July 1916), supplement, 1–8.

14. Patricia Bernstein, *The First Waco Horror: The Lynching of Jesse Washington and the Rise of the NAACP* (College Station: Texas A&M University Press, 2005); Rogers Melton Smith, "The Waco Lynching of 1916: Perspective and Analysis" (Master's thesis, Baylor University, 1971); James M. SoRelle, "The 'Waco Horror': The Lynching of Jesse Washington," *Southwestern Historical Quarterly* 86.4 (April 1983), 517–37; James M. SoRelle, "Jesse Washington Lynching," *The Handbook of Texas Online* (http://www.tshaonline.org/handbook).

15. Garna Christian, *Black Soldiers in Jim Crow Texas, 1899–1917* (College Station: Texas A&M University Press, 1993); James N. Leiker, *Racial Borders: Black Soldiers along the Rio Grande* (College Station: Texas A&M University Press, 2002); Ann J. Lane, *The Brownsville Affair: National Crisis and Black Reaction* (Port Washington, NY: Kennikat Press, 1971); John D. Weaver, *The Brownsville Raid* (New York: W. W. Norton, 1973). On the Brownsville affray see also James A. Tinsley, "The Brownsville Affray" (Master's thesis, University of North Carolina, 1948) and his article "Roosevelt, Foraker, and the Brownsville Affray," *Journal of Negro History* 41 (1956), 43–65.

16. Robert V. Haynes, "The Houston Mutiny and Riot of 1917," *Southwestern Historical Quarterly* 76 (1973), 418–39.

17. Robert V. Haynes, *A Night of Violence: The Houston Riot of 1917* (Baton Rouge: Louisiana State University Press, 1976); Haynes, "The Houston Mutiny and Riot of 1917," 418–39; C. Calvin Smith, "The Houston Riot of 1917, Revisited," *Houston Review* 13 (1991), 84–102; C. Calvin Smith, "On the Edge: The Houston Riot of 1917," *The Griot* 10 (Spring 1991), 3–12.

18. Fred L. McGhee, *Two Texas Race Riots* (Austin, TX: Fidelitas Publishing, 2012); Thomas Richard Adams, "The Houston Riot of 1917" (Master's thesis, Texas A&M University, 1972); Arthur E. Barbeau and Florette Henri, *The Unknown Soldiers: African-American Troops in World War I* (1974; New York: Da Capo Press, 1996), 26–32, 210–211; Martha Gruening, "Houston: An NAACP Investigation," *The Crisis* 15 (November 1917), 14–19; Phocion Samuel Park, Jr., "The Twenty-Fourth Infantry Regiment and the Houston Riot of 1917" (Master's thesis, University of Houston, 1971); Edgar A. Schuler, "The Houston Race Riot, 1917," *Journal of Negro History* 29 (July 1944), 300–338; C. D. Waide, "When Psychology Failed: An Unbiased Fact-Story of the Houston Race Riot of 1917," *Houston Gargoyle*, May 15, 22, 29, 1928; June 5, 12, 1928; Christian, *Black Soldiers in Jim Crow Texas*, 143–172, 203–207.

19. Kenneth R. Durham, "The Longview Race Riot of 1919," *East Texas Historical Journal* 18 (1980), 13–24; Kenneth R. Durham, "The Longview Riot of 1919," *The Handbook of Texas Online* (http://www.tshaonline.org/handbook); William N. Tuttle, Jr., "Violence in a Heathen Land: The Longview Race Riot of 1919," *Phylon* 33 (Winter 1972), 324–333.

20. Sarah Davis Elias, "Grimshaw's Ecological Analysis of the Longview Riot" (Master's thesis, Morgan State University, 1974); Sarah Davis Elias, *Recalling Longview: An Account of the Longview, Texas Riot, July 11, 1919* (Baltimore: C. H. Fairfax Company, 2004).

21. W. E. B. DuBois, "The Riot at Longview, Texas," *Crisis* 18 (October 1919), 296–298; Harry Krenek, "Race Riots at Longview and Sherman," in *The Power Vested: The Use of Martial Law and the National Guard in Texas Domestic Crisis, 1919–1932* (Austin: Presidial Press, 1980), 105–137; Annette Moye, "Longview," in "Major Race Riots in the Red Summer of 1919" (Master's thesis, Texas Southern University, 1971), 22–27; George Ohler, "Background Causes of the Longview Race Riot of July 10, 1919," *Journal of the American Studies Association of Texas* 12 (1981), 46–54; Lawrence Olsen, "Black Texans in the 'Red Summer' of 1919: The Longview Race Riot" (Master's thesis, Southwest Texas State University, 1974); William N. Tuttle, Jr., "Violence in a Heathen Land: The Longview Race Riot of 1919," *Phylon* 33 (Winter 1972), 324–33; Arthur I. Waskow, *From Race Riot to Sit-in, 1919 and the 1960s* (Garden City, New York: Doubleday, 1966), 16–20; Jared Wheeler, "Prelude to Anarchy: The Longview Race Riot of 1919," *The Texas Ranger Dispatch* 30 (Fall 2009), 4–14.

22. Bruce A. Glasrud, "Black Texans, 1900–1930: A History" (Ph.D. diss., Texas Tech University, 1969), 149–150; *Fort Worth Star-Telegram*, July 30, 31, 1910; Norris White Jr., "Bad Saturday: Revisiting the 1910 Slocum Massacre" (unpublished paper, Stephen F. Austin State University; copy in hands of this author); Linda Sue Stuard, "Racial Disorder in East Texas: The 1910 Slocum Incident" (unpublished paper, University of Texas-Tyler; copy in the hands of this author); E. R. Bill, *The 1910 Slocum Massacre: An Act of Genocide in East Texas* (Charleston, SC: The History Press, 2014), quote on 117.

23. Monte Akers, *Flames after Midnight: Murder, Vengeance, and the Desolation of a Texas Community* (Austin: University of Texas Press, 1999).

24. Carrigan, *Making of a Lynching Culture*, 192; Glasrud, "Black Texans," 166–167.

25. Edward Hake Phillips, "The Sherman Courthouse Riot of 1930," *East Texas Historical Journal* 25.2 (1987), 12–19; Robert M. Utley, *Lone Star Lawmen* (New York: Penguin, 2007), 133–140, quote on 134.

26. Donna J. Kumler, "'They have gone from Sherman': The Courthouse Riot of 1930 and its Impact on the Black Professional Class" (Ph.D. diss., University of North Texas, 1995); Mike Cox, "The Sherman Riot," in *Texas Ranger Tales II* (Plano: Republic of Texas Press, 1999), 193–205; Utley, *Lone Star Lawmen*, 133–140; Krenek, "Race Riots at Longview and Sherman," 105–37; Phillips, "The Sherman Courthouse Riot of 1930," 12–19; Durward Pruden, "A Sociological Study of a Texas Lynching" (Master's thesis, Southern Methodist University, 1935); Thomas Michael Murphy, "History of the Sherman Riot" (Master's thesis, Austin College, 1931); Arthur Franklin Raper, *The Tragedy of Lynching* (Chapel Hill: University of North Carolina Press, 1933), 319–55; Nolan Thompson, "Sherman Riot of 1930," *The Handbook of Texas Online* (http://www.tshaonline.org/handbook); Njoki McElroy, "The Ninth Day of May," in Suzanne Comer, *Common Bonds: Stories By and About Modern Texas Women* (Dallas: Southern Methodist University Press, 1990), 40–42.

27. James A. Burran, "Violence in an 'Arsenal of Democracy': The Beaumont Race Riot, 1943," *East Texas Historical Journal* 14.1 (1976), 39–51; James S. Olson and Sharon Phair, "The Anatomy of a Race Riot: Beaumont, Texas, 1943," *Texana* 11 (1973), 64–72; James S. Olson, "Beaumont Riot of 1943," *Handbook of Texas Online* (http://tshaonline.org/handbook); Tabitha C. Wang, "Beaumont Race Riot, 1943," *Blackpast Online Encyclopedia* (http://www.blackpast.org). See also James A. Burran, "The Beaumont Race Riot of 1943" (Master's thesis, Texas Tech University, 1973); Burran discussed the Beaumont Riot in his "Racial Violence in the South during World War II" (Ph.D. diss., University of Tennessee, 1977).

28. Burran, "Violence in an 'Arsenal of Democracy': The Beaumont Race Riot, 1943," 39–51; Olson and Phair, "The Anatomy of a Race Riot: Beaumont, Texas, 1943," 64–72; Olson, "Beaumont Riot of 1943."

29. For NAACP, see Michael L. Gillette, "The NAACP in Texas, 1937–1957" (Ph.D. diss., University of Texas at Austin, 1984); Neil G. Sapper, "The Fall of the NAACP in Texas," *The Houston Review* 7 (Summer 1985): 53–68. On Mansfield crisis, Robyn Duff Ladino, *Desegregating Texas Schools: Eisenhower, Shivers, and the Crisis at Mansfield High* (Austin: University of Texas Press, 1996); Alwyn Barr, *Black Texans: A History of African Americans in Texas, 1528–1995*, second edition (Norman: University of Oklahoma Press, 1996), 207.

On the sit-ins see Martin Herman Kuhlman, "The Civil Rights Movement in Texas: Desegregation of Public Accommodations, 1950–1964" (Ph.D. diss., Texas Tech University, 1994); F. Kenneth Jensen, "The Houston Sit-In Movement of 1960–61," in Howard Beeth and Cary D. Wintz, eds., *Black Dixie: Afro-Texas History and Culture in Houston* (College Station: Texas A&M University Press, 1992), 213–15; Donald Seals Jr., "The Wiley-Bishop Student Movement: A Case Study in the 1960 Civil Rights Sit-Ins," *Southwestern Historical Quarterly* 106 (January 2003), 419–40.

30. On the 1967 TSU episode, Bernard Friedberg, "Houston and the TSU Riot," in *Life Styles in the Black Ghetto*, edited by William McCord, John Howard, Bernard Friedberg, and Edwin Harwood (New York: W. W. Norton, 1969), 36–51. Also see Barr, *Black Texans*, 191–93.

31. Nick Davies, *White Lies: Rape, Murder, and Justice Texas Style* (New York: Avon Books, 1991).

32. Howard Swindle, *Deliberate Indifference: A Story of Racial Injustice and Murder* (New York: Viking Penguin, 1993).

33. Ricardo C. Ainslie, *Long Dark Road: Bill King and Murder in Jasper, Texas* (Austin: University of Texas Press, 2004); Joyce King, *Hate Crime: The Story of a Dragging in Jasper, Texas* (New York: Random House, 2002); Dina Temple-Raston, *Death in Texas: A Story of Race, Murder, and a Small Town's Struggle for Redemption* (New York: Henry Holt, 2002).

34. Nate Blakeslee, *Tulia: Race, Cocaine, and Corruption in a Small Texas Town* (New York: Public Affairs, 2005). See also Nate Blakeslee, "Bust Town," *Texas Monthly* (November 2002); Nate Blakeslee, "The Color of Justice," *The Texas Observer* (June 23, 2000). It was Blakeslee who first reported on the racial miscarriage of justice in Tulia.

1

Paris Is Burning

Lynching and Racial Violence in Lamar County, 1890–1920

Brandon Jett

From 1865 to 1920, the United States underwent vast transformations, especially in the South. New political, social, and economic systems emerged that transformed the South from a rural, slave-based society, to an increasingly urban, industrialized, free labor society. The changes to the social, political, and economic landscape of the South prompted an unprecedented era of racial violence throughout the region. From 1890 to 1920, lynching became the most visible and prevalent example of racial violence; at least 2,522 African Americans died at the hands of lynch mobs. Lynchings remained a continued threat for southern blacks throughout the Jim Crow era, however, the number of lynchings dropped steadily from the peak in 1892, and by 1920, lynchings became a relatively rare event. Historians have identified several reasons why lynchings declined during this period, including changes in the southern economy, increased pressure from outside anti-lynching organizations, and an increased reliance on the southern legal system to enforce compliance with Jim Crow customs and laws.[1]

An examination of these processes in Lamar County provides an understanding of the interconnections of these economic, social, and political transformations and the rise and decline of lynching in the New South. The county seat for Lamar County, Paris, exemplified the prototypical New South city. Paris became a major railroad hub and connected the county to larger markets for agricultural and manufactured products.

Although agriculture still undergirded the county's economy, by 1900, Paris housed a burgeoning manufacturing and industrial sector and was one of northeast Texas' most important cities. Despite the outward appearance of modernization, race relations remained mired in antebellum notions of

---

Originally published in the *East Texas Historical Journal* 51.2 (2013), 40–64. Reprinted with permission of the author and the East Texas Historical Association.

white supremacy and black subordination. White mobs in Paris lynched at least nine black men between 1890 and 1920. Most notoriously, Lamar County whites ushered in the era of spectacle lynchings in 1893 that terrorized southern blacks for the next thirty years. Lynchings continued to go unchallenged for thirty years until 1920, when prominent whites publicly condemned lynching for the first time.[2]

In 2001, Walter Buenger briefly discussed lynching in Lamar County in *The Path to a Modern South*. Buenger argued that the change in response to lynching was indicative of a larger cultural shift that occurred between 1890 and 1930 through which northeast Texans became less concerned with promoting the traditional southern ideals of the "Lost Cause" and states' rights. This cultural transformation, he stated, acted as the main catalyst to the region's changing attitudes regarding lynching.[3]

This chapter, "Paris is Burning," reexamines the rise and decline of lynching in Lamar County and focuses specifically on the role of prominent whites in Paris who initially propagated the continued use of and later hastened the decline of lynching locally. Following the heinous 1893 lynching of Henry Smith, local businessmen publicly expressed their empathy for the mob and condoned their actions. Because of their support, local mob participants faced no prosecution of any kind, even though Governor James Hogg pressured locals to bring the ringleaders to justice. Lynchers continued to enjoy local support until 1920. Following the public burning of two black men before a crowd of three thousand, the negative national press tarnished the image crafted by prominent whites in Paris. After a devastating fire in 1916 that destroyed much of the city, Paris city leaders promoted Paris as a modern and progressive city. The complete breakdown of legal and social order that made spectacle lynchings possible threatened the economic viability of Paris. In addition, thousands of local blacks fled the county in the aftermath of the lynching and forced city leaders to take steps to ensure the cheap labor supply remained in the county. Responding to those specific circumstances, prominent whites in Paris condemned the lynching publicly, encouraged local authorities to prosecute the lynchers, met with prominent blacks to encourage them to stay in the county, and ensured that lynching would no longer be a problem in Lamar County.[4]

The history of escalating racial violence in Lamar County dates back to the antebellum era. During the Civil War, a lynch mob murdered a slave named Rube. Allegedly, according to the *Dallas Morning News*, "five hundred people assembled and Rube was tied to a tree, rails were piled around him, set on fire and he slowly burned to death." This suggests that prior to emancipation, whites in the county were willing to go to extreme lengths to eliminate perceived threats to the racial caste system.[5]

Following emancipation, the Bureau of Refugees, Freedmen, and Abandoned Lands came to Texas to make emancipation a reality. The Bureau faced many problems in Texas. The central problems were a shortage of personnel and funds, bureaucratic regulations, and the violent resistance of white Texans to emancipation and black equality. During Reconstruction, white mobs murdered at least four hundred black Texans. Most of these lynchings allegedly resulted from the murder or rape of a white person at the hands of a freedman. The myth of the retrogressive and rapacious black man had begun.

In Lamar County, the Klan had organized by 1868 in response to federal efforts to help freedmen exercise their new rights. Bands of local whites resisted the Bureau's efforts violently and attempted to kill local bureau agent DeWitt C. Brown numerous times. These cabals also patrolled the county, murdering several white Republicans and "an untold number of freedmen." In this era, local whites realized that violence remained an effective way to limit black advancement and successfully thwarted the Bureau. By the end of 1868, Brown had resigned his post with the Freedmen's Bureau because he lacked federal support and left the county for good. One year later, it was clear to locals that the Bureau had failed, because blacks remained virtually enslaved to landholders and conservative whites had regained control of local political offices.[6]

With white Democrats firmly in control of the county, violence was less overt, but tensions remained. Paris housed a sizeable and well-established black middle class, with several African Americans serving as council members, including Harry Cunington in 1871, and Creed Taylor and Chris Johnson from 1882 through 1885. Like the national economy, Lamar County's economy grew tremendously during the last decades of the nineteenth century, accompanied by rapid population growth. The county's population more than doubled from 15,790 to 37,302 between 1870 and 1890, and the black population grew by more than two thousand people in the 1880s. The working-class character of recent black migration produced profound effects on local race relations, because white citizens of Paris, like those of most cities in the New South, pushed for economic improvement and growth while retaining traditions of white supremacy. Economic opportunities in the cotton trade in Lamar County prompted a mass influx of new, unknown blacks, causing black-white tensions to rise. For instance, local whites pushed for prohibition reform in the late 1880s and the early 1890s, a movement that pitted them against local blacks, who tended to be anti-prohibition. To many local whites, black opposition to prohibition signaled the retrograde nature of the new black migrants. The combination of recent black in-migration and blacks' resistance to prohibition reform increased racial tension in the county. By the 1890s, as Walter Buenger suggested, such conditions turned Paris into "a lynching site."[7]

In the summer of 1890, racial violence struck Paris again. Andy Young, a local black, became the first lynching victim after local whites accused him of having "difficulty with some white boys." The *Chicago Inter Ocean* described Young as "a hard-working Negro," but listed no additional reason for his murder. Young was in his early twenties and worked as a sharecropper on Nathan Grant's farm. The night of the lynching, a small group of six or seven whites found him at his residence, "called him up," and shot him as he came out of the door. Fitzhugh Brundage suggests that small-mob murders "can best be understood as a form of private vengeance." Young's murder did not fit the traditional image of spectacle lynching, but the mob sent a message to the rest of the black community by desecrating Young's dead body with a barrage of bullets. Andy Young's killing did not seem to upset the citizens of the community.

Evidence of black or white reactions is either nonexistent or lost to the historical record. The lack of reaction to the slaying is symptomatic of a lack of national attention to lynching and racial violence at the time. The absence of record might also suggest that blacks and whites generally accepted the lynching or felt they could not speak out against it because they too may become victims of violent reprisal.[8]

A similar lack of reaction by county whites occurred again in 1892, when a local white man, John Ashley, murdered local black sharecropper Jarrett Burns. Allegedly, Burns purchased a horse from Ashley but, according to Ashley, did not keep up the payments. Ashley took the horse from Burns because of his inability to pay. Burns then showed pragmatism and foolishness in the same instance. He went alone and unarmed to request the return of the horse in order to till his soil. Allegedly, during an ensuing altercation, Ashley killed Burns. In southern society, the value of blacks did not exceed even the most miniscule debt. Local authorities pursued no legal action against Ashley, suggesting that unpaid debts justified the murder of a black man at the hands of a white man in their eyes.[9]

This murder, however, sparked an unprecedented reaction from the county's blacks. The lack of legal action against Burns infuriated the black community in Lamar County, and they organized the "Colored Association" to voice their frustration. They expressed their dissatisfaction in a way that frightened many southern whites—through violence. Ashley claimed to have received numerous threats against his life from members of the "Colored Association," and they allegedly even poisoned his horses. The action considered most threatening to local whites was yet to come. According to the *Columbus Daily Enquirer*, local blacks attempted to enter Ashley's house a few nights after the murder of Burns. In defiance of all Jim Crow social rules, several local blacks rode around the Lamar County streets armed with guns.[10]

To combat the growing tide of black assertiveness, local whites organized for their own protection. Following the attempted break-in of Ashley's residence, members of the white community stood guard over Ashley's house to ward off any further black efforts at revenge. Additionally, local whites turned to the time-tested use of violence to send a message for blacks to leave the issue alone. Small groups of whites whipped numerous blacks in the ensuing days. Most disturbing to the black community was the attempted lynching of Jarrett Burns' niece, Ella Ransom. When the mob, including Ashley, attempted to lynch Ransom, she slipped the noose off and ran away while the men were "standing a little way off and while one of them was fixing the rope over a tree limb."[11]

Following the botched lynching of Ella Ransom, local blacks again asserted their manhood. Ella Ransom returned to Paris to report the attack to authorities under protection of several armed black men. Local whites refused to accept this assertion of dignity and violently expressed their disapproval. Three of the men who guarded Ella Ransom received beatings by a group of masked men, but the worst was yet to come. The racial tensions between the black and white communities came to a tragic culmination. On September 6, 1892, John Ransom, John Walker, and William Armor, three black men who protected Ella Ransom, were lynched. These black men who defended womanhood, the very thing that white southerners held so sacred, paid with their lives. Not one local white voiced any opposition or condemnation of the action.[12]

The triple lynching was meant to send a clear message to the black community. Twenty or thirty masked men rounded up the three men, placed nooses around their necks, and marched them into the woods. The next morning, two young boys discovered the bodies near a road and found that "Ransom was swinging clear of the ground, but the mob in its hurry had not hung [*sic*] Armor and Walker clear, and had to tie their feet up to clear the ground." According to reports, at least one of these black men belonged to the "Colored Association." Ransom, Walker, and Armor's bodies hung in public for all blacks to see with an oath signed by black members of the "Colored Association" attached to one of the dead bodies. This note, an obvious white fabrication, visibly linked the lynching with the recent black assertion of self-respect.[13]

At the time of the triple lynching, a new era of race relations was emerging throughout the South. Scientific racism became the guiding principle behind white southerners' attack of black civil liberties. According to proponents of scientific racism, African Americans were innately inferior to Anglo-Saxons and did not have the mental capability to operate effectively in civilized, white society. In fact, these proponents posited, African Americans had retrogressed from docile, humble, and hard-working under the civilizing institution of slavery back to their savage, violent origins following emancipation. The black male propensity to lust after and rape white women was the culmination of this process, according to racist ideology. Consequently, the popular notion of the black "beast" dominated southern thought and was often the justification for the violent treatment of blacks.[14]

In Lamar County, the new racist ideology and the obvious lack of punishment of previous lynchers brought about the era of spectacle lynching. In January 1893, Lamar County authorities found the dead body of a three-year-old white girl, Myrtle Vance. Days after her death, local authorities claimed the child had been raped and then choked to death. Based on unsubstantiated evidence, authorities quickly charged a local black man, Henry Smith, with the crime. Smith personified the stereotype of the retrograde character that local whites attributed to the newly arrived black population. Smith was a recent arrival to Lamar County, having lived there for only five years. He had limited family and community ties and a reputation as a drunk and a troublemaker. The circumstances surrounding the murder, alleged rape, and involvement of Smith were contested, but one detail stood out in the case. Months before the murder, local law enforcement official Henry Vance clubbed and arrested Smith, and upon his incarceration Smith allegedly vowed revenge against Vance, who was Myrtle's father. Upon the discovery of the young girl's body, Smith emerged as the prime suspect based on his low reputation and his vow to seek revenge against Vance.[15]

Smith fled the city, but authorities caught up with him at Hope, Arkansas, on January 31, 1893. The officers bound Smith in handcuffs and took the train back to Paris. Along the way, mobs of angry and belligerent whites met the party transporting Smith back to Paris and voiced their desire to see him lynched. When the train arrived at Texarkana, Texas, two thousand men gathered and expressed the desire to see Smith lynched. The mob demanded Smith be given over to them so they could lynch the "brute." However, the mob decided that the people of Paris deserved their vengeance. It was a foregone conclusion that, guilty or not, Smith was going to die.[16]

Whites in Paris were exhilarated at the chance to lynch Smith. In the 1890s, public burning became a popular form of lynching throughout the South. The *Dallas Morning News* reported a day prior to Smith's capture that "it is the almost universal sentiment that he will be publicly burned at the stake." On the day of the lynching, aroused citizens from all over northeast Texas and Arkansas came to view the spectacle. These onlookers filled almost every train destined for Paris. The railroad company even increased the number of passenger trains traveling to the city to accommodate the sheer number of curious whites. No one tried to stop the inevitable. Instead, locals prepared for the imminent lynching and assembled a large float box with the word "JUSTICE" painted across the front and a chair on top in order to secure Smith to the structure and parade him through the town. This spectacle would not be a quick murder. The impending lynching turned these religious, supposedly civilized people into a frenzied, insatiable mob that the entire community condoned.[17]

When authorities returned to Paris with Smith in hand, they quickly handed him over to the frenzied mob, and then the show began. The ringleaders paraded Smith up and down the main thoroughfares of the city. The lynching became a community event that thousands participated in, encouraged, and condoned. The mob of ten thousand men, women, and children followed the parade to a field just outside of the city center and watched as Henry Vance, his son, and two of Myrtle's uncles took their vengeance. According to the *New York Herald*, "hot irons were placed upon the soles of his [Smith's] feet, rolled over his quivering body, poked into his eyes and down his throat. A scaffold upon which he lay was then set on fire. His clothes and fetters burned off and he threw himself to the ground, he was tossed back into the flames again and again until death came to his relief." The mob watched and encouraged the torture until Smith's body burned to ashes. The *New York Herald* further stated, "Thousands looked at the death struggles with evident satisfaction and many of them with demonstrations of delight." For the time, civilization ceased.[18]

The level of brutality meted out against Smith captivated the nation and exposed millions of Americans to this unprecedented form of vigilante violence. Americans in all sections of the country had long accepted lynching as a necessary form of punishment in regions outside the control of the institutions of law and order, such as the West. Lynchings served as extralegal methods of punishment and mimicked legal executions. Victims usually admitted their crime and were hung in a matter-of-fact manner. The lynching of Henry Smith looked more like a medieval torture than a legal execution. It also occurred at a time when sensational newspaper reporting became the norm. Newspapers across the country reported the lynching in sensationalized form that captivated millions and exposed them to spectacle lynching for the first time. The *Philadelphia Inquirer's* headline read, "Tortured With Red-Hot Irons and Then Burned Alive-Thousands of Citizens of Paris Aid the Unparalleled Retribution." The *New Haven Register* also focused on the heinousness of Smith's prolonged death and printed the simple and straightforward headline, "Tortured Him to Death." Perhaps the most telling description of the Henry Smith lynching came from the *Chicago Daily Inter Ocean:* "The Texas Horror" ran across the headlines on February 3, 1893, and painted a violently negative picture of Lamar County.[19]

The extraordinary and unprecedented lynching piqued national interested and forced locals to defend their actions. Many citizens, according to an anonymous author, expected the event to come and go and "all seemed satisfied and went their way in peace." National attention, however, did not let the lynching fade quietly into history. Responding to a request for an explanation by the editor of the *New York Herald*, Editor A. P. Body of the *Paris News* replied, "I am not unmindful of the fact that such violence is a menace to the liberties of the people . . . and as a public journalist I do not generally indorse [*sic*] it." However, Boyd still believed the "sickening outrage" of the rape and murder of Myrtle Vance vindicated the actions of the citizens of Paris, and other locals expanded upon his argument.[20]

Prominent locals began a campaign to justify the mob's actions in various publications. Colonel J. C. Hodges, one of the leading criminal lawyers in the county, stated in the *Dallas Morning News* that, "When I think of Smith's fate and am disposed to protest against it I think of the little girl the torture imposed upon her when she was equally helpless, and I can find no word of condemnation for the manner in which Smith was put to death." Hodges' statements sought to redefine the "Paris Horror" as the rape and murder of Myrtle Vance, and not the torture of Henry Smith. In so doing he appealed to white men locally and regionally by claiming, "Smith's death was simply the will of the people. . . . The deed has been done and as good citizens we must indorse it."[21]

The most comprehensive defense of the lynching came in the form of a book published by prominent local businessman John M. Early, shortly after Smith's death. Entitled *Eye for an Eye* (1893), the book defended the action of the mob and attempted to justify the mob's incomprehensible brutality. Early emphasized that it was the sadistic rape and murder of the young girl that "incite[d]" the mob. The author blamed the brutal torture on the victim himself; Smith's actions alone led to the lynching, not some underlying racial motivation. Early described Smith as "the chiefest among sinners" who committed the most barbaric of crimes and argued that the "tardiness and uncertainty of punishment ha[d] stripped the law of its terror," and it therefore had not acted as a deterrent for heinous criminals such as Smith. According to Early, the lynching of Smith resulted from the inadequacy of the legal system to discourage violent crimes properly, which, in turn, forced the community to defend itself through extralegal means. In the eyes of the white community, the mob did not represent lawlessness. Instead, it was viewed as having acted responsibly and in a "very refined manner." In his attempt to save the reputation of the city, Early did not denounce the lynching but instead rationalized it as a necessary and justifiable punishment for atrocities committed by blacks against civilized society.[22]

Early's book expressed the pro-lynching defense, but it also had more personal motivations. Early was a successful local businessman with a wife and three children. More importantly, he was heavily invested in the city, so much so that in 1893 he built an elegant, two-story house just one mile outside the city center, complete with floor-length windows, ornate brass hardware, handmade doors, and a cherry wood stairway. Early did not want the lynching to discourage economic and population growth in Lamar County, and thus concluded his book with a statement describing the goodhearted nature of the community and the economic advantages of the city. Early described Paris as a place where economic prosperity was easily attainable, and he encouraged Americans to move to his town. He touted the community's economic potential and emphasized the availability of "thousands of acres of land at $2 per acre, rich as the Nile valley." Early explained the religious commitment of the city, its educational benefits, and the dedication of the citizens to protecting "at all hazards, the women and children, even though it takes a little fire."[23]

Prominent whites in Paris not only defended the actions of the mob, but they discouraged any type of prosecution of the lynchers. After the lynching, Governor James Hogg wired the local county attorney B. B. Sturgeon and asked him to "do your whole duty and prosecute every person engaged in the reported lynching of one Henry Smith at Paris. By all means preserve the names of the offenders and witnesses to the end that the guilty parties may be prosecuted." Hogg also wired Sheriff Hammond of Lamar County and asked him to pursue a similar course. He proclaimed, "Promptly make complaint before the proper officers against every person known to have been engaged in the lynching of the negro Henry Smith at Paris." Hogg's appeals to local law enforcement were not well received, and the *Dallas Morning News* reported that public sentiment regarded the governor's proclamations as "a joke." Despite pictures of the lynching and thousands of local witnesses, the county successfully avoided the issue and no prosecutions were made.[24]

After the 1893 lynching of Smith, the citizens in Lamar County never again resorted to such a large-scale, public lynching, but small-scale lynchings continued. Mobs killed two black men in Lamar County in 1895 and 1901, but little information about the lynchings exists. The lack of local accounts makes it necessary to rely on national newspapers that paid little attention to the murders, but the persistent acts of mob violence suggest continued community acceptance of lynchings. In 1895, whites in Paris lynched a black man named Jefferson Cole in the midst of increased White Cap violence. According to the *Kansas City Times*, "many outrages [were] committed by white caps in Texas" throughout the month of August 1895, but the report gave little indication why whites in the county resorted to violence against blacks. It stated that on August 23, 1895, Jefferson Cole, "an aged and inoffensive negro, was called out of his house and riddled with bullets" by a mob of whites. No reason was given for the murder of Cole, but the article noted that Cole owned land. Whites throughout the South reacted violently against black property owners because blacks who owned property "could be deemed disrespectful to certain elements of the white population." Local whites also attacked prominent members of the black community, including Reverend J. H. McClinton, who was murdered on December 25, 1901. The lynching did gain some national attention, but accounts only stated that the reverend was "shot to death by a crowd of men." From 1893 to 1920, lynching in Paris declined as the subordination of blacks hardened through legal and other less overt means.[25]

While lynching declined in Paris, Lamar County whites utilized another virulent form of subordination. White southerners implemented new laws that legally subordinated blacks in the 1890s and early 1900s. The Texas Legislature passed stringent laws legally segregating blacks and whites in the 1890s. In 1891, for example, the Texas Legislature passed a bill that required separate railroad coaches for blacks and whites.[26] The Supreme Court's decision in *Plessy v. Ferguson* (1896) officially gave southerners legal sanction to enforce segregation in nearly all public places as long as they followed the principle of "separate but equal."[27]

Legal segregation was accompanied by the removal of black political representation through disfranchisement measures. In 1903, the Texas legislature passed the Terrell Election Law, which required the payment of a poll tax in order to vote in Texas. The legislature amended the law numerous times between 1903 and 1923, and by 1908 had succeeded in eliminating almost all black voters. In that year, only one black voter attempted to vote. The Democratic Party's establishment of the white primary also played a role in eliminating the black vote. By 1910, Texans had firmly established a system of segregation that legally placed blacks below whites. Black disfranchisement had an obvious impact on the prohibition campaign. Earlier, in August 1902, Lamar County locals rejected a prohibition measure by a count of 4,046 for and 4,562 against. Undoubtedly, the votes of local blacks, who did not support prohibition, played an important role in this defeat. However, a year after the enactment of the poll tax, prohibition passed in the county, signifying the effectiveness of the poll tax in disfranchising blacks. The total number of votes cast had fallen by 3,000 since the previous election.[28]

Throughout the 1890s and the early 1900s, Lamar County experienced economic growth. Property values in northeast Texas steadily grew from 1900 to 1920, and Paris emerged as one of the largest cotton markets in the region. Throughout northeast Texas, farmers devoted more and more of their land to the production of cotton, especially after the outbreak of World War I in Europe. Demand for cottonseed oil, peanut seed oil, and other agricultural products grew as a result of the war, and local farmers answered the call. Agricultural production more than tripled between 1910 and 1920 as the overall value of all crops produced exploded from $5.5 million to $18.2 million. Investment in the manufacturing sector grew slowly between 1870 and 1880 from $43,750 to $74,970. However, the manufacturing economy expanded during the next two decades; by 1890 local capital investment blossomed by 600 percent to $439,350, and by 1900, it had more than doubled to just over $1 million.[29]

Wartime demand for agricultural and manufactured goods promoted economic growth in Lamar County during the 1910s, and the manufacturing sector doubled from 1914 to 1919. A devastating fire in 1916, which caused $11 million worth of property damage, did not stop economic growth in Paris, and locals came together and rebuilt the city. Economic growth encouraged population growth, and both blacks and whites migrated to the area for jobs. The total population grew from 46,544 in 1910 to 55,742 in 1920. The prosperity of Lamar County and the chance to rebuild after the 1916 fire allowed city leaders to promote Paris as a city of beauty and wealth.[30]

Despite the outward appearance of progress and growth, Paris was two different places. It was an idyllic place for whites, but underneath the veneer of progress there remained the ever-present threat of violence for local blacks. Although few lynchings occurred during this time, other, less widely reported instances of racial violence underlay race relations in the city. As historian Kidada Williams argues, rapes, whippings, assaults, and shootings became so commonplace in the late-nineteenth and early-twentieth century South that reports of these events rarely surfaced. Local blacks surely remembered the excessive punishment meted out against Henry Smith, thus more individualized acts of violence against local blacks probably were sufficient to ensure their cooperation within the confines of Jim Crow.[31]

World War I spawned economic prosperity, but it also profoundly affected race relations in Paris and throughout the country. Many returning black veterans vehemently opposed Jim Crow in an unprecedented assertive manner. Blacks across the country heeded the advice of W. E. B. DuBois to take up arms and join the army despite the "deep-seated feeling of revolt among negroes at the persistent insult and discrimination to which they are subject." DuBois hoped that blacks' loyal service in their nation's fight for democracy abroad would persuade white Americans to return the favor and grant equal rights at home. Nearly four hundred thousand African Americans followed DuBois' advice and enlisted in the armed forces. Upon the return of the black servicemen, the so-called "New Negro mentality" swept the nation. The New Negro asserted himself like never before as "on the national canvas and a force in the foreground of affairs" who emphasized the importance of black culture as separate from but equally important to white American culture. This new mentality encouraged many blacks to push for equal rights and challenge the American racial hierarchy.[32]

White Texans responded violently to the idea of a New Negro who rejected racial subordination. The Red Summer of 1919 represented the most evident impact of World War I on race relations in the United States. After fighting to make the world safe for democracy, returning black soldiers created tensions through their push for better treatment at home. Race riots erupted in twenty-two cities throughout the country from April 14 to October 1, 1919. Racial tensions boiled over in northeast Texas as well. In Longview, Texas, a race riot erupted when whites responded ferociously to the push by local blacks to "migrate, to start businesses, to vote, and to strive for equal rights."[33]

Although no riots erupted in Paris, the end of World War I brought an economic recession and the New Negro mentality to Lamar County. The county suffered when European production of agricultural and manufactured goods rebounded after the end of the war. The price of cotton dropped by more than fifty percent in 1920, and demand for other goods subsided as well. Accompanying the economic downturn, local black veterans returned from World War I with new ideas that threatened Jim Crow. To southern blacks, these valiant, uniformed men were a source of racial pride. However, these veterans struck fear into many southern whites. Southern whites viewed the New Negro as a threat, and as arrogant and impudent. Many feared violent clashes between southern whites and blacks because of the New Negro's assertion of manhood and willingness to fight for civil rights. In 1919, local whites alerted federal investigators that black veterans were conducting meetings with other black residents. Local whites feared these meetings would cause "trouble" because local black veterans urged their fellow blacks to fight for equal rights. Like blacks around the country, local blacks did not violently express their dissatisfaction with their subordination, and instead, many left the countryside and moved to cities to escape rural poverty and racial violence.[34]

In Paris, two young black tenant farmers decided to escape farm tenancy and move out of Lamar County's countryside. Herman Arthur, a twenty-six-year old World War I veteran who served in France, and his nineteen-year-old brother Irving, decided to leave. Along with many other blacks, they sought to escape from Jim Crow racial violence and find new economic opportunities in the emerging urban centers. Since cheap black labor was the backbone of the southern agricultural economy, many southern whites utilized a number of tactics to stem the flow of black migrants, and Lamar County was no exception. In the early afternoon of July 2, 1920, a wealthy farmer, J. H. Hodges, and his son Will confronted the Arthur brothers when they packed their limited belongings into a rented truck. The Arthurs allegedly owed J. H. Hodges money, but refused to acquiesce to Hodges' demands that they stay to work on his farm. An intense argument turned violent, and in the altercation, both J. H. and Will Hodges died of gunshot wounds. The Arthurs then took flight and headed north.[35]

In the wake of the Red Summer of 1919 and the race riot in Longview, Lamar County whites intended to send a message to the black community—the New Negro would not be tolerated. For several days, search parties fanned out over northeast Texas to capture the black fugitives. Four days after the murder of Hodges and his son, authorities in Valiant, Oklahoma, captured the Arthurs. Paris officials placed the brothers in jail to await trial, but quickly a crowd gathered, "stormed" the jail, and overpowered the authorities holding Herman and Irving. The mob quickly took the Arthurs to the fairgrounds, "where a stake and fuel had been prepared." At the fairgrounds, a crowd of around three thousand tied the defiant Herman and Irving to a stake and watched with ominous delight as the two men slowly burned. Herman and Irving, in the true spirit of the "New Negro," met their death bravely. When the mob's ringleaders asked Herman if he was sorry for killing Hodges, he replied, "[he] would kill any man, white or black, who assaulted [my] mothers and sisters." The defiant black men did not utter a single word while being burned alive. In a final act of desecration, the mob chained the charred bodies of the Arthurs to a truck and a "caravan proceeded to drive them through the streets and yards of the black sections of town." Although no blacks witnessed the lynching, the foul smell of burnt flesh, the rambunctious and boisterous crowd, and the dragging of the charred bodies through town reminded all of the city's blacks of the lengths to which whites would go to punish perceived transgressions.[36]

In light of the previous year's race riots, authorities feared a violent backlash from the black community. Following the mass burning of the two black men, city officials took "extraordinary precautions" to ensure no Longview-type race riots occurred. The mayor organized groups of armed volunteers and deputized squads that he then sent into the black section of town to quash any would-be rioters. In spite of the widespread fear of black reprisal, blacks did not organize a large-scale, violent response. Local blacks had no intention of retaliating violently. As Essex Reese, a ten-year-old black boy at the time of the Arthur lynching, remembered, "Most blacks had families and children; they weren't going looking for trouble." Thus, the organized bands of whites disbanded the following night with "quiet restored."[37]

Blacks did not respond to white violence with violence, but instead expressed their dissatisfaction through flight. Black flight was the safest and most common form of black discontent. Blacks in Lamar County fled on an unprecedented scale following the lynching. From 1920 to 1930, the number of blacks in Lamar County shrank from 12,970 to 9,382. Authorities released the remaining members of the Arthur family, and with the help of the Black Masonic Lodge and some sympathetic whites, they left for Chicago. Along with the Arthurs, "an exodus of black residents followed." The *Chicago Defender* sent a representative to report on the events unfolding in Paris. One of the newspaper's headlines read, "THOUSANDS OF RACE PEOPLE LEAVING BLOOD SOAKED DISTRICT." Census records support the newspaper reports and show that the migration led to a permanent and significant loss of black population.[38]

The exodus of blacks concerned white citizens of Paris, some of whom used a number of intimidation tactics to dissuade blacks from fleeing. The *Chicago Defender* claimed, "The only thing causing concern at the present time is the migration of hundreds of our people" from Paris. Whites understood black flight as a form of protest, but more troubling for southern whites was the threat to the region's agricultural economy posed by the mass migration of blacks. The lack of available farm labor threatened to cripple the manual labor workforce and damage an economy that, because of the devastating fire in 1916 that destroyed much of the city, was still in the process of rebuilding. Whites resorted to numerous, extralegal tactics to discourage blacks from moving out of the city. The *Chicago Defender* reported that banks "refused to allow the withdrawal of savings of the people who have already left or who are preparing to go" and hoped that blacks would not flee without their money. Whites also employed violent intimidation tactics to discourage blacks from leaving and patrolled the streets of Paris armed with revolvers and other guns to influence blacks to stay.[39]

J. M. Crook, mayor of Paris, demanded a meeting of leaders from the black and white communities to discuss the recent troubles and dissuade the city's blacks from fleeing. Thirty leading white citizens, such as Judge A. P. Park, Captain J. J. Dickerson, and Professor J. G. Wooten, led the white delegation. Reverend C. N. Hampton and Reverend Brackeen, two pastors from the leading black churches in Paris, led the black delegation. The purpose of the meeting, according to the white delegates, "was to impress on the colored people that it was very necessary for them to be discreet and temperate in speech and conduct." Local whites, once again, placed the blame for the lynching squarely on the black community. In this meeting, local businessman J. J. Dickerson announced to the black delegates the senselessness of leaving because blacks would receive similar treatment anywhere in the United States. Dickerson stated, "If they should go to Indiana, Chicago or other places in the North, they would receive summary treatment if they did not behave themselves." Dickerson's attempt to dissuade blacks from fleeing the city reflected the idea that blacks in general needed to respect the authority of whites, and if blacks continued to step out of place they would receive harsh treatment regardless of where they resided. Although prominent whites did not approve of the lynching, their demeanor towards the city's black population remained as ardently racist as in the 1890s.[40]

National media attention compounded the local problems caused by the Arthur lynching. The national black press and black organizations attacked the city, the state of Texas, and all American citizens for once again allowing a public burning of black men. The *Chicago Defender* blasted the city of Paris with a headline that read "Texans Rejoice as Men Burn: Paris, Birthplace of Stake Burning, Stands by Old Record." The NAACP denounced the lynching, and James Weldon Johnson criticized Governor William P. Hobby for his unwillingness to bring the members of the mob to justice. Johnson, in a public statement issued to the *Wichita Negro Star*, asked, "Christian America is there any justice within your power? How long will you burn human beings at the stake—what will be your end?"[41]

Most southern cities engaged in boosterism during this time, and city leaders of Paris promoted their city as vociferously as city leaders did in other major cities in the South. Groups of city leaders banded together and "sold" their respective cities to outside investors who could improve the economic capacity of their city. Boosters embellished the benefits of their city and downplayed the negative aspects, such as racial violence. Following the 1916 fire, Paris boosters sought to promote their city as modern and attractive to outside investment. The negative national attention that emerged following the Arthur brothers' lynching forced these boosters to respond to national criticisms. Whereas in 1893 city boosters defended lynching, this time, they moderated their response.[42]

Following the Arthur lynching, prominent whites condemned the mob's actions. A well-known minister, Robert Shuler, led the attack on lynching in a statement printed in the local newspaper. He claimed the lynching tarnished the city and the citizens and represented "a shameful defiance of civilized ideals and standards." Schuler further condemned mob violence, stating, "A mob never rights a wrong." He also expressed concern regarding the negative impact the lynching would have on the reputation of Paris. His public statement declared, "That our community will suffer beyond repair is proven by the fact that Wednesday afternoon there was published all over the North and East dispatches announcing that we had burned Negroes." Many other prominent members of Paris also worried the lynching damaged the respectability of their city during a crucial time. Focused on rebuilding their city, they worried that the unruly nature of the mob and turbulent race relations hurt chances for outside investment. As the *Paris Morning News* exclaimed, "The people of Paris will pay a heavy price for the orgy of anarchy." In light of changed national perceptions of lynching, the city leaders of Paris finally understood that lynching was bad for business.[43]

Following the pattern of previous lynchings, many locals deflected the responsibility for the lynching to blacks themselves. Even Schuler, the outspoken critic of mob violence, clung to the idea of racial subordination and exclaimed, "If the Negro race will show its appreciation by living as these good men [prominent white men of Paris] desire them to live, much of the errors of the past will be removed from the path of their race." He reminded blacks that in order to ameliorate the threat of violence against them, they needed to remain in their place and act according to the racial customs of the day. Schuler went further and claimed that the New Negro mentality brought on mob violence. He stated, "The attitude of many negroes toward farm labor and other work, their seething disposition not to assist the farms in earnest fashion and at fair remuneration, had much to do with the spirit of this mob." Shuler spoke out against lynching on legal grounds, but did not denounce the discriminatory and oppressive treatment of blacks, and instead placed the blame for extralegal violence squarely on the shoulders of local blacks.[44]

In response to local and outside pressure, authorities called a grand jury to investigate the Arthur brother lynching and bring the ringleaders to justice. According to news reports, a mass meeting of white citizens adopted a resolution insisting on a "thorough investigation" to look into who led the mob. The grand jury responsible for investigating the lynching consisted of some of the most influential members of the city, "the cream of the business and Chamber [of Commerce] crop of Lamar County, with a huge vested purpose to save the image of Paris, Texas." The grand jury attempted to identify the ringleaders, but had a difficult time finding locals who would testify against the alleged lynchers.[45]

Despite many impediments, the grand jury persevered and continued to investigate the matter diligently. After several days of interviews, the grand jury indicted local white farmers Wilber C. Clough, Ernest Coggins, Tom Dobbs, Charley Luckey, and T. D. Holderness for murder. Following a grand jury indictment, Judge Ben H. Denton decided to move the case because "the prejudice and excitement in this case in Paris would by its existence here be detrimental to a fair and just trial."[46] The trial took place in the 59th District Court of Grayson County in Sherman, Texas. A fire in 1930 destroyed most records of the trail, but it seems no convictions occurred because many of the people indicted continued to live in Lamar County.[47]

Although it appears no convictions came out of the trial, prominent citizens of the county considered the lynching an "outrage" and publicly supported the convening of the grand jury. The *Paris Morning News* printed a resolution signed by 198 prominent locals pledging "to render every assistance in our power" to the investigation into the Arthur brothers lynching. Although not every citizen spoke out against the lynching, prominent county whites assured the public that "There will never be another lynching in Paris." One can deduce, however, that violence remained a persistent threat to local blacks despite the fact that no lynchings were reported following the 1920 burning.[48]

From 1890 to 1920, whites in Paris consistently reaffirmed their dominance over local blacks through lynching. In response to an influx of working-class blacks and increasing black assertiveness, such as community defense in 1892 or the "New Negro" mentality in 1920, local whites utilized lynching as a method of ensuring conformity among the local black population. African Americans in Lamar County faced the threat of violence, and several local blacks who stepped out of traditional racial boundaries met their deaths at the hands of lynch mobs. Local whites used lynching to punish specific transgressions, but they also used lynching to send a message to the entire black community. Lynch mobs left their victims hanging in public, publicly tortured and burned them to death, and dragged them through black sections of town, all in an effort to intimidate the black community, remind them who ruled, and firmly reinforce white supremacy.[49]

Paris had an inveterate history of racial violence, but as white supremacist ideology grew in the 1890s, local whites became increasingly vociferous in their acceptance of lynching. Community participation in lynching increased steadily from the early 1890s and culminated in the 1893 lynching of Henry Smith before a crowd reaching upward of ten thousand people. As the number of mob participants increased, lynching became increasingly public and organized. When citizens in Paris lynched Henry Smith, the brutality and sheer size of the mob forced locals to defend their actions. Locals claimed such extreme forms of extralegal violence were necessary to deter rapacious blacks from raping white women and to counterbalance a slow, cumbersome legal system.

The national press, however, forced locals to respond to both the 1893 and 1920 lynchings. The responses from prominent locals changed from justifying lynching in 1893 to condemning it in 1920. Local attitudes reflected a broader national pattern. Lynching in the United States crescendoed in the early 1890s, when reports of lynchings proliferated more than in any other time in American history. Thus, when national attention focused on Paris following the lynching of Henry Smith, prominent citizens defended the actions of the mob as necessary due to the inability of the local legal system to protect the citizenry properly. By 1920, however, American perceptions of lynching had changed due to increased pressure from organizations like the Commission for Interracial Cooperation and the NAACP, the masses of blacks who migrated from southern states to the North, and the work of newspapers in painting lynching in a negative light. Therefore, in an effort to salvage their city's reputation and not appear backward and crude, prominent whites repudiated the actions of the mob in 1920, but by no means did they accept responsibility for mob violence. Following the lynching in 1893, locals blamed the lynching on the actions of Smith himself and not on the members of the mob. In 1920, locals blamed the entire black community for the lynching. Local whites hoped to maintain a sizeable black community for a cheap labor source and attempted to curb the flow of blacks fleeing the county, but they simultaneously argued that the local black community's inability to "behave themselves" was the root cause of mob violence.[50]

Following the 1920 lynching, blacks in Paris felt their vulnerability more intensely and took to flight. Their willingness to leave the county resulted in an increased recognition of the importance of the black community by local whites. In spite of Lamar County's history of lynching, the strength of the local economy outweighed the fear of violence, and the black population increased from 9,378 in 1890 to 12,970 in 1920. During the 1920s, however, the agricultural economy of Lamar County receded by an alarming rate; the total value of all crops produced during that decade dropped dramatically from an all-time high of $18.3 million in 1920 to $7.2 million in 1930. The economic downturn and the fear of violence caused black flight. The loss of a cheap source of labor threatened to damage the local economy further. This forced the local white power structure to begrudgingly recognize the local black community as a viable force in county affairs. Whereas negotiating with blacks was untenable in 1893, in the midst of massive black migration, prominent local whites called a meeting with local black leaders in 1920. Although they still did not see blacks as equals, local whites acknowledged the legitimacy of the local black community by inviting black community leaders to a meeting with the still all-white Chamber of Commerce.[51]

In summary, from 1890 to 1920, whites in Lamar County generally accepted lynching as a form of racial control. Locals repeatedly resorted to mob violence in an effort to establish racial subordination among a growing black population in Lamar County. From 1890 to 1920, mob violence continued unimpeded, but the changed national perception of lynching and the unprecedented exodus of thousands of local blacks forced prominent locals to rebuke mob violence to protect the reputation of their city and ensure that lynching in Paris was a thing of the past.

Notes

1. National Association for the Advancement of Colored People, *Thirty Years of Lynching in the United States: 1889–1918* (New York: NAACP, 1919), 29.

2. Amy L. Wood, *Lynching and Spectacle: Witnessing Racial Violence in America, 1890–1940* (Chapel Hill: University of North Carolina Press, 2009), 74.

3. Walter L. Buenger, *The Path to a Modern South: Northeast Texas between Reconstruction and the Great Depression* (Austin: University of Texas Press, 2001), 19–26, 165–173.

4. Buenger, *The Path to a Modern South*, xxv.

5. "The Triple Lynching," *Dallas Morning News*, September 9, 1892.

6. Jesse Dorsett, "Blacks in Reconstruction Texas, 1865–1877" (Ph.D. diss., Texas Christian University, 1981), 168–169; James M. Smallwood, Barry A. Crouch, and Larry Peacock, *Murder and Mayhem: The War of Reconstruction in Texas* (College Station: Texas A&M University Press, 2003), 50, 70; William L. Richter, "'The Revolver Rules the Day!': Colonel DeWitt C. Brown and the Freedmen's Bureau in Paris, Texas, 1867–1868," *The Southwestern Historical Quarterly* 93, no. 3 (January 1990): 332.

7. A. W. Neville, *The History of Lamar County (Texas)* (Paris: The North Texas Publishing Co, 1937), 201; Buenger, *Modern South*, 22–23; Dewey W. Grantham, *Southern Progressivism: The Reconciliation of Progress and Tradition* (Knoxville: The University of Tennessee Press, 1983), xvi.

8. "Savage Murder of a Negro," *Chicago Inter Ocean*, July, 21, 1890; Brundage, *Lynching in the New South*, 28.

9. Leon F. Litwack, *Trouble in Mind: Black Southerners in the Age of Jim Crow* (New York: Alfred A. Knopf, 1998), 15.

10. "Six Negroes Lynched: The Race Troubles in Texas Culminate in a Terrible Tragedy," *Langston City Herald*, September 24, 1892; "A Texas Lynching: Three Troublesome Negroes Swung to a Tree," *Columbus Daily Enquirer*, September 8, 1892.

11. "Backward Glances," *Paris Morning News*, July 29, 1937.

12. Jacquelyn Dowd Hall, *Revolt Against Chivalry: Jessie Daniel Ames and the Women's Campaign Against Lynching* (New York: Columbia University Press, 1979), 129–158; "Swung to a Limb: Three Negroes Taken out by a Mob and Hanged," September 6, 1892, Newspaper clipping attached to telegram, Vol. XXIX September 1–30, 1892, Letters Received, James Stephen Hogg Papers, Texas State Archives, Austin, TX, cited hereafter as "Swung to a Limb."

13. "Swung to a Limb"; "Recent Lynching," *Dallas Morning News*, September 14, 1892; "A Texas Lynching: Three Troublesome Negroes Swung to a Tree," *Columbus Daily Enquirer*, September 8, 1892.

14. Thomas Dixon Jr., *The Leopard's Spots: A Romance of the White Man's Burden-1865–1900* (New York: Doubleday, Page & Co., 1902; reprint, Ridgewood, NJ: The Gregg Press, Inc, 1967); James Kinney, "The Rhetoric of Racism: Thomas Dixon and the 'Damned Black Beast,'" *American Literary Realism, 1870–1910* 15, no. 2 (Autumn 1982): 147; Joel Williamson, *The Crucible of Race: Black-White Relations in the American South Since Emancipation* (New York: Oxford University Press, 1984), 180–89.

15. Ida Wells-Barnett, On Lynchings (Amherst, NY: Humanity Books, 2002), 77; P. L. James, *The Facts of the Case of the Horrible Murder of Little Myrtle Vance and its Fearful Expiation at Paris, Texas, February 1st, 1893, with Photographic Illustrations* (Paris, Texas: P.L. James, 1893), 3–5; Buenger, *Modern South*, 22.

16. "Texans Burn a Negro Murderer at the Stake," *New York Herald*, February 2, 1893.

17. "Myrtle Vance Murderer," *Dallas Morning News*, January 31, 1893.

18. "Myrtle Vance Murderer"; "Texans Burn a Negro Murderer at the Stake."

19. Waldrep, *The Many Faces of Judge Lynch*, 85–101; Wood, *Lynching and Spectacle*, 1–5, 10–12, 74; "Burned at the Stake: Awful Doom of a Negro Murderer in Texas," *Philadelphia Inquirer*, February 2, 1893; "Tortured Him to Death," *New Haven Register*, February 2, 1893; "The Texas Horror," *Chicago Daily Inter Ocean*, February 3, 1893.

20. James, *The Facts of the Case*, 66–67.

21. "The Paris Horror," *Dallas Morning News*, February 3, 1893.

22. J. M. Early, *An Eye for an Eye or The Fiend and the Fagot: An Unvarnished Account of the Burning of Henry Smith at Paris, Texas, February 1, 1893, and the Reason he was Tortured* (Paris, Texas: Marshall's Printing House, 1893), 5, 9, 41, 43; I. A. Newby, *Jim Crow's Defense: Anti-Negro Thought in America, 1900–1930* (Baton Rouge: Louisiana State University Press, 1965), 137–140.

23. See Texas State Historical Marker no. 277008191, J. M. Early House, Paris, Texas, dedicated 1967; Early, *An Eye for an Eye*, 71.

24. "The Paris Horror," *Dallas Morning News*, February 3, 1893.

25. Brundage, *Lynching in the New South*, 17–48; Stephen Kantrowitz, *Ben Tillman & the Reconstruction of White Supremacy* (Chapel Hill: University of North Carolina Press, 2000), 162–163; "Riddled With Bullets," *Kansas City Times*, August 24, 1895; Loren Schweninger, *Black Property Owners in the South: 1790–1915* (Urbana: University of Illinois Press, 1990), 228; "Texas Preacher Called Out And Shot To Death By The Mob," *Duluth News-Tribune*, December 26, 1901.

26. Alwyn Barr, *Reconstruction to Reform: Texas Politics, 1876–1906* (Austin: University of Texas Press, 1971), 108.

27. *Plessy v. Ferguson*, 163 U. S. 537 (1896).

28. Darlene Clark Hine, *Black Victory: The Rise and Fall of the White Primary in Texas* (Columbia: University of Missouri Press, 1979), 69–83; Jerry C. Drake, "'Something between Slavery and Freedom': The Evolution of Jim Crow in Texas, A Cultural History" (Master's thesis, Texas State University, 2003), 94–118; Leonard Brewster Murphy, "A History of Negro Segregation Practices in Texas, 1865–1958" (Ph.D. diss., Southern Methodist University, 1950), 91–97; Buenger, *Modern South*, 89.

29. Geospatial and Statistical Data Center, "Texas: Total Value of all Crops, 1910–1930," University of Virginia Library, http://mapserver.lib.virginia. edu/php/newlong3.php (accessed March 8, 2011); Buenger, *Modern South*, 149, 61, 138.

30. US Bureau of the Census, "Area and Population of Counties: 1890 to 1930," (http://www2. census.gov/prod2/decennial/documents/03815512v1ch10.pdf, accessed March 8, 2011), 1060; Buenger, *Modern South*, 149, 61, 138.

31. Kidada E.Williams, "Resolving the Paradox of Our Lynching Fixation: Reconsidering Racialized Violence in the American South after Slavery," in *Lynching Reconsidered: New Perspectives in the Study of Mob Violence*, ed. William D. Carrigan (New York: Routledge Press, 2008), 97–116.

32. W. E. B. DuBois, "Editorial," *The Crisis: A Record of the Darker Races* 14, no. 2 (June 1917): 61; W. Allison Sweeney, *History of the American Negro in the Great World War* (New York: G. G. Sapp, 1919; reprint, New York: Negro Universities Press, 1969): 77; Alain Locke, ed., *The New Negro: An Interpretation* (New York: Albert and Charles Boni, 1925): ix.

33. Lawrence Olsen, "Black Texans in the 'Red Summer' of 1919: The Longview Race Riot," (Master's thesis, Southwest Texas State University, 1974), 2. William M. Tuttle, Jr., Violence in a 'Heathen' Land: The Longview Race Riot of 1919," *Phylon* 33, no. 4 (4th Qtr. 1972): 324–33.

34. Buenger, *Modern South*, 147, 169; Steven A. Reich, "Soldiers of Democracy: Black Texans and the Fight for Citizenship, 1917–1921," *The Journal of American History* 82, no. 4 (March 1996): 1499; E. M. Beck and Stewart E. Tolnay, "Black Flight: Lethal Violence and the Great Migration, 1900–1930," *Social Science History* 14, no. 3 (Autumn 1990): 347–370.

35. "Negroes Kill Two Whites in Lamar County," *Fort Worth Star-Telegram*, July 3, 1920.

36. "Two Negroes Taken from Jail at Paris, Texas, and Lynched," *Tulsa World*, July 7, 1920; "Family Driven from South by Mob," *The Chicago Defender*, September 4, 1920; "Arthur Lynchings in Paris were 87 Years Ago," *Paris News*, July 6, 2007.

37. "Try to Prevent Texas Race Clash," *Greensboro (NC) Daily Record*, July 7, 1920; "Running North: A Family History," *Chicago Tribune*, February 12, 1998; "Quiet Restored after Lynching of Negroes," *Duluth News-Tribune*, July 9, 1920.

38. Neil R. McMillen, *Dark Journey: Black Mississippians in the Age of Jim Crow* (Urbana: University of Illinois Press, 1990), 272; US Bureau of the Census, "Composition and Characteristics of the Population, for Counties: 1920," (http://www2.census.gov/prod2/decennial/documents/41084484v3ch08.pdf, accessed October 20, 2010), 1003; US Bureau of the Census, "Population by Age, Color, Nativity, and Sex, for Counties: 1930," (http://www2.census.gov/prod2/decennial/documents/10612982v3p2ch09.pdf, accessed October 20, 2010), 961; "Arthur Lynchings in Paris were 87 Years Ago," *Paris News*, July 7, 2007; "Preacher Protests: White Member of Clergy Denounces Lynchers in Paris: Thousands of Race People Leaving Blood Soaked District," *Chicago Defender*, July 24, 1920.

39. "Preacher Protests: White Member of Clergy Denounces Lynchers in Paris: Thousands of Race People Leaving Blood Soaked District," *Chicago Defender*, July 24, 1920; Brundage, *Lynching in the New South*, 46; Herbert Lynn Hollis, *Paris Fire of 1916* (Wolfe City, TX: Henington Publishing Co., 1982); McMillen, *Dark Journey*, 272–73; Skipper Steely, "Paris, Texas: Living with a Bloody Past—The Lynchings," (unpublished manuscript, Paris Genealogical Society), 179.

40. "Made Talk to the Paris Negroes," *Paris Morning News*, July 13, 1920; Steely, "Paris, Texas: Living with a Bloody Past," 175.

41. "Angry Mob Burns Two at Stake in Paris," *Chicago Defender*, July 10, 1920; James W. Johnson, "Christian America is There any Justice Within your Power?," *Wichita (KS) Negro Star*, July 16, 1920.

42. Frances Dressman, "Visions for Houston: Booster Literature, 1886–1926," *The Houston Review* 9, no. 3 (1987): 137, 139.

43. "Rev. R. P. Shuler Made Statement about Lynching," *Paris Morning News*, July 10, 1920.

44. "Rev. R. P. Shuler Made Statement about Lynching."

45. "Declare Another Lynching Here is to be Impossible," *Paris Morning News*, July 10, 1920; Steely, "Paris, Texas: Living with a Bloody Past," 176, 180.

46. Typed interview given to Skipper Steely by Randy Rader, miscellaneous notes section, Steely Collection, Lamar County Genealogical Society, Paris, Texas.

47. Steely, "Paris, Texas: Living with a Bloody Past," 181–82.

48. "Special Grand Jury to Investigate Lynching," *Paris Morning News*, July 10, 1920; "Declare Another Lynching here is to be Impossible," *Paris Morning News*, July 10, 1920.

49. "Savage Murder of a Negro," *Chicago Inter Ocean*, July 21, 1890; Wood, *Lynching and Spectacle*, 2.

50. Walter White, *Rope and Faggot: A Biography of Judge Lynch* (New York: Alfred A. Knopf, 1929), 172–95.

51. US Bureau of the Census, "Composition and Characteristics of the Population, for Counties: 1910," (http://www2.census.gov/prod2/decennial/documents/36894832v3ch6.pdf, accessed October 20, 2010), 830; Geospatial and Statistical Data Center, "Census Data over Time, total Value of all Crops," University of Virginia Library; http://mapserver.lib.virginia.edu/php/newlong3.php (accessed March 8, 2011).

2

An "Exciting Occurrence"

The Lynching

Patricia Bernstein

The story of the Waco Horror begins with the discovery of a body. Just about sundown on the evening of Monday, May 8, 1916, near the town of Robinson,[1] eight miles south of Waco, twenty-one-year-old Ruby Fryer and her brother, fourteen-year-old George Fryer Jr., returned home from chopping cotton on the family's two hundred-acre farm.[2] In the heavy heat and quiet of the late afternoon, they noticed that their mother, Lucy Fryer, was not in the house as usual. Just as George was going out to look for her, Ruby peered through the window and saw Lucy lying in a pool of blood in the doorway of the seed house, about thirty steps away.[3]

A neighbor, Cris Simon, had been away from home all day and had just come back through the big gate at the main road when he heard Ruby and George screaming and crying over their mother's body. It was probably Simon who ran for George Fryer Sr., who had been working in a different part of the field from the children, about a mile from the house. The *Waco Times Herald* reported that when George Fryer Sr. learned that his wife was dead, he "was overcome."[4]

According to Lucy Fryer's granddaughter, Lucy Wollitz Kirkland, who still lives in Robinson, there was a quiet romance connected to the history of George and Lucy Fryer—a story of suffering, separation, and exile for the sake of true love, which may have made George Fryer's grief at the loss of his wife all the more terrible. George and Lucy Fryer grew up in central England. George was said to have been a stable boy on a large estate while Lucy was the daughter of the upper-class family who employed him. Lucy's parents did not want the young couple to marry, so George crossed the ocean,

Originally published in *The First Waco Horror: The Lynching of Jesse Washington and the Rise of the NAACP* (College Station: Texas A&M University Press, 2005), 87–118, 218–23. Reprinted with permission of the author and Texas A&M University Press.

entering the United States at Galveston in 1882. He settled in Cottonwood, Texas, and worked for four years to earn enough money to send for Lucy.[5]

There is some evidence that this often-told tale of two lovers divided by class may not be strictly accurate. According to United Kingdom birth records, a Lucy Davis was born on July 1, 1860, the same birth date recorded for Lucy Davis Fryer in Fryer family records and on her death certificate. This Lucy Davis was born in Callaughton Wenlock, County of Salop (now part of Shropshire), the daughter of Henry Davis and Elizabeth Pope Davis. But Henry Davis, Lucy's father, is identified in the official birth record not as a lord, merchant, or landowner, but as an "agricultural labourer."

Whatever the true story of their births and original circumstances, George Fryer and Lucy Davis did immigrate to the United States from England and were married in McLennan County on April 30, 1890.[6] At the time of their marriage, Lucy was twenty-seven and George was within a couple of weeks of his thirtieth birthday.

The couple settled in the Lorena area in the southern part of McLennan County. Their first child, Ruby, was born in 1894. In 1898, they had another little girl named Beatrice Pearl, who died in 1907 at the age of nine and was buried in the Lorena cemetery.[7] George Jr. was born in 1901.

At the time of Lucy's murder, the Fryers had been living in Robinson for six to eight years and were "among the most highly esteemed and respected residents of the Robinson community," according to the newspapers.[8] The couple had just celebrated their twenty-sixth wedding anniversary. Lucy was fifty-three. But all that was past now.

Lucy Fryer lay in the doorway of the seed house "almost brained and criminally assaulted."[9] Her skull had been bashed in at several points and her clothing was disheveled. Dr. J. H. Maynard examined her and reported at the trial that "a quantity of brain had escaped from the cranial vault" and at least two of the six wounds on her head, made with a heavy, blunt instrument, could have killed her.[10]

Deputy Sheriffs Lee Jenkins and Barney Goldberg arrived on the scene first and were followed soon after by Sheriff Samuel S. Fleming, Constable Leslie Stegall, and Deputy Phil Hobbs. Both Stegall and Jenkins were highly regarded peace officers. Jenkins began his career in law enforcement as a Texas Ranger in 1880 at the age of eighteen and was elected constable in 1883. Later he served as deputy sheriff, detective, and chief of police. When he died in 1929, he was described as "the best criminal detective the Lone Star state has known."[11]

About fourteen years younger than Jenkins, Stegall also began his career as a peace officer as a very young man when he became a deputy sheriff in 1897. He served Waco as constable from 1912 to 1922, and then was elected McLennan County sheriff for the next ten years. Stegall, like Jenkins, was described by admirers as "a detective type officer [who] used modern methods of detection in the days when strong arm methods were prevalent."[12] Stegall and Jenkins have important roles to play in this story. Together they helped to turn the tide of Waco's ugly history.

At this point in their illustrious careers, however, both men were subordinate to friendly, accommodating Sheriff Fleming. Although Fleming got most of the credit for solving the murder of Lucy Fryer, it was Lee Jenkins, according to at least one newspaper report, who immediately found evidence that pointed to a suspect. The "evidence" may simply have been the fact that Cris Simon had that morning seen a black farm laborer, seventeen-year-old Jesse Washington, planting cotton about 250 yards from the Fryer house—closer to the house than either Mr. Fryer or the children and close enough to know that after the noon meal no one else was around.[13] As Simon arrived home that evening, he saw Jesse Washington coming in from the field and going to the mule lot near the seed house just a few minutes before the children cried out.

Jesse Washington, with his mother and father, Henry and Martha, and at least one brother, William, possibly about sixteen, had been living and working on the Fryer farm for only five months or so, since the beginning of the year.[14] According to Elisabeth Freeman's account of the lynching, there were also some younger children in the family.[15] Jesse Washington was a large, strong young man, but was illiterate and possibly retarded. When Freeman went to Waco to investigate the lynching for the NAACP, one of Washington's teachers told her that no one had ever been able to teach Jesse to read or write.[16]

One lifelong resident of Robinson, Thomas Hague, claimed in an interview that he was told by his father, Hugh Hague, who was a close friend of George Fryer Sr., that Jesse Washington was not retarded, but "a little bit thickheaded" and "just plain ol' lazy." The elder Hague tried to get Jesse Washington to help him with some carpentry work, but the task seemed to require more effort than Washington wanted to put out.[17] (Or perhaps carpentry was simply beyond Jesse's abilities.)

During this period, there were other black men who allegedly committed crimes and were lynched who fit the same pattern as Jesse Washington: "illiterate and feeble-minded," as lynching victims were often characterized in the literature of the Association of Southern Women for the Prevention of Lynching.[18] Henry Smith, the victim of vicious, prolonged public torture and burning in 1893 in Paris, Texas, was "out of his head for weeks" at a time, suffered from attacks of delirium tremens, and should have been in an asylum, according to a local black minister.[19] George Hughes, the victim of the burning of the courthouse in Sherman, Texas, in 1930, was also said to have been illiterate and feeble-minded.[20] Lynch mobs, which were coagulations of cowards and bullies, naturally tended to focus on the most defenseless and friendless black men they could find.

One of the best indications that Jesse Washington was "absolutely deficient," as Elisabeth Freeman puts it in her report, is not, according to her reasoning, the fact that "he attacked an old woman of 53 when this young girl [Ruby] was in the family." [21] Enough is known about rape now to know that the impulse is not activated by the victim's sexual appeal. The more revealing detail is, rather, the fact that, after Jesse Washington supposedly raped and killed Lucy Fryer, he went placidly back to planting cotton as if nothing had happened and made no effort to escape or to cover up his crime other than hiding the hammer that was later said to have been used in the attack. Freeman reports that when Jesse Washington was arrested, he was frightened at first, but then "curled up in the automobile and went fast to sleep."[22]

Freeman also reports a rumor she was unable to verify, which, if true, would indicate that, in the context of the times, Jesse Washington was a hothead with very poor judgment. Freeman was told by one of Waco's leading black men that the Saturday night before the murder, Washington went to Rosenthal, another small town south of Robinson, and, while there, accidentally stepped on the toes of a white man. "The white man smashed him," writes Freeman in her report to the NAACP. Washington fought back until finally the white man said, "If you get in my way again, I will blow your damned head off." On his way home, Washington supposedly drove into the man's yard and said, "Now blow my head off." [23]

Whatever the intelligence or temperament of the alleged assailant, as soon as word of the murder of Lucy Fryer got out, a general hue and cry arose in the Robinson neighborhood. The male residents, "thoroughly aroused and greatly incensed over the terrible crime," reports the *Times Herald*, organized to try to help the officers find the culprit.[24]

From the first, the *Herald* seasoned news stories about the murder with incendiary language designed to make the tale more dramatic. Helpful asides include the following: "That Mrs. Fryar [*sic*] had made desperate resistance against the brute who assaulted her and then completed his fiendish crime by killing her, was unmistakable" and, "That she was given no chance for her life is apparent, and the lustful brute waited until he was absolutely sure no help was in sight before he attacked his helpless victim."[25]

Fortunately for Jesse Washington, the officers found him before the men of Robinson did. He was sitting in his yard, unconcernedly whittling a piece of wood.[26] Lee Jenkins later testified that he found blood on Jesse Washington's clothes, undershirt, and pants.[27] Washington claimed the blood had come from a nosebleed, but Jenkins arrested him on the spot. By then it was about nine o'clock in the evening, only three hours after the body was found.[28] Jesse's brother William, and later his parents and a woman named "Moore" who lived with them, were all arrested along with Jesse. Officers stated that they had arrested family members not because anyone other than Jesse had participated in the crime, but so that "no avenue of obtaining information may be lost by the officers."[29] The real reason was probably to apply more pressure on Jesse to confess.

Jesse was taken to Waco, where he was questioned by both Lee Jenkins and County Attorney John B. McNamara. At first, he "denied, stoutly" that he had had anything to do with the rape and murder of Lucy Fryer.[30] Later he told McNamara that he had indeed beaten Lucy Fryer with a "piece of iron"; finally, he admitted that he had killed her with a blacksmith's hammer.

The most incriminating element in Washington's confession, according to newspaper reports, was that he told his questioners exactly where he had hidden the hammer. While Washington was being interrogated, a group of officers was turning the Fryer farm upside down trying to locate the murder weapon—they even replowed ground in the area where Washington had been working—but they failed to find what they sought.[31]

The hammer was finally discovered right where Washington said it would be, at the end of the rows where he had been plowing, in some high brush and weeds near a hackberry tree along the main Robinsonville road. According to testimony at Washington's trial, it was covered with blood and bits of cottonseed lint.[32]

Sheriff Fleming knew, of course, that the citizens of Robinson and the vicinity were on the prowl and would soon hear that Jesse Washington had been arrested. Fleming made arrangements to transfer him, the very night he was arrested, to the jail in Hillsboro, some thirty-five miles north of Waco. Sometime on Tuesday, the Waco newspapers were informed that Jesse Washington had confessed to the crime to Sheriff Fleming on Tuesday morning in the Hillsboro jail.

Fleming could see that Hillsboro was not far enough away, so he had Jesse moved again, this time to the Dallas County jail, a further sixty-five miles from Waco. In Dallas, Washington repeated his confession before witnesses. The confession was officially recorded and read back to him. Washington signed with an X.[33]

In the meantime, there were ominous developments in McLennan County. On his way out of town to serve some papers Tuesday night, Sheriff Fleming encountered "a determined body of citizens from Robinson, Rosenthal and other towns in the southern part of the county" on their way into Waco to get Jesse Washington.[34] Another lawman might have taken a different approach to this challenge to his authority, but Fleming's method of dealing with the crisis was to get out of his car, gather the men around him, and talk to them earnestly in the middle of the road. He pleaded his case to about five hundred angry citizens, reminding them that he had solved the crime, arrested the culprit, obtained a confession in less than twenty-four hours, and was now obligated by his oath of office to protect the man in his custody. He told the men that Jesse Washington was out of their reach in Dallas, but encouraged them to come into Waco and search the jail if they did not believe him. A long line of "grim-visaged farmers" took Fleming up on his offer, caravanning into town in a line of "buggies, autos and men on horseback," after the leader of the group declared, as reported in the *Times Herald*, "When we left home tonight our wives, daughters and sisters kissed us good bye and told us to do our duty, and we're trying to do it as citizens."[35]

The newspaper coverage, however, leaves no doubt of the general climate of sympathy for the would-be lynchers. "It was admitted by the officers last night," reports the *Waco Morning News*, "that if there ever was a justification for the formation of a mob, the Robinson crime was one of them." The *News* even compares the mob to their glorious forebears who had fought the Redcoats for freedom from Great Britain: "Resembling the forefathers who dared anything for their country's sake, the determined band of farmers and neighbors last night declared to the sheriff that they didn't want trouble, but that their blood would not stand for a fiendish brute to trample the chastity and sacredness of life and their women folk."[36]

What ensued, however, was hardly the "shot heard 'round the world"; it more closely resembled a farcical episode from one of the popular traveling vaudeville shows that occasionally passed through Waco. Sheriff Fleming led the delegation of farmers into town and encouraged the entire group to search the jail—which they proceeded to do most thoroughly, climbing on the steam radiators to be sure no one was hiding on top of the cells, exploring the section where demented prisoners were kept, and even clambering up into the belfry.

When they were done, Fleming helpfully suggested that they might want to search the Hillsboro jail and even offered to "pay their way" to Hillsboro. But by now, it was very late, and the men, exhausted from their exertions in the name of good citizenship, decided they had had enough excitement for one night. The five hundred outraged citizens went home.[37]

In the midst of all this commotion, Lucy Fryer's burial went almost unnoticed—a couple of paragraphs at the end of stories that feature lengthy descriptions of Washington's confession, the Robinson mob, the confrontation between Fleming and the mob on a rural highway, and the search of the jail. There was a simple ceremony at the Fryers' home, and Lucy was buried in the Lorena cemetery near a daughter who had died in childhood.[38] One of the men who officiated at Lucy's funeral had earlier said that there was "no better woman living" than Lucy Fryer, but Lucy's tale was not told in the Waco papers.[39] One of the sad consequences of the chaos and turbulence that surrounded the Waco Horror was that the story of Lucy Fryer's life was lost. She was remembered only as the inert, "almost brained" victim of a "negro brute."

Waco's newspapers then proceeded—all three of them—to publish Jesse Washington's confession in full. Even bowdlerized of the worst of the original language, the confession is disturbing and a fine exemplar of what Jacquelyn Dowd Hall calls the "acceptable folk pornography" of newspaper descriptions of the alleged crimes of "black fiends" during this period.[40] The modern reader may find the confession disturbing in other ways, as well. Portions in brackets show the words in the original confession that were changed or eliminated in the newspapers to make the piece fit for public consumption. The italicized words are the substitutions for the original language:

> On yesterday May 8th, 1916, I was planting cotton for Mr. Fryar near Robinsonville close to Waco, Texas, and about 3:30 o'clock p.m.[41] I went up to Mr. Fryar's barn to get some more cotton seed. I called Mrs. Fryar from the house to get some cotton seed, and she came to the barn and unfastened the door and scooped up the cotton seed. I was holding the sack while she was putting the seed in the sack, and after she had finished, she was fussing with me about whipping the mules, and while she was standing inside of the door of the barn, and still talking to me, I hit her on the side of the head with a hammer that I had in my hand. I had taken this hammer from Mr. Fryar's home to the field that morning, and brought it back and put it in the barn at dinner. I had picked up this hammer and had it in my hand when I called Mrs. Fryar from the house, and had the hammer in my right hand all the time I was holding the sack.
>
> When I hit Mrs. Fryar on the side of the head with the hammer she fell over, and then I *assaulted her* [pulled up her clothes and crawled on her and screwed her. By screwing her I mean that I stuck my male organ into her female organ, and while I was going (doing?) this she was trying to push me off. When I got through screwing her I got off of her and]. I then[42] picked up the hammer from where I had laid it down, and hit her twice[43] more with the hammer on top of her head. I saw the blood coming through her bonnet.
>
> I then picked up the sack of cotton seed and carried it and the hammer to the field, where I had left the team. I left the sack of cotton seed near the planter and went about forty steps south of the planter and the mules, and put the hammer that I killed Mrs. Fryar with in some woods under some hackberry brush.
>
> I knew when I went to the barn for the cotton seed that there wasn't anybody at the house except Mrs. Fryar, and when I called her from the

> house to the barn, I had already made up my mind to knock her in the head with the hammer and then *assault* [screw] her.
>
> I had been working for Mr. Fryar about five months, and first made up my mind to *assault* [screw] Mrs. Fryar yesterday morning and took the hammer from the buggy shed to the field with me, and brought it back and put it in the barn at dinner time, so that I could use it to knock Mrs. Fryar in the head when I came back for seed during the afternoon.
>
> I planted cotton the rest of the afternoon, then put up the team and went home *to* [at] my daddy's house where I was arrested. There wasn't anybody else who had anything to do with the killing or *assaulting* [raping] of Mrs. Fryar except myself.
>
> Signed Jess Washington X, his mark [Signed by arrested party][44]

The first thing one notices about this ugly tale of premeditated violence blended with common daily routine—besides its being published in full in three newspapers where it would certainly be read by every literate potential juror in McLennan County—is the strange combination of the grossest vernacular with rather stilted speech that probably does not represent the way Jesse Washington really talked. But Jesse Washington could not read the confession he was told to sign.

Oddly, while the whole city of Waco had read Jesse's confession and knew that he was supposed to have "criminally assaulted" Lucy Fryer, there was no testimony about the rape at the trial. Even Dr. Maynard, who testified about the wounds to Lucy's skull, was not asked about the rape, which makes one wonder if there was any solid evidence, other than Washington's confession (which was probably coerced), that Lucy was raped at all. But, in the context of the times, it was the rape story more than the murder that inflamed the populace and served as a pretext for the lynching. Elisabeth Freeman initially accepted the story of the rape,[45] but after investigating the Washington lynching exhaustively, came to believe that Lucy Fryer had not been raped.[46]

Why did Jesse Washington suddenly attack Lucy Fryer on May 8, 1916? Apparently, until that day Washington had never given any member of the Fryer family any reason to distrust him. Lucy did not seem to fear Jesse's temper. She did not hesitate to berate him for whipping the mules; she did not anticipate that he might react violently. Maybe Jesse killed Lucy simply on an impulse because he was angry that she had scolded him. Maybe no rape was ever involved.

There is also, of course, the possibility that the attack appeared to be unanticipated and inexplicable, and that Jesse Washington plowed all afternoon after Lucy Fryer's murder because he was, in fact, innocent and knew nothing of what had happened. What if the blood on his clothes really did come from a nosebleed, as he claimed? What if Fleming's men found the hammer or placed it in the brush and *then* forced Jesse to "tell" where he had put it? What if Jesse only "confessed" because, as he said when asked by his defense attorneys if he was concerned about the possibility of a mob coming after him, "They promised they would not if I would tell them about it."[47] In other words, Washington claimed that the officers of the law who questioned him promised that if he "confessed," they would protect him from being lynched.

Nona Baker, the great-niece of Sank Majors, a Waco lynching victim 11 years earlier, has suggested that Jesse Washington might have been brutally interrogated and beaten in three different jails—in Waco, where he was initially taken along with his whole family; in Hillsboro, where he confessed; and in Dallas, where he "signed" a confession he couldn't read.[48] Defense attorney Joe Taylor Jr. later told Elisabeth Freeman that "the boy had not had the third degree."[49] But there may have been no need to beat Jesse Washington into confessing; he was no match for his interrogators.

There is also an odd story that has lingered for more than eighty years in the little town of Robinson. According to this tale, George Fryer killed his wife or hired Jesse Washington to do it.[50] The origin of this rumor was most likely an article that appeared in the *Chicago Defender* on June 10, 1916, declaring that "the truth has come to light that this woman's husband is the murderer," but that "not one word has been sent to the daily papers; not one word has gone out to the Associated Press." The article does not detail how the truth supposedly "came to light" or what this new "truth" is exactly, but the author cries out against Waco for lynching an innocent and demands to know if the true perpetrator of the murder will now be tried and hanged.[51]

The *Chicago Defender* story drifted south to Waco and was reprinted locally on June 17, 1916, by twenty-seven-year-old A. T. Smith, managing editor of the *Paul Quinn Weekly*, the newspaper of Paul Quinn College, one of Waco's two colleges for black students.[52] After the story was published in the *Paul Quinn Weekly*, Smith was indicted for criminal libel. Although the NAACP was notified about the Smith case, the organization, which picked its causes with care from among the great swamp of injustices committed against blacks across the South, did not involve itself in Smith's problems, because, as NAACP secretary Royal Freeman Nash, put it, "He [Smith] must have known it was untrue, at least the charge that Mr. Fryar had been arrested."[53]

Elisabeth Freeman, while in Waco, heard a rumor that George Fryer had confessed to the crime, had gone insane, and had been confined in a local hospital. She visited the hospital and did not find Fryer, but later did meet and speak with him: "He was very quiet and reserved," she reports, "and said little or nothing. He did not talk about his troubles—and a man who does not talk about his troubles is not likely to talk about his crimes."[54] Freeman eventually concluded that Jesse Washington was probably guilty of murdering Lucy Fryer. She was convinced primarily by the discovery of the hammer precisely where he had allegedly left it and the absence of hard evidence pointing to anyone else.[55]

Even those who repeat the tale that George Fryer might have murdered his wife have no knowledge of any friction between husband and wife or of any other motive for murder. Martha Kettler, a lifelong resident of Robinson who was six when Lucy Fryer was killed, characterized Lucy Fryer as "just a normal nice little lady." Kettler described George Fryer, who never married again and lived in Robinson until his death in 1938, as "average, friendly, neighborly."[56]

The violent death of Lucy Fryer and the maelstrom of violence that destroyed Jesse Washington provided rich soil for the sprouting of rumors and suppositions. The darkest crimes never seem to be forgotten. They blight the locale where they occur. Buildings may be torn down and replaced, fields replanted, thousands of sweet, ordinary days may pass after the one day of monumental evil, but the shadow, however faded, lingers.

The methods used by the justice system of the time also encourage endless speculation about Washington's guilt or innocence. In that poisoned climate, it would have been up to Jesse Washington to prove he was innocent, and Jesse had only the dimmest understanding of what was going on. For the purposes of this story, however, it makes little difference in the end whether Jesse Washington was innocent or guilty. Nothing he could have done would have justified what happened to him.

On Thursday morning, May 11, the grand jury convened in special session and within thirty minutes indicted Jesse Washington for the murder of Lucy Fryer. A special venire of fifty men was summoned for possible service as jurors in Jesse's trial. "It is not expected," remarked the *Times Herald*, "that the trial of the negro, who is charged with the heinous crime, will occupy much time."[57]

The whole idea was to rush through the trial and the execution as speedily as the arrest and confession, in order to convince the public that the evildoer would be punished almost as fast by legal means as by lynching—and, therefore, there was no need for the upheaval and disorder of a lynching. Jesse Washington was to be put on trial for his life on Monday morning, May 15, 1916, one week to the day after the murder of Lucy Fryer. He would be tried in the 54th District Court, presided over by fifty-eight-year-old District Judge Richard Irby Munroe.

A wiry little man, Munroe was a unique character well known in Waco for his dry, salty wit. He grew up in Florida, one of a family of twenty-one brothers and sisters. The Florida Munroes must have been famous hell-raisers. Munroe was fond of telling a story that when he first arrived at Emory College in Atlanta, one of his professors peered at him over the top of his glasses and asked him, "Are you one of the Florida Munroes?" Munroe admitted that he was, and the professor replied, "Then God help your soul."

Munroe came to live in Waco in 1881, served as city attorney, wrote an early Waco city charter, and, while in private practice, appeared before the US Supreme Court in a complex probate case. By 1916, he had already served on the bench of the 54th District Court for eight years. He would serve in the same court for fifteen more years, until his retirement in 1931.

Munroe spoke his mind in and out of court and was fond of leavening his remarks with folksy maxims that must have seemed endearing when he was eulogized as an exemplar of days-of-yore local color in his 1942 obituary. He had a habit of referring to friends and foes alike, in fun, as "horse thieves" and once described an acquaintance as "a cross between a dried apple and a cracklin."[58] On one occasion, a lawyer practicing in Munroe's court was disgusted with the bail set for his client and remarked sarcastically, "Why don't you set it at a million dollars?" Munroe did. On another occasion Munroe set bail for a poor black defendant at one penny.[59]

When Elisabeth Freeman inquired about Judge Munroe in Waco in 1916, she heard less appealing descriptions. "The judge is a rotter . . . a reprobate . . . His moral character is unspeakable," she reported. "He has been a gambler and drunkard and of low repute—but a splendid criminal lawyer, though representing only the liquor interests and their victims—respectable people would not have him as their lawyer."[60]

Was Munroe an amusing but honest judge, or the disreputable creature of those who had put him in office? He speaks for himself later in this story and may be judged on that basis.

Six very young and inexperienced lawyers were appointed to represent Washington: Joe Taylor Jr., known to all as "Little Joe" because of his small size, was the leader of the group. Taylor was twenty-seven and had been practicing law for about six years. He was the son of one of Waco's most prominent attorneys, Joe Taylor Sr. His mother, Sally Sears Taylor, was the daughter of early Waco pioneers and for many years one of Waco's most-admired social luminaries. In 1873, when Sally Sears was a dazzling eighteen-year-old beauty, she had hosted the inaugural ball on the arm of the newly installed governor, Richard Coke.[61]

The other young attorneys appointed as defense counsel were Frank Fitzpatrick, C. H. Machen, Kyle Vick, Percy Wilie, and Westwood Bowden Hays Jr. Fitzpatrick was twenty-five and had been practicing law for all of two years. He had just recently been appointed secretary of the county Democratic Executive Committee,[62] and was described as "one of the very prominent among the younger members of the bar here" in Waco newspaper articles that appeared in June 1916,[63] when he announced that he was running for "flotorial" representative to the Texas Legislature representing McLennan, Falls, and Limestone counties.

Chester Machen was about thirty at the time of the Washington trial.[64] Kyle Vick was twenty-four, had barely received his law license, and did not even open an office in Waco until the following year.[65] Hays was only about twenty-three—another socially prominent young attorney, son of the founder of an important fire insurance business in Waco and grandson of a pioneer settler of Waco.[66] Only five years later, Hays was implicated in one of the first violent acts by the Ku Klux Klan in Waco, the abduction and tarring and feathering of a local man, allegedly for selling dope to Baylor University students.[67] Many of Waco's most prominent citizens, including Kyle Vick, offered to provide bail for Hays and the other culprits.[68]

The youthful defense attorneys were allowed a grand total of two days to prepare for a capital murder trial.[69] Jesse Washington was not to be returned to Waco until Sunday night; there is no record that any of the defense attorneys went to Dallas to talk with him before the trial.

The young attorneys were probably appointed to the case because they were viewed as manageable fellows who would take their elders' advice and not make too much of a fuss about defending Jesse Washington. Some of Waco's leaders apparently had not forgotten that the Sank Majors lynching had been triggered because defense attorney George Barcus convinced the judge that the jury had not been charged properly, thus forcing the judge to grant Majors a new trial.

Times had changed, according to one newspaper report. Defense attorneys had learned to be less finicky about constitutional rights and suchlike: "There has been a complete change in the manner of handling cases of this kind, by common consent in Texas, and after parties charged with criminal assault get a fair hearing in the trial court and are found guilty, there being no reasonable doubt of guilt, then attorneys withhold further effort, no technical points are raised or delays occasioned and executions take place quickly. This has had the effect of stopping many of the lawless demonstrations which formerly characterized the commission of the diabolical crime of which Washington stands accused and to which he has confessed."[70]

One bystander commented before the trial, "I hope he [Washington] waives his thirty days [before hanging] and allows the officers to hang him at once; otherwise I fear trouble."[71] In other words, Jesse Washington himself was to prevent his own prospective lynching by voluntarily giving up whatever bit of life was left to him. The practice of lynching was to be ended by hustling defendants through fast-paced trials and straight on to eternity in record time—in effect, converting illegal lynchings into legal ones.

Sheriff Fleming did take one more precaution—or seize one more opportunity to be seen doing his duty. On Saturday morning, May 13, he went to Robinson to address farmers from the area again, this time at Joe Swayne's store. Fleming and other local leaders pointed out to the assembled crowd, one more time, that the criminal had been identified, apprehended, and charged as quickly as was humanly possible, and that the trial would take place immediately. They asked their audience to let the law take its course.

Fleming was received respectfully. Members of the Robinson community urged "calmness and forbearance" on their fellow citizens. At that point the situation appeared to be under control.[72]

But a vapor of unrest and anxiety continued to hang in the air. Some citizens felt that Jesse should have been granted a change of venue to avoid trouble. Despite all the assurances of the men of Robinson, "the feeling of uneasiness was found pretty general," says the *Waco Morning News*.[73]

In a brief paragraph buried in the lower left-hand corner of the editorial page on Friday, May 12, the *Waco Times Herald* makes its own plea to the citizens of McLennan County—which suggests that the newspaper's editors were not convinced, despite Fleming's efforts, that all was well and that the danger of mob action had been averted: "The *Times Herald* begs the citizenship of McLennan County to at this time put their confidence in the judicial tribunals of their own creation. Judge Lynch has no proper place in a community where courts are properly organized and conducted. Let the law be supreme. Let the law take its course."[74]

On Saturday, May 13, it seemed that McLennan County just might squeak by without another "lawless demonstration." But events on Sunday, May 14, should have set off warning bells for those who hoped to maintain order. All day Sunday and into early Monday morning, people poured into Waco from the outlying areas. "The railroad trains," says the *Waco Morning News*, "brought in a good many people from practically every town within twenty-five miles of Waco."[75] At that point Fleming should have seen that, with so many curiosity seekers thronging the city and anticipating excitement, the situation was likely to get out of hand. On Sunday, Fleming or Mayor Dollins or Chief of Police Guy McNamara, brother of County Attorney John McNamara, should have considered bringing in reinforcements to help local officers or asking Judge Munroe to postpone the trial and possibly to consider a change of venue.

But Fleming did nothing and, apparently, no other city leader suggested that he should. Instead, late Sunday night Jesse Washington was brought back to Waco from Dallas and secreted in Judge Munroe's little office behind the courtroom. "Attorneys for the defense," says the *Waco Morning News*, "remained with Washington until nearly midnight Sunday, hearing his gruesome tale, looking for some mitigating circumstances. They declared they found none. One declared that he told the negro that there was no possibility of his life being saved, and it was suggested that he had better spend the night in prayer. The negro seemed unmoved, they declared."[76]

Such was Jesse Washington's defense—a suggestion that he should pray. This late-night interview appears to have been the first time that any of the six rookie lawyers saw or spoke with their client.

The crowd that surrounded the county jail the next morning hoping to get a glimpse of Washington "was the largest ever seen," said the *News*.[77] The *Waco Times Herald* estimated that as many as twenty-five hundred people crowded into Judge Munroe's courtroom,[78] "churning around the chamber for an hour, flooding the balconies and standing two persons high wherever a railing or a bench permitted."[79]

There were hundreds more milling around inside and outside of the courthouse, including a number of black people who, reported the *Morning News*, were "quiet and seemingly not much excited."[80] It seems more likely that they were terrified and trying to attract as little attention as possible. Sure enough, in local photographer Fred Gildersleeve's best-known photograph of the lynching, there are a few black faces on the fringes of the crowd. Their expressions are unreadable.

The reporters did not interview any of the black spectators, so it is impossible to know if members of the Washington family were among them. Freeman comments in her report that "the family has been arrested and taken away from Robinson."[81] This is the last mention found in the record of Washington's relatives.

The courthouse was so packed with people that a farmer named Brown fainted in the crush in the corridor on the first floor and had to be taken outside. The solemnity of the crowd might be gauged by the remark of a young white girl, about eighteen, who had managed to force her way up to the third floor but could not get inside the courtroom: "I would just give anything to see that negro," she declared.[82]

A path had to be cleared for the judge to get into his own courtroom. The court reporter, Warren Hunt, barely found a place to sit, and the defense counsel and the county attorney, John McNamara, who was prosecuting the case, abandoned all thought of getting chairs. Spectators occupying the chairs in the jury box had to be cleared out so the jury could be seated.[83] Some witnesses and some of those called for jury duty had to be lifted over desks and people to the front of the courtroom.[84]

As proceedings were about to begin, Sheriff Fleming begged the crowds to stand back if they possibly could: "It's not *if* you possibly can," said Judge Munroe, less deferentially, "but you must, else there won't be any court today."

"We don't need no court," someone yelled, but no one paid any attention to him.[85]

Munroe made no effort to clear the courtroom but did repeatedly demand that the boys in the balcony quiet down and all "gentlemen" present remove their hats.[86] He did not ask anyone to remove their guns, however. When Jesse Washington, wearing overalls and a calico shirt and looking no older than the seventeen years he claimed, was brought into court, a young man in the crowd reached for his revolver, muttering, "Might as well get him now."

"Let them have their trial," admonished an older man sitting near him. "We'll get him before sundown and you might hurt an innocent man."[87]

By some accounts, Washington seemed unmoved by the spectacle he saw—the mass of white humanity glaring at him, all those eyes fixed on him with barely controlled rage. But one reporter noted that "the negro's heavy lips were trembling and he seemed to be muttering to himself."[88]

The trial began about 10:00 a.m. A jury was seated quickly; the six young defense attorneys did not challenge a single juror. The foreman was W. B. Brazelton, a leading citizen. Brazelton was a longtime, prominent Waco lumberman and a member of the school board.[89] After the jury was impaneled, Judge Munroe read the charge and asked Jesse Washington if he wanted to plead guilty or not guilty. Jesse, who must have been entirely lost, did not answer at first and plainly did not understand the question. The judge explained the charges and the consequences of pleading guilty. "Washington's plea of guilty" said the *Morning News*, "was a muttered 'Yeah.'"[90]

Prosecutor McNamara then called Dr. J. H. Maynard to the stand. Dr. Maynard described the battered condition of Lucy Fryer's body, but did not testify that she had been raped. A succession of officials then testified either to having heard Jesse Washington making his confession in Hillsboro or to having witnessed him signing the confession with his X in Dallas. Cris Simon told how he had arrived home, glimpsed Jesse Washington walking into the mule lot, and heard the Fryer children crying over their mother's body. Fleming, Jenkins, and Stegall all testified as to how they had identified Washington as a suspect, how they had arrested and interrogated him, and how the murder weapon had finally been found after he had told them where it was.

The only question asked by defense counsel was put to Sheriff Fleming by Joe Taylor: "Who were present when the hammer was found?" Fleming replied that John McNamara and deputy sheriffs Lee Jenkins and Joe Roberts were present, along with Fleming himself. Jenkins added in his testimony that, before the hammer was picked up, the group had stopped a passing car; the driver, Mr. Reeder, plus another man who lived nearby, a Mr. McCullough, were asked to come and see where the hammer had been found.[91]

Washington's confession was formally introduced into evidence; then, finally, he was allowed to speak on his own behalf. According to the court record, he said only, "I ain't going to tell them nothing more than what I said . . . that's what I done." Then he mumbled something that could not be heard by the court reporter. Joe Taylor interpreted the mumble for the court as, "He says he is sorry he did it." Taylor then asked Washington if there was anything else he wanted to say. There was no answer. Taylor said, "That is all."[92]

John McNamara made use of his summation to pat everyone on the back and made a special point of congratulating the defense attorneys for doing their duty. Then, declaring that "the prisoner has been given a fair trial as fair as any ever given in this court room," he demanded that Jesse Washington be assessed the death penalty.[93] The crowd broke into loud applause and yells. The defense contributed no final argument.

Outside, as soon as the cheer was heard in the courtroom, voices cried, "Let's go in and get him"; "Throw him out of the window"; "They're goin' to take him out the other way—we'll have to watch all sides for him"; and "Oh, we'll get him; they can't keep him from us." One reporter describes the increasing tension in the scene outside, with men and boys "running here and there with straining eyes and faces growing more excited each minute. Boys not more than fifteen years of age were running wildly around and around the building, either to get a view through curiosity or else to have some part in the gruesome work ahead . . . [they] were running with the speed of wolves or hounds it seemed, almost, and were frantic lest the officers should manage to spirit the negro away."[94] There were also girls and women on the courthouse lawn. They seemed more nervous and more serious than the men, but, says the same reporter, as they got used to the situation and relaxed, they began laughing and chatting, though their faces were still pale.

The jury retired for a total of four minutes and then returned to the courtroom. Foreman W. B. Brazelton read the verdict: "We the jury find the defendant guilty of murder as charged in the indictment and assess his penalty at death." By then the time was 11:22 a.m.[95] Jesse's entire trial had taken a little over an hour. "Is that your verdict, gentlemen?" asked Judge Munroe. The members of the jury answered that it was. Munroe began writing in his docket, "Plea of guilty and verdict of guilty, and pun . . ."[96] The actual document remains in the old courthouse files; it is obvious that the judge broke off at "pun . . ." and added the remaining " . . . ishment assessed at death" in haste afterward. "As he wrote there was a hush over the entire court room. It was a moment of hesitation, but just a moment," wrote the reporter for the *Waco Semi-Weekly Tribune*.[97] The officers were preparing to take Jesse Washington away.

Suddenly, all hell broke loose. A tall young farmer at the back of the room put his hands on the heads and shoulders of the people in front of him and lifted himself over them, leaping on a table as someone cried, "Get the nigger!" A man standing by the judge looked up and said, "They are coming after him," and "the wave of people surged forward."[98]

According to Elisabeth Freeman's report, by then Sheriff Fleming and the court stenographer, Warren Hunt, who both knew what was coming, had slipped out of the courtroom. One deputy, Barney Goldberg, pulled his revolver. He had not heard that Fleming had given orders to his men to let the crowd get Washington. A rumor later made the rounds in Waco that Goldberg had struck two men in the mob with his gun, injuring one of them severely. Members of the mob threatened revenge.

Goldberg was apparently so afraid of the public's reaction if it became generally known that he had made even a feeble attempt to stop the lynching that he convinced several friends to swear out affidavits and publish them in the newspapers claiming that he had never left his grocery store all day and was not even present at the trial.[99] It seems unlikely that Goldberg did anything more than draw his gun and stand there for a moment until he realized that he was all alone.

The unidentified "tall man" grabbed the collar of the terrified Jesse Washington, and the mob carried him down the back stairs behind the courtroom and out into the alley, tearing off his clothes as they went. The lynchers paused for a moment on the east side of the courthouse, long enough to put a chain around Jesse's neck, and proceeded to drag him down Washington Street.[100] "Then," wrote one reporter, "he became the plaything of the mob."[101]

At first, Washington fought them, "squealing like a crazed animal," according to one newspaper account. He managed to bite one man's finger "almost to the bone," but released him when another man "stamped him in the face."[102] Freeman reports she was told that Jesse cried out, "Haven't I one friend in this crowd?"[103] By this time, men in the crowd had begun slashing at Jesse with their knives so that "he was covered in blood long before the square was reached."[104]

Now that they had their chance, it seemed that nearly every man in Waco wanted to take his turn at Jesse Washington. Along the way, people in the crowd beat him with shovels, bricks, clubs, and anything else that came to hand.[105] One paper reports that "a yellow negro boy who was raised here in Waco" hit Jesse on the head and cried, "'You're getting just what's coming to you, you d——rascal."[106] Despite their delicacy in not printing words like *damned* in full, the Waco newspapers spared their readers none of the details of the lynching. Such details became as much a part of the "folk pornography" of the time as details of rapes.[107]

Part of the crowd surged toward the bridge, thinking Jesse would be hanged where Sank Majors had been hanged eleven years earlier, but the ringleaders already had another plan in mind. Hanging would be too easy a death. They turned on Second Street to take Jesse to the town square by City Hall and burn him alive. Piles of kindling and wood had been left along the way; dry goods boxes and inflammable material like excelsior seemed to appear out of nowhere.

"The shouts attracted attention,'" reports the *Tribune*. "They were shouts like those a crowd will give when leading a triumphal procession from a ball game that has been a big victory."[108] The *Times Herald* takes refuge in a kind of imperial passive voice, as if the lynching had been ordained by some abstract overlord or deity: "Others from Waco followed the crowd to the place where it *had been decreed* that Jess Washington should pay with his life the penalty for the terrible crime of which he admitted he was guilty."[109] But it was individual men who killed Washington. They can be seen doing their work in Gildersleeve's picture.

Jesse was pulled over the fence around City Hall and the chain attached to his neck was flung across the limb of a tree in the rear of the building. "They drew the chain over the tree and the boy grabbed it. They then cut off his fingers so that he could not hold the chain," reports Elisabeth Freeman.[110] "Fingers, ears, pieces of clothing, toes and other parts of the negro's body were cut off by members of the mob that had crowded to the scene as if by magic when the word that the negro had been taken in charge by the mob was heralded over the city," says the *Times Herald*.[111]

Leona Lester, a young manicurist at the Goldstein Migel Department Store—"a child," Freeman calls her—told Freeman during a manicure that she had seen someone in the mob "unsex" Jesse Washington. "Men state that they did not do anything of the kind and would swear to it," says Freeman in her report, "but others say they did and that they were carrying the proof around in a handkerchief showing it as a souvenir."[112]

Thomas Hague, third-generation resident of Robinson, claimed to have seen years ago a by-then thoroughly moth-eaten shirt full of blood that was supposed to have been taken from Jesse Washington. A friend's father had purchased it.[113] Nona Baker remembered that a friend, now deceased, had picked cotton on a white man's farm when he was a boy. One day the boy's employer showed him a finger in formaldehyde in a jar and told him it was Jesse Washington's finger.[114] According to one report, children were occasionally even given these relics to play with and show their friends.[115]

Thousands of people came rushing to the town square to see the sight. "Not all approved, but they looked on because they had never seen anything of the kind," reports the *Tribune*.[116] Before the fire was lit under the tree on the town square, Jesse Washington, "half alive and half dead," was propped briefly against the tree and then suddenly yanked up by the chain around his neck and dangled in the air, his tongue protruding from his mouth and his face smeared with blood. He was cut in so many places, "his body was a solid color of red, the blood of the many wounds inflicted covered him from head to foot."[117] Freeman comments that just as the chain was jerking Washington into the air, "the big man" smashed him on the back of the neck with a knife; this violent blow may have been "practically the death blow."[118]

By now all the kindling material that had been gathered was piled into a huge dry goods box placed at the base of the tree. Washington's body swayed in the air and then was gradually lowered into the box. Coal oil was poured over him. "No sooner had his body touched the box than people pressed forward, each eager to be the first to light the fire, matches were touched to the inflammable material and as smoke rapidly rose in the air, such a demonstration of people gone mad was never heard before. . . . Shouts of delight went up from the thousands of throats."[119]

After that, Washington's body was lowered into the fire several times and then raised again. Unfortunately for him, he was a strong young boy—"from the pictures, a wonderfully built boy," says Freeman.[120] Death had not yet come to him. He even managed at one point during the burning to kick himself free of his funeral pyre, but his executioners quickly grabbed the chain and pulled him back into the fire.[121]

Estimates of the number of spectators range between ten thousand and fifteen thousand, "crowding the city hall lawn and overflowing the square, hanging from the windows of buildings, viewing the scene from the tops of buildings and trees. . . . Onlookers were hanging from the windows of the city hall and every other building that commanded a sight of the burning."[122] A number of small boys had climbed into the top of the tree from which Jesse was hanged and into other trees nearby.[123] At least one little boy had to be removed from the tree from which Washington was hanging when it got too hot for him to stay there.[124]

Mayor John Dollins and Chief of Police Guy McNamara observed the proceedings in comfort from the mayor's office on the second floor of City Hall. Gildersleeve was advised ahead of time where the lynching would take place and had his photographic equipment set up and ready to go in the mayor's office. He took photographs of the waiting crowd during the trial and photographed Washington's body up close at various points during the burning, just as he would have shot the high school football team before the big game, just as he had shot the pictures of Waco's Prosperity Banquet in 1911. To Gildersleeve, it was one more slice of life in Waco. Freeman declares in her account that the picture-taking was a "cooked business" between the mayor and Gildersleeve and implies that the mayor was getting some kind of "rake-off" from the sales of the photos afterward.[125]

"Many turned away [from the scene of Jesse's torture]," reports the *Tribune*, "but many lingered to talk about it and to watch it. Some stayed in the outskirts of the crowd not caring to rest their eyes upon the actual scene."[126] Some watched with more enthusiasm than others: "Two tall farmers held on their shoulders a man said to have been George Fryer so that he could see the assaulter and murderer of his wife burn. There were probably fifteen thousand people in the crowd, many of them women, and one well dressed woman clapped her hands when a way was cleared so that she could see the writhing, naked form of the fast dying black." There were also boys and girls about, who had left school to go home for lunch. Some of these children actually saw the burning.[127]

Jesse Washington's body burned and smoldered for about two hours until there was nothing left but a skull, a torso, and the stumps of limbs. Even then the crowd was not satisfied. Spectators searched the area for bits of charred bone, links of the chain, and pieces of the tree that could be kept or sold as souvenirs. Links of the chain sold for twenty-five cents.[128]

"And then the worst happened," says the *Waco Semi-Weekly Tribune* with unintended irony, although by now Jesse Washington was dead.[129] About midafternoon, a horseman came along, lassoed what was left of Washington's body and began to drag it around the square and then through the streets of town while waving his hat in the air. Somewhere along the way the skull bounced loose from the rest of the body and was placed on the doorstep of a prostitute on "Two Street," where it was picked up by a group of small boys who extracted the teeth and sold them for five dollars each.[130] The rest of the body, now tied behind a car, was dragged all the way to Robinson, put in a sack, and hung from a telephone pole in front of a blacksmith's shop for everyone to see. Toward the end of the day, Constable Les Stegall went out and picked up the sack and brought it back to town, where the little that was left of Jesse Washington was buried in the local potter's field. The Washington family was either gone or so terrorized that even after Jesse was dead, they were afraid to claim his remains.[131]

Some of the good citizens of Robinson were actually embarrassed by this last excess. One Robinson man called the *Morning News* and a group of men visited the offices of the *Times Herald*, in each case to say that the people of Robinson condemned—not the lynching—but the dragging of the body through the streets.

And thus ended the Waco Horror.

There are suggestions at the very end of the long article about the lynching in the *Waco Morning News* that not every resident of Waco approved of what was done that day. Under the paragraph header, "Some Grave Faces in the Frantic Crowd," the reporter notes: "Here and there—but rarely—some man walked with sober stride, downcast head and grave expression, talking in a subdued voice of his regret over what was taking place, declaring that if it had been at all possible every step should have been taken to spare the community the cataclysm of human passion which was turned loose within a few minutes' time."[132] But the same reporter immediately follows that comment by noting that the vast majority of spectators seemed "satisfied" with what was going on or at least passive about it. Note, also, that these "grave" men spoke of "sparing the community," not of sparing the victim the ordeal that was visited upon him.

An "old Confederate veteran" was said to have commented before the uproar began that any spark would set off the crowd. "It would be wrong, of course," he said, "but that is what would happen if a movement should start."[133] Another observer described by the reporter only as "a man connected with the courts," speaking before the lynching, blamed the sheriff for having "conferred too much with the citizens of Robinson, though it was well meant." This observer thought the people of Robinson should just have been told firmly that "the negro" would be legally tried and legally executed.

There is a little picture offered here by this same "man of the courts," who seems to have a very good opinion of his own insights. He notes that wherever a group of eight men gathered in the days before the lynching, one or two expressed a hope that the incident would end legally and in good order, but the others said nothing. This sketch suggests in a thumbnail the comparative ratio of those who wanted Jesse Washington to be legally convicted and legally hanged to those who either wanted him lynched or did not care.

One poignant note in the *Morning News* story implies in a more oblique way that some folks were horrified by what had been done: The reporter repeats a conversation between two men which he overheard after the lynching. One man said "he would not have had his son, fourteen years old, witness the incident for all the money in Waco." The other answered that he would have been glad to have his son "witness the tragedy"—as a salutary moral lesson perhaps? "Each was sincere," adds the reporter, "just a different viewpoint."[134]

So much for the more thoughtful crowd in Waco. No doubt, some citizens were deeply troubled by the lynching of Jesse Washington, but no one took any action to stop it.

The *Waco Morning News* responded to the lynching by running a poem on the editorial page composed by editor E. G. Senter. Salient passages of "Vengeance Is Mine, Saith the Lord" (apparently originally written in 1905 in response to a different lynching) include the following:[135]

The maddened crowd its fury feeds with fame,
Nor reeks of God, nor feels the sinful shame.
Thou fool- the serpents which thy passions breed
In whirling fury on thyself shall feed . . .

Who is the doubter of God's justice? Tell
Him of the dark abyss that curtains Hell.
Man's fitful wrath adds nothing to the woe
Of guilty wretch about to leap below.
'Round the avenger shadows grimly draw,
Father, forgive him—he forgot thy law.

Senter was new to the position of editor at the *News* and probably new to Waco, as well. He had been introduced to the business community at a Young Men's Business League event in early April, at which time he had forecast "a splendid future for this city" and also a splendid future for the *Waco Morning News*, which he intended to make a "great statewide" newspaper.[136] But Senter apparently did not stay in Waco long enough to appear in even one edition of the *Waco City Directory*. In 1917, Charles Marsh and E. S. Fentress, who had come to Waco from Des Moines, took over both the *Waco Morning News* and the *Waco Semi-Weekly Tribune* and created the *News-Tribune*, which competed for ten more years with the *Times Herald* until Fentress's company acquired that paper, as well.[137]

At the time of the Waco Horror, however, before the Fentress/Marsh takeover, the *Times Herald* was a much stronger paper than the *Morning News*. According to E. S. Fentress's son Harlan Fentress, "The morning paper had been kicked around a good bit, various ownerships, none of which had made any particular success." The owner of the *News* in May 1916 was Artemas R. Roberts who, at his death in 1933, was remembered principally as the man who had erected the Amicable skyscraper. His ownership of the Waco newspaper seems to have lasted only about two months, after which he sold his stock back to the previous owners.[138]

It was natural, then, that the weaker daily, the *Morning News*, should take refuge in the oblique, symbolic language of a poem as a way of making a faint effort at a critical commentary on the lynching. Elisabeth Freeman met a director of the *Morning News* who "deplored the whole thing,"[139] but she reports that the Waco newspaper owners she interviewed were, for the most part, afraid that a strong criticism of the lynching would "injure their circulation."[140]

The *Waco Semi-Weekly Tribune* was something of an exception. It was owned by old-time journalist A. R. McCollum, who had founded his first newspaper in Waco in 1878 and had been running some sort of paper in the city ever since.[141] The *Tribune*, published only twice a week, was also probably the weakest of Waco's three newspapers. McCollum was sixty-seven and in poor health at the time of the Waco Horror and would expire in 1918, only a year after selling his last newspaper venture to Fentress and Marsh.

Elisabeth Freeman reports that, in May 1916, A. R. McCollum was almost blind and said "anything he please[d]."[142] He was also, however, a state senator running for reelection.[143]

McCollum's *Tribune*, like the *Waco Morning News*, published a poem on the editorial page—an anonymous poem contributed by an unknown citizen of Waco. The poem, entitled "The Mob,'" ends dramatically:[144]

Then burn your laws, your bill of rights,
Your constitution and your code,
Proud guaranties that were your lights
Whose searching rays swept clear the road.
You do not need their guidance now,
A tyrant's hand is on the reign,
And subjects, self-enslaved must bow
And follow blindly in his train.
Disdainful of your valiant past,
Without a sigh or muffled sob,
Plunge on—while on your skies is cast
The grinning shadow of the Mob.

But McCollum dared to print an editorial as well, the only newspaperman in Waco who did so immediately after the lynching. "The Work of the Mob" is a fascinating artifact of its time because it so plainly illustrates the mental contortions of a man who thought he was a good person, a serious person, a man who loved his community. Clearly, McCollum (assuming he wrote the piece himself) was steeped in the near-universal racism of his time, but he was still uncomfortable about what had happened. He was attempting somehow to simultaneously excuse what the mob had done and express his discomfort.

McCollum begins, as many similar editorial writers of the period did, with a half-jocular personification of the lynching that seems highly offensive to the modern reader: "Judge Lynch held assizes in Waco last Monday, displacing the tribunal that the people of the state had established for the orderly and sure processes of justice." He goes on to say that everyone was expecting the lynching, it would have been next to impossible to avert it, and Sheriff Fleming and his deputies should not be blamed, but rather should be given credit for preventing the lynching for as long as they did. As was customary in these pieces, McCollum expends a lot of energy reviling the murderer and the horrors of his crimes and makes the usual nod to "the sacredness of our womanhood," a "consideration that overshadows all others." He never describes or decries the vicious sadism of the lynchers. "We cannot repress regret, though," he adds, "that the men who took execution of the law into their hands had not forborne and allowed the law to take its course." He goes on to warn that "the influences of mob action must ever hold menace and danger to morals and civilization." McCollum acknowledges that some argue that lynching is a deterrent to crime, but he comments, after listening to this argument "in a respectful spirit," that the so-called deterrent effect of lynching has not been proved and can probably never be proved.

In closing, McCollum congratulates the city by insisting on the silver lining, also mentioned repeatedly in the *Tribune's* coverage of the event. The saving grace for Waco, as McCollum sees it, is the fact that no black people other than Jesse Washington were injured or threatened in any way, unlike in such places as "Springfield, Illinois," and "Canton, Ohio," (it is no accident that he mentions "northern" cities) where, after initial violence directed at one or two men, many blacks were attacked or driven out of town. In Waco, says McCollum, "there is no evidence of hostility to the negro simply because of his race, and we should feel regret if it were otherwise."[145]

The editorial is a self-serving piece, designed primarily to uphold the good name of the community, and McCollum's criticism of the mob action is muted to the point of ineffectuality, but at least it is there. At least, he made some effort to face the facts and take a look at them.

And what of the paper that Harlan Fentress called the strongest in Waco at the time, the *Times Herald*, run by George and Fred Robinson? Much-admired veteran newspaperman E. M. Ainsworth was probably working for the *Times Herald* at this time.[146] Elisabeth Freeman comments in her report to the NAACP that "Mr. Ainsworth of one of the newspapers seemed the only man who wanted to start a protest."[147] But Ainsworth's admirable impulses must have been overruled by higher-ups.

The day after the lynching, the *Waco Times Herald* published a very short wrap-up story covering the judge's failure to complete his entry on the docket because he was interrupted by the mob action, the burial of the pitiful remains of Jesse Washington, and a defense of the young attorneys assigned to represent Washington for doing their duty. After that, the *Times Herald* never published another word about the Waco Horror. The three-paragraph story, buried on page five, ends with the hopeful conclusion, "Yesterday's exciting occurrence is a closed incident."[148] The author of those words could not possibly have known how mistaken he was.

Notes

1. Details vary in newspaper coverage of the Waco Horror. Even official court documents are not entirely reliable. Robinson is sometimes called Robinsonville, the town's original name. The Fryers' neighbor, "Chris Simon," is referred to in a variety of ways. In one news story, Ruby Fryer is called "Lucy" Fryer, and the Fryer name is frequently misspelled as "Fryar." I have tried to use correct spellings and verify details wherever possible. Ruby Fryer was born on November 8, 1894; George Fryer Jr.

was born on September 3, 1901, according to my interview with Lucy Wollitz Kirkland, age seventy-six, July 4, 2000. "Lucy Bee," as Lucy Wollitz Kirkland is known, is the granddaughter of the Lucy Fryer who was killed on May 8, 1916, in Robinson, and the daughter of Ruby Fryer Wollitz. The "Bee" stands for Beatrice. Lucy Bee was named after her grandmother and the aunt who died at the age of nine.

2. Elisabeth Freeman, "Waco Lynching," NAACP Archives, NAACP Administrative File, Subfile under Lynching: Waco, Texas, 1916, Group 1, Box C-370, Library of Congress, 7; "Negro Confesses to Terrible Crime at Robinsonville," *Waco Times Herald*, May 9, 1916, 5.

3. Freeman, "Waco Lynching," 8; "Statement of Facts" (transcript of trial testimony), testimony of Leslie Stegall, *State of Texas* v. *Jesse Washington*, No. 4141, 54th District Court, McLennan County, March Term A. D. 1916, 7, from NAACP Archives, NAACP Administrative File, Subfile under Lynching: Waco, Texas, 1916, Group 1, Box C-370, Library of Congress (hereafter "Statement of Facts").

4. "Negro Confesses to Terrible Crime at Robinsonville," 1.

5. Author's interview with Lucy Wollitz Kirkland, June 23, 2000.

6. McLennan County, Texas, Marriage Records, vol. 2 (January 1871—July 1892): 125.

7. Gravestone of Beatrice Pearl Fryer, Lorena, Texas, cemetery.

8. "Negro Confesses to Terrible Crime at Robinsonville," 5.

9. "Murder of Robinson Woman Breaks McLennan Records for Fiendish Brutality," *Waco Morning News*, May 9, 1916, 1.

10. "Statement of Facts," testimony of Dr. J. H. Maynard, 1–2.

11. "Lee Jenkins' Vivid Career Comes to End," *Waco Times Herald*, June 10, 1929. 1.

12. "Ex-Sheriff Leslie Stegall Dies in Waco," *Waco News Tribune*, October 12, 1953. 1.

13. "Statement of Facts," testimony of Criss [*sic*] Simon, 6.

14. "Negro Confesses to Terrible Crime at Robinsonville," 5.

15. Freeman, "Waco Lynching," 7.

16. Ibid., 10.

17. Author's interview with Thomas Hague, age sixty-nine. Hague told me that Robinson or Robinsonville was originally a settlement of primarily German immigrants, established only three years after Waco was founded. The Germans of Robinson tended to stick together, and English immigrants like the Fryers and the Hagues also tended to stick together. Lucy Fryer, according to Hague's father, was "an extremely beautiful woman." Judging from available photos of Lucy, she may well have been a beauty as a young woman. But a photo taken of her in middle age records the image of a rather ordinary-looking, roly-poly little person, her early loveliness dimmed perhaps by years of hard farm work and the pain of losing a beloved child at a tender age.

18. Hall, *Revolt against Chivalry*, 207.

19. Ida B. Wells-Barnett, *Southern Horrors and Other Writings: The Anti-lynching Campaign of Ida B. Wells, 1892–1900*, ed. Jacqueline Jones Royster (Boston: Bedford/St. Martins, 1997), 96. For an abridged version of the story of the lynching of Henry Smith, see chapter 1, note 66.

20. Hall, *Revolt against Chivalry*, 129.

21. Freeman, "Waco Lynching," 7.

22. Ibid., 8.

23. Ibid., 17–18. Washington was probably "driving" a buggy or wagon.

24. "Negro Confesses to Terrible Crime at Robinsonville," 5.

25. Ibid.

26. Freeman, "Waco Lynching," 8.

27. "Statement of Facts," testimony of Lee Jenkins, 5.

28. "Statement of Facts," testimony of Leslie Stegall, 7.

29. "Negro Confesses to Terrible Crime at Robinsonville,"' 5.

30. Ibid.

31. Freeman, "Waco Lynching," 10.

32. "Statement of Facts," testimony of Sam Fleming and Lee Jenkins, 4–5.

33. "Sheriff's Alertness Saves Negro's Life," *Waco Times Herald*, May 10, 1916, 7; "Sworn Confession by Jesse Washington," *Waco Times Herald*, May 10, 1916, 4; "Grand Jury Indicts Slayer of Mrs. Fryar," *Waco Times Herald*, May 11, 1916, 5.

34. "Sheriff's Alertness Saves Negro's Life."

35. Ibid.

36. "Farmers from Robinson Form Mob and Search Jail for Black Brute," *Waco Morning News*, May 10, 1916, 1.

37. Ibid.

38. "Sheriff's Alertness Saves Negro's Life"; "Special Session of Grand Jury Called to Consider Robinson Murder Case," *Waco Morning News*, May 11, 1916, 5.

39. "[Illegible] Body on a Robinson Farm," *Waco Semi-Weekly Tribune*, May 10, 1916, 5.

40. Hall, *Revolt against Chivalry*, 150. "The myth of the black rapist reached pathological proportions at the turn of the century, in part because of its congruence with the exaggerated sexual tensions of a dying Victorianism," says Hall (48).

41. The misspelling "Fryar" appears often in the newspaper accounts of the crime. In the court transcription of the confession, the name is also consistently misspelled, but as "Frier."

42. Several phrases that don't appear in the actual transcribed confession were added to the newspaper version: "I then" was added at this point to make sense of the edited sentence. The phrase "and went about forty steps south of the planter" was added in the next paragraph, and the word "woods," which appears a little later in the same sentence, is a substitution for "weeds," which appeared in the transcribed confession.

43. Transcript of confession says "twist."

44. Original confession appears in "Statement of Facts," 8–9. The published confession appears in "Sworn Confession by Jesse Washington"; "Special Session of Grand Jury Called to consider Robinson Murder Case"; and "Murderer of Mrs. Lucy Fryer to Be Tried Next Monday," *Waco Semi-Weekly Tribune*, May 13, 1916, 2.

45. See Elisabeth Freeman to Royal Freeman Nash in [undated] series of letters. The letters and wires exchanged between Nash and Freeman about her investigation in Waco are found in the NAACP Archives, NAACP Administrative File, Subfile under Lynching: Waco, Texas, 1916, Group 1, Box C-370, Library of Congress (hereafter Freeman/Nash Letters).

46. Freeman implied during her NAACP-sponsored speaking tour to publicize the story of the lynching of Jesse Washington that she believed that the rape "was written into the lad's confession." See "Phillip Peabody Gives $20,000 to Fight Lynching," *Chicago Defender*, August 5, 1916.

47. Freeman, "Waco Lynching," 11.

48. Nona Baker, letter to editor of *Waco Tribune Herald*, undated [summer 1998].

49. Freeman, "Waco Lynching," 4.

50. Author's interviews with Bill Wuebker, age seventy-three, and with Martha Frosch Kettler, age ninety.

51. "[Illegible] White Man for Crime Which Boy Was Lynched," *Chicago Defender* (June 10, 1916), 7.

52. On his death certificate, A. T. Smith's birthday is listed as January 24, 1888, which would have made him twenty-eight when Jesse Washington was lynched. But A. T. Smith describes himself in an interrogatory in one of the libel suits related to his publication of the *Chicago Defender* story as age twenty-seven. The interrogation was probably completed during the fall of 1916.

53. Royal Freeman Nash memorandum to J. E. Spingam, August 11, 1916, Anti-Lynching Campaign. There is a longer discussion of the fate of A. T. Smith and of George Fryer's lawsuits for libel in Bernstein's chapter 9.

54. Freeman, "Waco Lynching," 6, 11.

55. Ibid., 11–12.

56. Kettler interview. Kettler told me that after the lynching of Jesse Washington, black children in Robinson made up a rhyme that went, "I never did and I never will/Pick cotton for Old Man Fryer in Robinsonville."

57. "Grand Jury Indicts Slayer of Mrs. Fryar."

58. "Colorful Career of Noted Jurist Closed by Death," *Waco News Tribune*, February 6, 1942, 1.

59. Ibid.

60. Freeman, "Waco Lynching," 4, 17.

61. "J. W. Taylor Jr., Veteran Lawyer of Waco, Is Dead," *Waco News Tribune*, August 28, 1947, 1; "J. W. Taylor Is Dead; Funeral Service Today," *Waco Times Herald*, August 28, 1947, 1; "Society of Yesterday," *Waco Tribune Herald*, centennial special section, October 30, 1949. Death certificate of Joe Willis Taylor.

62. "Frank M. Fitzpatrick Sr. Dies; Longtime Lawyer," *Waco News Tribune*, January 31, 1973, 8B; "Rites Thursday for Longtime Waco Attorney," *Waco Times Herald*, January 31, 1973, 1A; death certificate for Frank Minnock Fitzpatrick Sr.; "Deserved Compliment for Frank Fitzpatrick," *Waco Times Herald*, April 12, 1916, 12.

63. "Frank Fitzpatrick to Make Race for Floater," *Waco Times Herald*, June 11, 1916, 6; "Frank Fitzpatrick," *Waco Semi-Weekly Tribune*, June 14, 1916, 12.

64. "C. H. Machen, Lawyer and Veteran, Dies," *Dallas Morning News*, February 19, 1943, 2–4.

65. "Kyle Vick's Last Rites Here Today," *Waco News Tribune*, October 17, 1956, 18; "Veteran Waco Attorney Dies Early Today," *Waco Times Herald*, October 16, 1956, 1; death certificate of Kyle Vick Sr.

66. "Bowden Hays, Jr., Dies from Injuries in Auto Accident," *Waco News Tribune*, August 7, 1922, 1; "Injuries Fatal for Bowden Hays," *Waco Times Herald*, August 7, 1922, 3; "Attendants Announced for the Hays-Campbell Wedding," *Waco Times Herald*, December 25, 1921, 3.

67. Katherine Kennis Kuehler Walters, "The Great War in Waco, Texas: African Americans, Race Relations, and the White Primary, 1916–1922" (Master's thesis, Southwest Texas State University, 2000), 63.

68. The story of the incident is told in the following *Waco Times Herald* articles: "Wife Rescues Man from 5 Masked Men," June 7, 1921, 1; "Alleged Whitecappers Placed under Bond; Cummings Is Tarred," July 9, 1921, 1; "Man Tarred and Feathered Says He'll Leave Waco," July 10, 1921, 3; "Whitecapping Cases Will Come Up Wednesday," July 12, 1921, 3; "One Dismissed in Whitecap Cases, $1000 Bond for Three; Make Rush to Sign Bonds," July 13, 1921, 1. Also see Walters, "Great War in Waco," 62–64. I am much indebted to Katherine Walters for sharing information on this subject and also providing me with copies of court documents relating to George Fryer's libel lawsuits over the article published in the *Paul Quinn Weekly*, reprinted from the *Chicago Defender*, that announced Fryer's "arrest" for the murder of his wife.

69. "Grand Jury Indicts Slayer of Mrs. Fryar"; "Negro Indicted for Murder of Robinson Woman: Trial Monday," *Waco Morning News*, May 12, 1916, 8; "Murderer of Mrs. Lucy Fryer to Be Tried Next Monday," *Waco Semi-Weekly Tribune*, May 13, 1916, 2.

70. "Robinson Gives Assurance Will Not Molest Murderer," *Waco Morning News*, May 13, 1916, 6.

71. "Swift Vengeance Wreaked on Negro After Jury Brings in Death Penalty," *Waco Morning News*, May 16, 1916, 5.

72. "Will Permit Law to Take Its Course in Negro Boy's Trial," *Waco Times Herald*, May 13, 1916: 3.

73. "Robinson Gives Assurance Will Not Molest Murderer."

74. [No headline], *Waco Times Herald*, May 12, 1916: 8.

75. "Swift Vengeance Wreaked on Negro," 5.

76. Ibid., 1.

77. Ibid., 5.

78. "Mob Takes Negro from Court House," *Waco Times Herald*, May 15, 1916, 1.

79. "Swift Vengeance Wreaked on Negro," 1.

80. Ibid., 5.

81. Freeman, "Waco Lynching," 7.
82. "Swift Vengeance Wreaked on Negro," 5.
83. "Mob Takes Negro from Court House," 1.
84. "Swift Vengeance Wreaked on Negro," 1.
85. "Mob Takes Negro from Court House," 1.
86. Ibid.
87. "Swift Vengeance Wreaked on Negro," 1.
88. Ibid.
89. See "Three Outstanding Waco Business Men Claimed by Death," *Waco Tribune Herald*, June 17, 1934, 1. W. B. Brazelton was the grandfather of noted pediatrician Dr. T. Berry Brazelton, the "Dr. Spock" of America in the 1980s, author of numerous books on child development, and host of the TV show *What Every Baby Knows*. Dr. Brazelton, who was born in 1920, has vivid and unpleasant memories of his early childhood in Waco. Every Friday night the Ku Klux Klan burned a cross on the hill above his parents' home, and his father would leave the house and hide out somewhere. (Brazelton's father was considered a liberal and was, therefore, a Klan target.) Dr. Brazelton told me that while his father was gone, he, his brother, his mother, and a black woman who worked for the family hid under the bed (author's interview with Dr. T. Berry Brazelton).
90. "Swift Vengeance Wreaked on Negro," 5.
91. "Mob Takes Negro from Court House," 1, 5; "Statement of Facts," testimony of S. S. Fleming and Lee Jenkins, 4–6.
92. "Statement of Facts," testimony of Jesse Washington, 10.
93. "Swift Vengeance Wreaked on Negro," 5.
94. Ibid.
95. "Negro Burned to a Stake in the Yard of the City Hall," *Waco Semi-Weekly Tribune,* May 17, 1916, 7.
96. "Court's Entry Not Finished," *Waco Times Herald*, May 16, 1916, 5.
97. "Negro Burned to a Stake."
98. Ibid.
99. "As to Barney Goldberg," *Waco Semi-Weekly Tribune*, May 17, 1916, 7; "No Part Taken in Guarding Negro by Barney Goldberg," *Waco Morning News*, May 16, 1916, 2; Freeman, "Waco Lynching," 12.
100. "Mob Takes Negro from Court House," 1; "Swift Vengeance Wreaked on Negro," 1.
101. "Negro Burned to a Stake."
102. "Swift Vengeance Wreaked on Negro," 1.
103. Freeman, "Waco Lynching," 13.
104. "Swift Vengeance Wreaked on Negro," 1.
105. "Mob Takes Negro from Court House," 1.
106. "Swift Vengeance Wreaked on Negro," 5.
107. See note 40 in this chapter.
108. "Negro Burned to a Stake."
109. "Mob Takes Negro from Court House," 1; emphasis mine.
110. Freeman, "Waco Lynching," 14.
111. "Mob Takes Negro from Court House," 1.
112. Freeman, "Waco Lynching," 14. When I first read Faulkner's *Light in August*, I thought the castration of the dying Joe Christmas by army Capt. Percy Grimm was a stunning example of over-ripe southern gothic melodrama. As it turns out, Faulkner's account of a lynching and castration is mild compared to the lynchings that were actually occurring in the South during the period the novel covers.
113. Hague interview.
114. Baker interview, June 19, 2000.
115. Sandra Denise Harvey, "Going Up Bell's Hill: A Social History of a Diverse, Waco, Texas,

Community in the Industrial New South, 1885–1955" (Master's thesis, Baylor University, 1995), 70. Harvey obtained this information from a 1994 interview with Helen Geltemeyer, an elderly Waco resident.

116. "Negro Burned to a Stake."

117. "Mob Takes Negro from Court House," 1.

118. Freeman, "Waco Lynching," 15.

119. "Mob Takes Negro from Court House," 1.

120. Freeman, "Waco Lynching," 16.

121. "Swift Vengeance Wreaked on Negro," 1.

122. "Mob Takes Negro from Court House," 1.

123. "Negro Burned to a Stake."

124. Freeman, "Waco Lynching," 24.

125. Freeman, "Waco Lynching," 15. Freeman's syntax is confusing at this point. The "rakeoff" to which she refers may simply mean that she felt she personally was overcharged for the photographs. She says the Gildersleeve pictures were going for ten cents apiece to the general public, but she had to pay fifty cents each.

126. "Negro Burned to a Stake."

127. "Swift Vengeance Wreaked on Negro," 1.

128. Freeman, "Waco Lynching," 16.

129. "Negro Burned to a Stake."

130. Freeman, "Waco Lynching," 16.

131. "Court's Entry Not Finished."

132. "Swift Vengeance Wreaked on Negro," 5.

133. Ibid.

134. Ibid.

135. E.G. Senter, "Vengeance Is Mine, Saith the Lord," *Waco Morning News*, May 16, 1916, 4.

136. "New Editor of News Is Speaker," *Waco Morning News*, April 5, 1916, 6.

137. Harlon Morse Fentress, interview by Thomas L. Charlton (Baylor University Institute for Oral History), 24–25. The Waco newspapers acquired by Marsh and Fentress became the headquarters of a chain headquartered in Waco that owned thirteen daily newspapers at its peak.

138. "Artemas R. Roberts Sells His Holdings in Morning News," *Waco Morning News*, June 4, 1916, 2.

139. Freeman, "Waco Lynching," 20.

140. Ibid., 6

141. "Funeral Today 4:30 p.m. Editor A. R. McCollum," *Waco Times Herald*, November 10, 1918, 7.

142. Freeman, "Waco Lynching," 6.

143. "Statements by Senator A. R. M'Collum," *Waco Semi-Weekly Tribune*, June 17, 1916, 6.

144. "The Mob," *Waco Semi-Weekly Tribune*, May 17, 1916, 6.

145. "The Work of the Mob," *Waco Semi-Weekly Tribune*, May 17, 1916, 6.

146. "E. M. Ainsworth's Death Ends Long Newsman Career," *Waco News Tribune*, November 26, 1940, 1.

147. Freeman, "Waco Lynching," 18.

148. "Court's Entry Not Finished."

3

The Houston Riot of 1917

C. Calvin Smith

Black Americans, and especially black soldiers, have always been committed to the American creed of freedom and democracy for all. Anytime the nation has found itself threatened by a foreign enemy, black men have been among the first to volunteer their services in its defense. Black soldiers took pride in their military record and the black community accorded them a place in the highest level of social respectability. However, many whites, especially in the South, believed blacks were inferior and should not be allowed to wear the uniform of the armed forces that they held so dear. Whites were also disturbed by the attitude of pride and self-worth exhibited by black soldiers that they interpreted as arrogance and a threat to Jim Crowism. Black soldiers were not wanted in the South because, as Senator James K. Vardaman of Mississippi put it, "Whites are opposed to putting arrogant, strutting representatives of the black soldiery in every community."[1]

In 1916, with United States entry into World War I almost a certainty and the induction of large numbers of blacks into the military likely to follow, Vardaman and a group of southern congressmen sponsored a bill to prevent the enlistment of blacks in the armed forces or the reenlistment of those already in uniform. The measure, however, was defeated because of the strong opposition of Newton D. Baker, the secretary of war, who argued that passage of the statute would be unwise since "black soldiers have performed brave and often conspicuously gallant service for the nation since the American Revolution."[2] Baker, more informed than the congressmen, knew the United States was destined to enter the European war and that all available manpower would be needed. Veteran black soldiers serving in the

Originally published in the *Houston Review* 13 (1991): 84–102. Reprinted with permission of the *Houston Review*.

armed forces in 1916 were not unaware of the efforts of white southerners to oust them, but they were men who were proud of their record in the armed forces and were determined to live up to the standards established by their predecessors. They were also aware that the nation, especially white southerners, had little respect for their service and treated "no other friend so ill."

Of all the places where black soldiers served, the documented record of "ill treatment" and lack of respect was greatest in Texas. Perhaps that was because Texas served as one of the border states between the United States, unstable Mexico, and the revolution-racked republics of Central America. In the 1890s and early 1900s, US troops were sometimes dispatched from Texas to wars and hot spots in those countries, and a significant number of those soldiers were black. Following the Spanish-American War of 1898, the all-black 10th Cavalry, which had served with distinction during the war, was transferred to Texas for duty. While traveling by train between Huntsville and San Antonio, the soldiers suffered unprovoked sniper fire from resentful white civilians. The frequency and intensity of the attacks were so great that their white commanding officer was forced to request the War Department to provide a military escort for his troops so they could "pass through an area which they were supposed to protect without danger from hidden assassins."[3]

The unwarranted attack upon black soldiers in 1898 was not an isolated incident; in fact, it was part of a recurring pattern of hostility toward black troops in Texas. In 1906, 167 members of the all-black 25th Infantry, stationed at Brownsville, Texas, were dishonorably discharged and imprisoned after being accused of conducting a random and unprovoked raid upon the city. The fact that the raiders were never identified by any investigative body, civilian or military, and that the white commanding officers of the accused testified that a roll call during the incident revealed that all their men were in camp with clean, unfired weapons made little difference in their fate.[4] To the local community, justice had been done. Their views were succinctly expressed by a local newspaper editor when he wrote: "Whatever may be the value of black troops in wartime, in peacetime they are a curse to the country."[5]

The attitude of Texans toward black soldiers had changed little when the United States entered World War I in April 1917. Following passage of the Selective Service Act in May of that year, which removed the army's quota system that limited black enlistments to their percentage of the total population and opened the service to the mass enlistment of blacks, military officials recognized the potential for conflict if black recruits were sent into Jim Crow southern communities for training. Initially, army officials decided against sending black recruits into the South for training and tours of duty, especially those from the North, because they feared "embarrassing difficulties will arise in places of public entertainment from the demands of these troops who are associated with white contingents in Northern states, and are accustomed to a situation which they are sure not to find in the neighborhood of Southern camps."[6] This decision was revoked in early August by Baker, who believed it conflicted with established military tradition. However, Baker was cognizant of the potential racial problems that could arise from his decision and ordered commanders of southern camps to "exercise discretion and judgment to prevent any difficulty from arising from this cause."[7]

Hoping to minimize the potential for racial conflict between black troops and local white communities in the South, the War Department ordered the all-black 3rd Battalion, 24th Infantry, United States Army, to Houston, Texas, for a tour of guard duty during the construction of nearby Camp Logan. They arrived July 28, 1917. It was an assignment that neither the black troops nor their white officers wanted, because of the reputation Texans had in regard to their treatment of black soldiers. Col. William Newman, battalion commander, tried to get the order revoked because:

> I had already had an unfortunate experience when I was in command of two companies of the 24th Infantry at Del Rio, Texas, in April 1916, when a colored soldier was killed by a [Texas] ranger for no other reason than that he was a colored man; that it angered Texans to see colored men in the uniform of a soldier.[8]

Newman's view was shared by many of his officers. "Every time we have been in Texas we have had trouble," commented Capt. Lindsey Silvester, commanding officer of Company K of the 24th.[9] And Cecil Green, a black sergeant with the battalion, said the troops "expected trouble in Houston from [white] mobs" from the very beginning.[10] Newman's superiors attempted to allay his fears and those of his men by informing them that the Houston Chamber of Commerce had assured the War Department that black troops would be received by the citizens of Houston "in a spirit of patriotism."[11]

When the 3rd Battalion, 24th Infantry, arrived in Houston it entered a community that was already rife with racial tension caused by the strict enforcement of Jim Crow laws, police brutality, and white civilian resentment of the troops because they were replacing a detachment of the all-white Texas National Guard. Black citizens in Houston, in all walks of life, had little to say that was positive about race relations in the city. "Having a home [in Houston] is all right," a black Houston physician told a National Association for the Advancement of Colored People (NAACP) reporter, "but not when you never know when you leave it in the morning if you will really be able to get back to it at night." Similar sentiments were expressed by Elijah C. Branch, a black Houston minister, who said, "Law abiding citizens feared the police in getting over the city at night more than they feared the highwayman."[12] The soldiers of the 24th were not welcomed and were expected, by local authorities and civilians, to behave in the same fashion as local blacks, accepting brutality, harassment, and insulting racial epithets without retaliation or comment. According to the battalion's commander, the general attitude among local police and white civilians was that the men's status as soldiers was negated by their race. He reported that white construction workers at Camp Logan "lost no opportunity to refer to the 24th Infantry as 'niggers;' the city police and people generally did the same . . . and no efforts were made in any respect to discourage the use of this appellation?"[13]

The common use of the word "nigger" by local civilians and police was particularly offensive to the men of the 24th, the majority of whom had spent the previous two years in the Philippine Islands (Manila), Columbus, New Mexico, and Cheyenne, areas where they faced little or no racial discrimination. Colonel Newman knew his men would have a difficult time in Houston since "the Texan's idea of how a colored man should be treated was just the opposite of what these 24th Infantrymen had been used to."[14] News from Waco, Texas, of an almost violent confrontation between black soldiers and white civilians in that city on July 29, the day after the 24th arrived in Houston, did little to reduce growing racial tension. In an effort to reduce white hostility toward his troops, Newman ordered all of his men disarmed, including the battalion's military police, and stored the arms under lock and key. He believed the unarmed troops would be viewed as less of a threat to local whites and reduced the possibility of retaliation on the part of the soldiers for acts of injustice and humiliation. The only members of the 24th allowed to carry weapons were the guards on duty around the outskirts of Camp Logan, and they were allowed only their rifles and five rounds of ammunition.[15] Newman's early efforts to reduce white hostility toward his troops did little good. Capt. David E. Van Natta, one of the troops' white officers, wrote: "At different times since August 17, the date of my arrival at Camp Logan [the troops had arrived on July 28], I have heard various people talking about the colored troops being here. The sentiment was very strongly against them or any more colored troops being sent here for any purpose."[16] Less than a month after their arrival in Houston, the incident most feared by the War Department and the officers and men of the 24th Infantry occurred. On the night of August 23, 1917, soldiers from the 24th clashed with white police and civilians in Houston, a confrontation that resulted in the death of twenty people: two black soldiers, five white police officers, and thirteen white civilians.

Professional historians have devoted little time to analyzing the causes and consequences of the Houston incident. The first published accounts were written by biased and emotionally charged journalists and other individuals who were more interested in presenting their interpretation of the incident rather than a balanced account.[17] In recent years more balanced accounts have been written. Arthur E. Barbeau and Florette Henri's *The Unknown Soldiers: Black American Troops in World War I* (1974) is one of the more interesting historical treatments of the incident. However, the most definitive studies published to date are "The Houston Mutiny and Riot of 1917" (1973) and *A Night of Violence: The Houston Riot of 1917* (1976), both by Robert V. Haynes.[18]

All studies of the Houston incident agree on most of the basic facts: a small group of soldiers from the 24th were involved in a violent confrontation with white police and civilians of Houston, sparked by police brutality and the use of the term "niggers." However, Haynes accepts the military authorities' conclusion that the violence grew out of a planned conspiracy, carefully concealed by a manufactured fear of a white mob attack, of revenge against the police on the part of experienced soldiers." Haynes argues that the cry heard in the soldiers' compound, "They are coming! The mob is coming," moments before the outburst of gunfire from the camp was a signal for the attack upon Houston to begin. He also argues that Sgt. Vida Henry, who apparently committed suicide after the attack on Houston, was the plotter and leader of the conspiracy. Haynes's arguments depend on his acceptance as fact the testimony given during the trials: testimony from white civilians, police, white officers of the battalion, and from black soldiers who were alleged participants in the affair and served as witnesses for the prosecution in return for immunity. A careful reading and analysis of the official documents relative to the Houston incident clearly shows both bias on the part of many of the witnesses and distortion of the testimony on the part of the military. Reexamination of the circumstances and the conflicting stories of those involved suggests instead that the conspiracy theory was a convenient measure to place exclusive blame on the soldiers and not actual fact.[19]

The night of August 23, 1917, was indeed one of violence, but it did not grow out of a planned attack on the white police of Houston by angry, revenge-seeking black soldiers; rather, it was a spontaneous outburst triggered by weeks of having to endure insulting racial epithets, by police brutality, and by the fear in the camp of an imminent mass mob attack by angry white Houstonians and the belief that such an attack had been launched. The fuse that ignited the explosion of that tragic night was lit at approximately 2:35 p.m. when Cpl. Charles W. Baltimore, a black military policeman, approached two city policemen, Lee Sparks and Rufus Daniels, and inquired about the brutal arrest of a black soldier earlier that day. According to Baltimore, he asked, "in what I thought to be a respectful tone of voice what had been the trouble with the [black] soldier they had just arrested."[20] Patrolman Sparks, who had a reputation as a bully and "negro baiter," answered Baltimore's inquiry by shouting, "Don't you like it?" Before the startled soldier could explain, Sparks attacked him with his service revolver. In an attempt to escape the rain of blows, Baltimore ran, was fired at, pursued, caught, and severely pistol-whipped. Sparks later justified his actions on the grounds that the victimized soldier had approached him roughly and was using profanity. However, Rufus Daniels, Sparks's partner, refused, in sworn testimony, to confirm Sparks's story. He said that he had not heard any profanity while Baltimore was talking to his partner.[21]

Following the Baltimore incident, rumors quickly spread that the soldier had been killed and that a white mob was planning an attack upon Camp Logan. The rumors of Baltimore's death and the resulting tension in Camp Logan attracted the attention of Maj. Kneeland S. Snow, who had assumed command of the 24th Battalion on August 20. According to Snow, he and his white officers immediately "realized we were sitting on a powder-keg" and began "doing everything in our power to keep it from being touched off." Snow, accompanied by Capt. Haig Shekerjian, who was in charge of military police, proceeded to police headquarters to investigate the Baltimore affair. There they found Baltimore severely beaten, but alive. Subsequently, they were able to secure his release by convincing Chief of Police Clarence Brock that the injured soldier had been carrying out his duties as a military policeman when he questioned the arrest of another soldier. Brock also promised the officers that Patrolman Sparks would be suspended for his unwarranted attack upon Baltimore, and that he would order his men to refrain from referring to the soldiers as "niggers" since that appeared to be the source of most of the friction.[22]

During their return to Camp Logan, Snow informed Baltimore of Brock's promise and requested that he relay the information to the men. Snow also informed his white officers of Brock's promise. To prevent an accidental clash between his men and white Houstonians, Snow canceled all passes for the evening and posted extra guards to make sure that no one left camp without authorization. After taking these precautions, Snow and his officers believed they had defused the explosive situation and that the camp would be back to normal the next day.[23] Tension, however, remained high in the camp since many of the inexperienced soldiers and their black officers feared that they had been disarmed so that they could not defend themselves from the white mob attack they believed would occur at any moment.

The cause of widespread fear in Camp Logan of a white mob attack has never been fully explained. Haynes has argued that this fear was part of a planned conspiracy and was manufactured by those involved in planning the attack upon Houston, in order to create panic and give their plans a reasonable chance for success. He draws this conclusion from conflicting testimony given to the Houston Civilian Board of Inquiry, which was organized after the incident to investigate its causes, and to military courts by frightened black youths, revenge-seeking white police and civilians, and military officials who were trying to clear themselves of any and all responsibility for the incident.[24] It was upon these highly questionable sources that Haynes constructed his conspiracy theory. These people, by Haynes's own admission, and according to the report of one of the army's chief investigators of the incident, Col. G. O. Cress, were asked leading questions with suggested answers by prosecutors who wanted to prove the incident was premeditated and not a spontaneous reaction to weeks of humiliation and an imminent fear of physical violence.[25]

A careful analysis of the official report by military investigators reveals that the soldiers' fear of a white mob attack was genuine and that there was no conclusive proof the fear was deliberately created by alleged conspirators against the city of Houston to mask their plans. From the moment the 24th arrived in Houston, the soldiers were under immense pressure because, according to Colonel Newman, "There was a disposition on the part of the citizens not to respect a uniform [when worn by a black soldier] and that the situation was much more trying than they had ever been made to face."[26] Newman's views were shared by Colonel Cress, who reported that "the attitude among . . . the white citizens generally is, in substance, that a nigger is a nigger, and that his status is not effected by the uniform he wears."[27] These attitudes often resulted in acts of brutality against the defenseless soldiers by police and civilians when, according to Colonel Newman, "it was clearly not the soldier's fault."[28]

To understand the fear of attack felt by the men of the 24th on the night of August 23, an examination of the events surrounding the suspension of Patrolman Sparks and his reaction is necessary. Long before the arrival of the 24th in Houston, Sparks had developed a reputation as a "brutal bully" and a "negro baiter" who was not satisfied with the socioeconomic advantages whites enjoyed over blacks. He was a man who missed no opportunity to use brutality to put those he viewed as "uppity" blacks in their proper place. This sadistic conduct was apparently endorsed by Sparks's superiors since there is no evidence to indicate any effort was made to alter his behavior.[29] Since Sparks had never been disciplined for his treatment of blacks, he was shocked when informed by Chief Brock that he was being suspended due to the Baltimore incident, and he angrily accused Brock of being a Negrophile. "Any man that sticks up for a nigger," Sparks yelled at his supervisor, "is no better than a nigger."[30]

Sparks's suspension was not only a blow to his ego, but it also threatened him economically. He had only recently returned to duty after a 10-day suspension, without pay, for "improper remarks made to a white woman," and could not afford another one.[31] Sparks was clearly not a man who hid his feelings, and he faulted the black soldiers for his fate, publicly berated his chief, and talked of getting even. In a city where public hostility toward black troops was at an all-time high, the angry explanations of his position, which Sparks undoubtedly would have made to white civilian associates to garner their support, could easily have led to rumors of retaliation among them. Since whites often disregarded the presence of black onlookers, such as servants, when discussing racial issues or airing hostility towards other blacks, it is quite possible that black civilians informed the men of the 24th about the threats of revenge against them: thus accounting, in part, for the soldiers' heightened fear of attack.

The intense fear of an attack by a mob of white Houstonians engulfing Camp Logan on the night of August 23 cannot be dismissed, as it is by Haynes and some military investigators, as something generated by a small group of revenge-seeking black soldiers to conceal their plans for an attack upon the city. Nor can the charge that the cry, "They are coming! The mob is coming," be interpreted as a covert, coded signal to the men to begin such an attack. "That those who went out of camp employed this alarm, 'the mob is coming,' as a means of starting the riot," reported Col. G. O. Cress, "could not be ascertained, but all circumstances point to the fact that the men left back in camp . . . were obsessed with the idea that a mob of citizens from Houston would attack them."[32] The cry was followed by gunfire and by a mad scramble for weapons and a mass exodus from camp by approximately 150 frightened and inexperienced soldiers, but the evidence indicates that the camp was indeed fired upon by outside forces.

The men left in camp, after the first shots were fired, clearly believed they were under attack and seized their weapons and began to return fire indiscriminately. According to one of their white officers, "The only way to get the men to stop shooting was to shake them and make them realize that they were actually shooting at each other and not some mythical mob of white citizens."[33] The soldiers had only army rifles at their disposal but the initial shots fired near Camp Logan, testified L. E. Gentry, a local white policeman, "didn't sound like rifles to me." An examination of those wounded in and near Camp Logan also revealed that "these wounds resulted from gun shot [weapons of nonmilitary issue] and not rifle fire."[34] An examination of bullets fired into homes near Camp Logan on the night of the "alleged riot" also revealed that they had been fired from nonmilitary weapons.[35] This, combined with the examination of bullets in the camp and Gentry's testimony, substantiates the statement by soldiers left in the camp that those who disobeyed orders and left the camp did so in order to form a skirmish line around the camp to meet their attackers.

The conspiracy theory is further weakened by the testimony of R. E. Lewis before the Houston Civilian Board of Inquiry. According to Lewis, a local attorney who lived near Camp Logan, a small group of men passed his home after the initial shooting and he inquired of them "What was going on?" One of them replied, "Oh we are shooting up the whites; we haven't but a little time to stay here; (but) we are no negroes." Lewis then testified that "one of the men raised his rifle and said, 'You know how far and how fast one of these magazine rifles can shoot?'"[36] Lewis did not identify the men he talked to on that dark and rainy night as black or white. However, the fact that they left Lewis unharmed clearly indicates that they were not an angry group of black soldiers on a mission of revenge against whites. Were these men, armed with rifles, members of the Texas National Guard, which the 24th replaced, along with other whites (Haynes's "mythical" white mob)? Was the attack upon Camp Logan an attempt to duplicate the Brownsville incident of 1906? The evidence is clear that Camp Logan had been fired into by outside forces and that the frightened soldiers panicked, seized their weapons, and left camp to meet their assailants. It was not an organized or planned exit since the soldiers left camp "hollering and yelling like a mob."[37] Such an exit does not indicate that it was one planned by experienced or veteran black soldiers.

Haynes has argued that Sgt. Vida Henry and a small group of supporters planned and organized the attack upon Houston. This view was first advanced by military authorities who, Haynes admits, deliberately distorted the sworn testimony of the two chief officers of the 24th Battalion, Commander Snow and Chief of Military Police Captain Shekerjian, in order to produce a conspiracy theory. Both men testified that Sergeant Henry was the one who warned them of possible trouble on the night of August 23, but in order to identify Henry as the organizer of the incident and leader of the rebellious men, top army officials concluded that the officers had made a mistake and that someone else had given the warning. Accepting the distorted military view, Haynes goes on to argue that Henry was indeed the principal conspirator, that he deliberately deceived his superiors, tricking them into seizing all weapons in camp in order to create fear among the men, arranged for the cry "the mob is coming" to be shouted in camp as a signal for action on the part of his followers, and planned to use his position as a first sergeant to lead more men from the camp into Houston on a mission of revenge.[38]

The argument that Sergeant Henry led the men in such a conspiracy is unsupported either by reliable, documented evidence or by Henry's character and attitudes. Based upon his military record prior to the incident, Henry was one of the few members of the 24th who was enjoying his stay in Houston. According to Col. William Newman, who was in command of the 24th until August 20, Henry told him that he was fond of the city because "he had met more high-class colored people in Houston than he had ever seen before."[39] Newman described Henry as a man of unquestioned loyalty who had been given responsibilities that were beyond his capabilities. "I thought he was unoffensive and not forceful enough to be a First Sergeant of a company," said Newman. Major Snow, Newman's successor, held similar views of Henry, whom he described as illiterate but courteous. Snow also testified that it was Henry who first warned him of trouble.[40] In light of the sworn opinions of Colonel Newman and Major Snow, it is inconceivable that Sergeant Henry had the desire, courage, or ability to organize a full-fledged rebellion against military authority and the city of Houston.

All who identified Sergeant Henry as the leader of the soldiers' attack upon Houston were frightened men who testified under grants of immunity from prosecution or promises of leniency from military prosecutors. The witnesses responded to questions that were worded to elicit a preconceived response.[41] It is beyond question that Henry participated in the incident. However, his decision to do so was made after failing to prevent the troops from seizing weapons and from disobeying orders to remain in camp. According to Colonel Cress's investigation and report on the incident, the soldiers who bolted the camp after the initial shooting "were not in any formation when they left but appear to have halted and, at least partially, organized on the street just east of camp."[42]

In all probability Henry was among the men who panicked and, once outside the camp, realized that a serious military offense had taken place that would bring the severest of punishments. He, therefore, decided to make the crime fit the harsh punishment that surely awaited the men when the camp returned to normal and made the decision to direct their actions. This was a spur-of-the-moment decision rather than a coldly premeditated plot. Once the decision had been made, Henry realized its gravity, which explains why he took his own life on the streets of Houston rather than give the army the pleasure of dictating his execution.

The other soldiers who participated in the Houston confrontation were not as fortunate as Henry. In the aftermath of the disturbance, the entire 3rd Battalion, 24th Infantry, was immediately transferred to Camp Furlong in Columbus, New Mexico, where 118 men were arrested, charged with murder and mutiny, and held for trial by general court-martial. The purpose of a court-martial, as the history of such events has shown, is to convict—and 110 of the accused were ultimately convicted. The men were tried in three groups: sixty-three on November 1, 1917; fifteen on December 17, 1917; and the last forty on February 18, 1918. The trials resulted in twenty-eight death sentences, thirteen of which were secretly carried out on December 11, 1917, before the cases could be reviewed and without notification to the respective families. President Woodrow Wilson reluctantly commuted ten of the remaining death sentences to life imprisonment after his office was flooded with letters protesting the earlier executions and requesting leniency for those who remained on death row. Those not given the death penalty were sentenced to the federal prison in Leavenworth, Kansas, to serve terms that ranged from two years to life.

When the fate of those soldiers sentenced to death because of their alleged involvement in the Houston affair became public knowledge, the black community reacted with fury. Blacks on the street openly talked of revenge and the nation's black press refused to condemn what the white press described as "one of the most disgraceful mutinies of American troops in our history."[43] Instead, black newspapers angrily attacked what they believed to be military injustice. *The Crisis*, the journal of the NAACP, which served as the organization's national voice, described the executed soldiers as "martyrs for the cause of democracy."[44] Similar views were expressed by the *Baltimore Crusader*, the *Messenger*, a socialist publication in New York City edited by Asa P. Randolph and Chandler Owen, and the *New York Age*, a publication founded by the well-respected T. Thomas Fortune. Fortune was a strong supporter of the philosophy of Booker T. Washington and counted among his supporters prominent politicians such as Senator Thomas C. Platt of New York and former president Theodore Roosevelt. An editorial in the *Age* angrily declared that "strict justice has been done, but full justice has not been done. And so sure as there is a God in heaven, at some time and some way full justice will be done."[45]

All of the 110 men sentenced to death or imprisonment by the military courts-martial proclaimed their innocence. The night of the incident was dark and rainy, making it impossible for the white officers of the 24th to identify individual participants.[46] Nor did the courts-martial produce any evidence to identify individuals. Subsequently, the accused were convicted upon military speculation and the conflicting testimony of seven frightened black soldiers, one of whom was so scared that he "defecated in his breeches" on the night of the incident.[47] These men were pressured to admit that they were participants in the affair and were promised leniency in return for their testimony against other suspected participants. The goal of army prosecutors was to prove that the Houston incident was unprovoked, premeditated, and that the white officers of the 24th bore no blame. With the aid of the seven black soldiers, the prosecution was able to ensure that all the white officers of the battalion were officially relieved of any responsibility for the incident.

If the white officers bear no responsibility, who was responsible for the Houston incident? The easy answer is that the soldiers were responsible since they disobeyed orders and took up arms against civilians. This was the official position taken by the War Department. In his studies of the incident, Haynes accepts the War Department's position but also broadens the responsibility. He argues that local business leaders and public officials shared some of the responsibility due to economic greed (the profits to be made from the construction of Camp Logan) and an unwillingness to sacrifice political popularity to guarantee fair treatment to soldiers. Haynes also criticizes Chief of Police Brock for his inability to control his men and eliminate police brutality. But Haynes's hardest indictment is reserved for the soldiers, whom he denounces for their decision to fight violence with violence. The urge to defend oneself when under attack, a natural urge propelled by intense fear, is not a factor in Haynes's analysis, since he dismisses their reactions to the attack of their encampment by an irate mob in favor of a conspiracy theory. There is no question that some of the inexperienced soldiers from the 24th, reacting to what the evidence indicates was a mob attack, panicked and reacted with violence toward their attackers. That, however, was a reaction to violence and not its cause. The ultimate responsibility, therefore, rests with those who deliberately set in motion the forces that ended in violent confrontation.

The War Department and the white officers of the 24th bear much of the responsibility for the bloodshed in Houston. The secretary of war, Newton D. Baker, reversed a decision made by army officials not to send black troops into the South for military training and tours of duty, in full recognition of the potential problems. Top army officials and lesser officers then failed to carry out his directive that they "exercise judgment and discretion" to prevent clashes between their men and the local white population. Conflict between black soldiers and whites in Houston was assured when the War Department decided to send 65 experienced, noncommissioned officers from the 24th to commission officer training school at Fort Des Moines, Iowa. According to Brigadier General J. L. Chamberlain, these men were "the very best material among the non-commissioned officers of the regiment and included the Regimental Sergeant Major, the Battalion Sergeant Major, the First Sergeant, and three other Sergeants from Company I, the company in which the mutiny started." Subsequently, "many of the non-commissioned officers and many of the men left with the regiment were new men," not experienced soldiers as Haynes and others have charged.[48] Those elite noncommissioned officers from the 24th who were attending officer training school believed that if they had been with their men, the Houston incident would never have occurred. They even volunteered to "give up their prospects for commissions so as to return to the regiment and redeem its reputation."[49]

The War Department was also responsible for transferring command of the 24th from Col. William Newman, an officer with experience in commanding black troops, to Maj. Kneeland S. Snow, an inexperienced officer, who, according to Haynes, was more concerned about his golf game and Houston's nightlife than he was with the welfare of his men.[50] Snow took command of the 24th two days before the tragedy of August 23 and miserably failed to execute Baker's directive to use "judgment and discretion" to prevent trouble between black troops and the local white population. Due to these actions, significant responsibility for the Houston tragedy must fall on the shoulders of the War Department, which, blinded by military tradition and racism, ignored an excellent opportunity to play a major role as an agency of model race relations and progressive social change.

In view of the economic importance of Camp Logan to the Houston economy, Baker and army officials could have forced local officials to treat the men of the 24th with dignity and respect, even within the confines of a Jim Crow community. However, the War Department did not believe that its duty was to work for improved race relations in the civilian community or the army. This was clearly communicated to Emmett J. Scott, Baker's black assistant for minority affairs, in the aftermath of the Houston incident when he asked Baker to implement more humane racial policies in the army. "There is no intention on the part of the War Department," Baker replied, "to undertake at this time a settlement of the so-called race question."[51] Despite the War Department's lack of concern and poor decision-making, however, the ultimate responsibility for the Houston incident rests on the shoulders of local police, the business community, and political leaders.

It was the Houston business community that successfully lobbied the War Department for Camp Logan and it was the construction of the camp that ultimately brought the all-black 24th Infantry to the city. Camp Logan was an economic boon for Houston, contributing approximately $60,000 weekly to the local economy.[52] Local leaders wanted more and were negotiating with the War Department for an aviation school. In fact, the announcement that the city had been awarded the school was made on August 21, 1917, one day before the incident. During the negotiations, business leaders were aware of growing problems between white civilians, police, and the black troops at Camp Logan but refused to report them to the War Department for fear of losing the aviation school and having the operations of the camp severely restricted.[53] This was clearly revealed in an unsigned editorial in the Houston *Post* following the explosion at Camp Logan. According to the editorial, "The only explanation of toleration of this insolent and disorderly conduct [any display of pride and independence by blacks was viewed as insolent and disorderly conduct by many local whites] is that those who knew of it thought it best to endure patiently rather than run the risk of losing the camp by flooding the War Department with complaints."[54]

The Houston business community, represented by the local chamber of commerce (which had assured the War Department that the black soldiers would be treated with respect by local whites), allowed the pursuit of profits from government wartime expenditures to override its civic responsibility. Treating black soldiers with respect would not have seriously challenged the local Jim Crow laws, which the white community cherished. Had business and political leaders pressured local police authorities into reining in a brutal, out-of-control police force, clashes might have been minimized and violence averted. Instead, business leaders not only failed to intervene but refused to report problems with the 24th to the War Department in order to protect their profits. It was this failure of courage and political leadership, fueled by greed, that paved the way for what is commonly known as the Houston Riot of 1917.

In 1921, Congressman D. R. Anthony of Leavenworth, Kansas, introduced a resolution into the US House of Representatives requesting Secretary of War John W. Weeks to review the cases of the 63 soldiers still imprisoned as a result of the Houston tragedy to determine if they were eligible for pardons or clemency. Weeks reported that the cases of the imprisoned soldiers had been reviewed in the spring of 1920 by the Department of Psychiatry and Sociology at the US Disciplinary Barracks, Fort Leavenworth, Kansas, and that the prison psychiatrists had issued a negative report. According to the report:

> Practically all of these prisoners deny participation in the mutiny or events occurring in the city of Houston on August 23, 1917. It seems to us that the conspiracy continues among these men. In view of the serious nature of the offenses of which these men were convicted, it is believed that it would be distinctly prejudicial to discipline and the interest of the services to grant any clemency at this time.[55]

In denying clemency, the army refused to consider the fact that the accused had not been positively identified by anyone as actual participants in the Houston affair. The protests of innocence might have been truth, rather than an obstinate conspiracy. Nor did the army consider the mitigating circumstances that led to the incident.

In the aftermath of World War I, the war fought to "make the world safe for democracy," the vast majority of black Americans readily agreed with

Emmett Scott, Baker's assistant secretary of war for black affairs, when he commented in 1933: "As one who recalls the assurances of 1917 and 1918 . . . I confess personally a deep sense of disappointment, of poignant pain that a great country in time of need should promise so much and afterward perform so little."[56] And the remnants of the 24th who bravely fought and died in the war while their brothers languished in prison could say to America with conviction that "you treat no other friend so ill."

Notes

1. Quoted in David M. Kennedy, *Over Here: The First World War and American Society* (New York: Oxford University Press, 1980), 159.

2. Mary F. Berry and John W. Blassingame, *Long Memory: The Black Experience in America* (New York: Oxford University Press, 1982), 308.

3. Ibid.

4. For detailed accounts of the Brownsville incident see John D. Weaver, *The Brownsville Raid* (New York: W. W. Norton, 1970); Ann J. Lane, *The Brownsville Affair: National Crisis and Black Reaction* (Port Washington, New York: Kennikat Press, 1971); and Lewis N. Wynne, "Brownsville: The Reaction of the Negro Press," *Phylon* 33 (Summer 1972): 153–60.

5. Berry and Blassingame, *Long Memory*, 311. In 1972, more than sixty years after the incident, the army cleared the records of those accused of raiding Brownsville and declared their original conviction a gross injustice.

6. Newton D. Baker, secretary of war, to President Woodrow Wilson, August 17, 1917, *The Papers of Woodrow Wilson*, vol. 43 (Washington, DC: Library of Congress, 1955), 506.

7. Ibid.

8. The comments of Col. William Newman are included in an investigative report on the Houston incident of 1917 by Col. G. O. Cress entitled "Investigation into the disciplinary conditions in 3rd Battalion, 24th Infantry, while on duty in Houston, Texas, July 26 to August 25, 1917." The report is dated October 5, 1917. See Record Group 407, Records of the Adjutant General's Office, 1917–1925, Box 1277, Folder 4, National Archives. Cress and a number of other military officials filed multiple reports on the Houston incident, hereafter cited by name of correspondent, date, and record group number.

9. Robert V. Haynes, *A Night of Violence: The Houston Riot of 1917* (Baton Rouge: LSU Press, 1976), 53.

10. Statement of Sgt. Cecil Green to Col. G. O. Cress, August 30, 1917, in an investigative report by Colonel Cress entitled "Investigation of the Trouble at Houston, Texas, Between the Third Battalion, 24th Infantry, and the Citizens of Houston, August 23, 1917," Record Group 393, US Army, Southern Department, Box 364, File 370.61, National Archives.

11. See Newman's statement in Cress Report, October 5, 1917, RG 407.

12. Martha Gruening, "Houston: An N.A.A.C.P. Investigation," *The Crisis* 15 (November 1917): 19; Haynes, *A Night of Violence*, 85.

13. Cress Report, October 5, 1917, RG 407.

14. Report of Col. William Newman to Inspector General of the Army, September 20, 1917, Record Group 407, Records of the Adjutant General's Office, 1917–1925, Box 1277, National Archives.

15. Ibid.

16. Report of Capt. David E. Van Natta, 2nd Illinois Infantry, to Inspector General of the Army, September 25, 1917, Record Group 393, US Army, Southern Department, Records of the Judge Advocates General, Box 364, File 370.61, National Archives.

17. See *The Outlook*, September 5, 1917; *Literary Digest*, September 29, 1917; Gruening, "Houston," 14–19.

18. Robert V. Haynes, "The Houston Mutiny and Riot of 1917," *Southwestern Historical Quarter*, 76 (1973); Haynes, *A Night of Violence.*

19. Haynes, "The Houston Mutiny," 430 n53.

20. For the sworn statements of Lee Sparks and Charles Baltimore, see Cress Report, September 13, 1917, RG 393.

21. Ibid.

22. Cress Report, October 5, 1917, RG 407.

23. Major Snow's account of events leading up to the confrontation on the night of August 23 is located in Cress Report, September 13, 1917, RG 393.

24. See testimony of Chief of Police Clarence E. Brock in Newman Report, September 20, 1917, RG 407; and the testimony of Cleo Lockhart, age 15, Edna Topper, age 13, and Flassy and Bessie Chancey, ages 15 and 16 respectively, Record Group 153, Records of the Judge Advocate, NNG-73-543, General Court Martials, Federal Records Center (Microfilm), Suitland, Maryland.

25. Cress Report, October 5, 1917, RG 407.

26. Newman Report, September 20, 1917, RG 407.

27. Cress Report, September 13, 1917, RG 393.

28. Colonel Newman's comments are quoted in Cress Report, October 5, 1917, RG 407.

29. Haynes, *A Night of Violence*, 93.

30. Ibid., 102.

31. Testimony of Chief Clarence C. Brock before the Houston Civilian Board of Inquiry, August 24, 1917, p. 217 of transcript, Record Group 393, US Army, Southern Department, Box 364, File 370.61, National Archives. Haynes has argued that Sparks was suspended for using abusive language in front of a black housewife while arresting her teenage son. This appears very unlikely in view of the record of unrestrained police brutality blacks endured in Houston. By Haynes's own admission, Sparks's supervisors had made no effort to control his abusive behavior prior to the Baltimore incident *(A Night of Violence*, 93.) Furthermore, Sparks apparently continued his career of brutality toward blacks. Three days after the Camp Logan tragedy, Sparks shot and killed a black Houstonian. Although indicted for murder, Sparks was quickly acquitted by the jury (Haynes, "The Houston Mutiny and Riot of 1917," 478 n76).

32. Cress Report, September 13, 1917, (5), RG 393.

33. Haynes, *A Night of Violence*, 125.

34. Testimony of Patrolman L. E. Gentry before the Houston Civilian Board of Inquiry, p. 25 of transcript; Maj. K. S. Snow to Brig. Gen. John A. Hulen, "Report on Circumstances Attending the Mutiny," August 24, 1917, Record Group 393, US Army, Southern Department, Box 364, National Archives.

35. Haynes, "The Houston Mutiny," 429 n49.

36. Testimony of R. E. Lewis before the Houston Civilian Board of Inquiry, p. 97 of transcript, August 24, 1917, RG 393.

37. Haynes, *A Night of Violence*, 136–139.

38. Haynes, *A Night of Violence*, 136–139.

39. Statement by Newman, October 1, 1917, in Cress Report, October 5, 1917, RG 407.

40. Testimony of Maj. K. S. Snow, September 27, 1917, Record Group 407, Records of the Adjutant General's Office, Box 1277, Folder 4, National Archives.

41. Haynes, *A Night of Violence*, 258.

42. Cress Report, September 13, 1917, RG 393.

43. *The Outlook*, September 5, 1917, 10; *Literary Digest*, September 29, 1917, 4–5.

44. *The Crisis*, October 17, 1917, 284–285.

45. These papers are quoted in John Hope Franklin, *From Slavery to Freedom: A History of Negro Americans* (New York: Knopf, 1980), 330.

46. Cress Report, September 13, 1917, RG 393.

47. Haynes, *A Night of Violence*, 261–262, 277, 304.

48. Brig. Gen. J. L. Chamberlain, Inspector General, US Army, to Adjutant General, September 26, 1917, Record Group 407, Records of the Adjutant General's Office, Box 1277, National Archives.

49. Ibid.

50. Haynes, *A Night of Violence*, 91.

51. Newton D. Baker, secretary of war, to Emmett J. Scott, September 30, 1917, quoted in Kennedy, 159.

52. Edgar A. Schuler, "The Houston Race Riot, 1917," *The Journal of Negro History* (July 1944): 304.

53. Ibid.

54. Ibid.

55. John W. Weeks, secretary of war, to the Honorable Julius Kahn, US House of Representatives, December 6, 1921, Record Group 233, House Committee on Military Affairs, 67th Congress, Houston Riot Cases, HR67A-F28.1, National Archives.

56. Quoted in Kennedy, 284.

4

Violence in a Heathen Land

The Longview Race Riot of 1919

William M. Tuttle Jr.

Meeting at the Olivet Baptist Church on Chicago's South Side were four deeply troubled men. Two were fugitives from the law of Longview, Texas; two were officials of the National Association for the Advancement of Colored People; all were civil rights activists at a time when the rights and even the lives of black people were being repeatedly violated. Dr. C. P. Davis and Mr. S. L. Jones, the fugitives, had come to Chicago to seek the aid of the NAACP. Secluded at the church, they recounted their story of suffering and courage to Mr. John R. Shilladay, the white executive secretary of the NAACP's national office, and Dr. Charles E. Bentley, a black dentist who was serving as president of the organization's Chicago chapter. The date was August 18, 1919, the midpoint in America's "Red Summer" of racial violence.[1]

In the six-month period from April to early October 1919, race riots bloodied the streets of twenty-five towns and cities throughout the country, among them Charleston, South Carolina, Longview, Washington, DC, Chicago, and Omaha. As many as 120 people of both races died in these riots in the first year of peace after World War I. Wars always bring change, domestically as well as internationally, and trailing in the wake of World War I were not only deep suspicion and fear of foreigners and alleged radicals, but violent race hatred as well. In 1919 the epithet "Bolshevism" became an effective instrument for damning all sorts of opposition and contrary beliefs; Communism was a phantom that conjured up a myriad of demonic images, and these images inspired a host of aggressive impulses. By midyear, government at all levels had succumbed to the emotional tide. Several states had enacted red flag, criminal anarchy, syndicalist, and sedition laws; and the federal police powers, led by Attorney General A. Mitchell Palmer, were mounting, leading to the grossest abuses of the "Red Scare." But the

Originally published in *The Phylon Quarterly* 33 (Winter 1972): 324–33. Reprinted with permission of Clark Atlanta University and *Phylon*.

most highly susceptible objects of prejudice in postwar America were its black men and women, not because they were radicals or new arrivals to the country, but because they threatened the nation's race system of white superiority and black inferiority. Having helped as soldiers and war workers to win the war for worldwide "democracy," blacks entered the year 1919 with aspirations for a larger share of democracy at home. Tensions mounted—and racial violence erupted—as these aspirations collided with the general white determination to reaffirm the black people's prewar status on the bottom rung of the racial ladder.[2]

Also in 1919 lynch mobs murdered 78 black people, an increase of 15 over 1918 and 30 over 1917. However, the toll might have been even higher had it not been for the determination of many blacks to stand fast and even retaliate against white violence. Too often, historians have depicted black people as anonymous, faceless figures. Yet black men and women were actors in the tragedy of bloodshed of 1919. Not mere passive victims, these "New Negroes" fought back.

> If we must die—let it not be like hogs
> Hunted and penned in an inglorious spot,
> While round us bark the mad and hungry dogs,
> Making their mock at our accursed lot.
> If we must die—oh, let us nobly die,
> So that our precious blood may not be shed
> In vain; then even the monsters we defy
> Shall be constrained to honor us though dead!
> Oh, Kinsmen! We must meet the common foe;
> Though far outnumbered, let us show us brave,
> And for their thousand blows deal one death blow!
> What though before us lies the open grave?
> Like men we'll face the murderous, cowardly pack,
> Pressed to the wall, dying but fighting back![3]

So wrote Claude McKay in the summer of 1919. And his was not a solitary voice calling for self-assertion, manliness, and resolute self-defense. Two other black men who felt the same way were C. P. Davis and S. L. Jones, both of Longview.

Longview, the center of population of an east Texas county of 8,500 whites and 8,200 blacks, had been uneasy with racial tension during the spring and early summer months of 1919. For one thing, members of the local branch of the Negro Business League had set up cooperative stores whose products competed with those of the white merchants. For another, these same black leaders—men such as Davis and Jones—had urged black farmers to bypass the white cotton brokers in Longview by selling directly to the buyers in Galveston. Then, on June 17, there was a lynching. Lemuel Walters allegedly had been discovered in a white woman's bedroom. He was arrested, but the next day his nude, bullet-riddled body was found lying near the railroad tracks at a desolate spot known as Foote's Switch, four miles south of Longview. On June 22, Jones, who was the local "agent for colored papers . . . and was accustomed to go to the jail on Sunday to bring papers to colored inmates," visited the jail and talked with its one white and three black prisoners. While there, as Jones later recalled in Chicago, the prisoners described how on the evening of June 17, "ten men came to the jail and got Walters and took him away. The mob jammed five pocket handkerchiefs in the lad's mouth, had a key to the jail, unlocked the door and when they had taken the prisoner, they locked the door with the same key."[4]

Anxiety gripped the black community, and Davis and Jones, leading a delegation of eleven men, made a call on the county judge, Erskine H. Bramlette, "to place the matter before him and to ask his advice and help . . . in bringing the matter properly before the authorities." The judge, after hearing the story, asked the black men for the names of the prisoners from whom Jones had gained this information. He also advised silence, saying that "there [should] be no talking as talking would interfere with locating the culprits." Days passed, but no arrests were made, and it appeared to the black men that law officials were not only not investigating the lynching but that they were even using this time to remove evidence that would prove the guilt of the murderers. The black delegation again called on Judge Bramlette, and on this visit, as during the first, the judge advised "no talking." And three days later, when Jones returned to the jail, he found that "the prisoners had been taken away."[5]

An important weekly event in Longview's black community was the arrival on the train of the Chicago *Defender*. Sold at the Quick Grocery, Benton's Market, McWilliams' Restaurant, and Leroy's Fountain, the newspaper was also peddled by boys like the doctor's son, C. P. Davis Jr., who in the paper was once commended as "the popular little Defender agent" of Longview. "Every Race man and every lover of justice," the signs in Longview's black grocery and drug stores proclaimed, "should read the Defender." The *Defender* not only emphasized pride in race and the need for solidarity, it was equally emphatic in its denunciation of the South. To the persistent rumor that blacks would freeze to death if they migrated to the North, the *Defender* countered that this was "all 'bosh.' IF YOU CAN FREEZE TO DEATH in the north and be free, why FREEZE to death in the south and be a slave, where your mother, sister and daughter are raped . . . where your father, brother and son are . . . hung to a pole, [and] riddled with bullets. . . ." What probably heightened its appeal and persuasiveness even more was the outrage it caused among whites. The whites of Madison County, Mississippi, adopted a resolution claiming that the *Defender* was German propaganda designed to "revive sectional issues and create race antagonism," and they thus "condemned its circulation in the county." Other whites confiscated copies locally, and one rural community would permit no correspondence between its black residents and the newspaper.[6]

The July 5, 1919, issue of the *Defender* was of special interest, for it had a story with the dateline "Longview, Tex., July 4." "Despite the fact that every effort has been made by officials here to keep the outside world from learning of the lynching of Lemuel Walters at this place June 17, the news has leaked out." "Walters," the article continued, "was taken from the Longview jail by a crowd of white men when a prominent white woman declared she loved him, and if she were in the North would obtain a divorce and marry him." Not only had no charges been preferred against Walters, but "the sheriff of the jail [had] gladly welcomed the mob. . . . Walters was taken to the outskirts of the town and shot to pieces. His nude body was thrown near the roadside. He was buried by the people of his Race." The *Defender* concluded by suggesting another motive for the white people's anger—the fact that "our people have been leaving this part of Texas in droves, and since this lynching all the farm hands have left."[7]

What follows is the account of Jones and Davis (as told to John Shilladay and Dr. Bentley) of the bloodshed that erupted on July 10, the Thursday after publication of the *Defender* article.[8]

> Jones "was in town and had left his automobile when, upon returning to it, he was accosted by three white men," two of whom were brothers of the woman whose name, whites felt, had been defamed. One of the men grabbed Jones, while another pulled a wrench out of his coat and struck him a heavy blow on the head. "Other blows followed. Jones felled one of the men with a blow with his fists . . . and then all three jumped him. Jones ran, but ran into a wire obstruction and fell. While on the ground he was accused of having written the Defender article, which he denied, and [he] was [then] beaten, and [sustained a] cut on the head. Getting away from his assailants, he went to Dr. Davis' office and had the doctor dress his wounds.
>
> "Deputy sheriff John Harrison told an old colored man of the 'good nigger' type that there was going to be trouble that night. A colored boy came to Dr. Davis and told him that Prof. Jones was going to be lynched before 12 [o'clock] that night if he was still in town. Davis then went to see some of the prominent white citizens of the town. . . . Mayor G. A. Bodenheim at 6:30 sent a boy to Dr. Davis . . . to tell Davis and Jones to get out of town at once. Davis refused to do so. The latter then went to about 25 colored

men and told them what had been said and what was threatened. They all agreed to stand by him and Prof. Jones.

"Davis learned that the mayor, other officials and some citizens were holding a meeting at the city hall. He went there and asked to know what they planned to do and to have a chance to state the case for Prof. Jones and himself. By this time he had been included in the charge of having written the Defender article, which he denied. . . . At the meeting he was told to take off his hat. He refused saying. 'Yes! that's all "you all" say to a colored man who comes to talk serious business to you: "Take off your hat." I am not going to do it. I want to know what protection we colored citizens are going to have tonight.' The mayor replied 'You will have to take your chances.' Chief of Police Sam Matthews, who was drunk . . . walked over to Davis and said 'Now I've always been your friend. You'd better be careful or you mightn't get back where [you] came from.' The mayor ordered Matthews to sit down. Tom Flanagan, who was the leader of the mob which afterward attacked Prof. Jones' house, followed Davis out of the city hall and demanded to know who wrote the Defender article. Davis told him he didn't know—that neither he nor Prof. Jones had anything to do with it. All this time Davis refused to allow Flanagan to get behind him. Davis went to his Ford car and keeping Flanagan in a safe position (Davis was armed) rode away.

"The colored guard gathered around Jones' house and pledged their lives in his defense. Davis assumed charge and posted men where they could safeguard every side from which an attack could be made. The men were instructed what to do and not to fire before Davis did and under no circumstances to shoot into white people's houses.

"After 11 p.m., Davis went to the city hall, taking precautions, and saw cars, guns and men gathered there, using the fire department as headquarters. He returned to Prof. Jones' house and, rounding up the men, told them what he had seen and offered to allow any of them who did not feel like risking his life in defense of Prof. Jones to retire, and nobody would think any the less of them. Every man stayed and said he was prepared to take what might come.

"Soon afterward and approaching midnight, the mob came down through a back street. The colored men kept quiet and held their places, waiting until Prof. Jones' house was approached or attacked. Four white men came on the back porch of the house and called to Jones to come out. There was no response from within. When it became evident that they intended to force their way in, Davis fired the first shot and a general melee began. The colored men were so located on the defensive, that they had the advantage. . . ."

More than a hundred shots were fired in half an hour, and four whites fell with serious wounds, causing the rest of the mob of about a dozen whites to retreat to the town square. Minutes later, automobiles sped down the street leading to Jones's house, white men hopped out, picked up the wounded, and sped away.

After the mob had retreated, Davis sneaked to the downtown district again. He saw the survivors, and he heard "talk of going back but no leader could be found to start the trip. The colored guard stayed where it was for a time and then disbanded. On the way back Davis heard crying in the homes of white people, some women saying, "I told them not to go down where them niggers were." Throughout the night, a fire bell was sounded, eventually summoning about one thousand white men to the town square. Until almost daybreak the leaderless crowd simply milled around; then, at the first sign of daylight, men began smashing their way into the hardware store and helping themselves to rifles, pistols, and ammunition. Thus armed, a mob headed back to Jones's house. Davis recounted later that he was "where he could see what was going on." The men of the mob "cautiously moved around Jones' house and, when they were assured it was unoccupied, they set it afire. They then went directly across the street, shot the householder and his wife and set their house afire. From there they went to Davis' office and after carefully surrounding it, broke in, destroyed the contents and burned the building. They then went to Davis' house and set it afire also. They had kerosene oil behind them in a buggy. Davis' wife and children were in the house. After some talk, they allowed a colored man to go in and take the woman and children away.

"Davis went to the home of his mother-in-law which was searched twice while he was there by men seeking to find him. In one case he was behind some large cans, in the second, in the attic looking down through a crack at them and, armed, ready to shoot when necessary. His father-in-law told the searchers that he was not there and, when they looked at the attic, offered them a ladder to go up. They replied, 'Well! If you say he ain't here we'll take your word for it.' The father-in-law had a Winchester and pistol and was prepared to assist if it were needed.

"Davis started to get away at about daylight. He sent a boy over to a neighbor's for a soldier's uniform . . . [put on the uniform] and started for the railroad track. When he attempted to get on the train as it was going a trainman asked him where he was going. He replied that he was going home and that he lived down near 'Camp Switch' which was a short distance away, and where the train slowed down for an upgrade. . . . He jumped off at Camp Switch, waved his hand at the trainman who waved back, and then went off in the direction of the settlement. There he found friends. When he finally came to get on a train he found that the first train left at after 7 [o'clock] instead of near 5 as he had at first been told. Know-

> ing that anyone looking for him would be looking for a doctor, he bought some popcorn, some red pop and some other refreshment and walked around the railroad track and toward the station, throwing the bottle in the air, drinking from it ostentatiously and eating and singing, like a simple 'darky.' Arriving at the station, he tackled a white boy to shoot craps with him. After much effort he lost fifteen cents to the white boy and said 'that cleans me. I ain't done got no more money.
>
> "When the train came along there were some colored soldiers in it. He rushed up to the window, grabbed the hand of one and greeted him as a comrade, whom he had not seen since they were in France, then stepped into the car and seated himself next to one of the men and told him to move over quickly and ask him no questions as he was in trouble. The fellow said, 'Are you one of the Longview fellows,' to which he replied that he was whereupon they told him they had heard about the trouble there. Davis was given an overseas cap and a gas mask and the crowd pledged to 'take care of him.'"

A few hours later, his head bandaged, Jones also eluded the mob and the police and left town. Also that day, however, tragedy struck again. The sheriff and a deputy returned to the home of Davis's 60-year-old father-in-law, Marion Bush. Bush, frightened, fired five shots and then, clutching his rifle, he fled. Bloodhounds were soon in pursuit; it was not the sheriff, but armed white citizens, who a day later gunned Bush down in a cornfield three miles south of town.[9]

On July 12, the governor, at the request of Mayor Bodenheim, put the town under martial law and dispatched to the scene two hundred national guardsmen, a dozen Texas Rangers, and, for some reason, five airplanes, only three of which arrived. One crashed en route, slightly injuring the pilot, who proceeded the rest of the way by train; the other's engine gave out halfway between Dallas' Love Field and Longview. Although the aviators did little to effect the restoration of calm, the soldiers and the Rangers were very effective. The guardsmen, for example, established receiving stations for weapons, ordering even the Boy Scouts to turn in "their little rifles," and the Rangers arrested twenty-three whites, charging seventeen of them with assault with intent to commit murder and charging all of them with arson. The Rangers also removed to Austin for safekeeping the twenty blacks who had been arrested. Two weeks later half of these men were freed, and, according to newspaper reports, their return elicited "no resentment" and "was considered entirely proper by white people." These were not the blacks, however, who had fired on the mob. The men of Dr. Davis's "army" were imprisoned without charges until August 13, when they were freed "under condition that they would not return to Longview."[10]

After the killing of Marion Bush there was no more bloodshed. Yet that day and night of rioting had left one person dead, several badly wounded, and many homeless. Both blacks and some whites deplored the white vigilantism, but the whites did so only after condemning the "scurrilous [*Defender*] article" about "a respectable white lady." "We will not," some of Longview's "leading citizens" declared in adopting a post-riot resolution, "permit the negroes of this community and county to in any way interfere with our social affairs or to write or circulate articles about the white people of our city or county . . ."[11]

In mid-August, a little more than a month after the riot, Davis and Jones were interviewed in Chicago by Shilladay and Bentley. Over three weeks before the interview, however, newspaper articles had emanated from Topeka that "the great State of Kansas was stirred as never before or since the days of old John Brown, of Harper's Ferry fame, when Dr. C. P. Davis of Longview, Tex." had arrived in town to surrender himself to the governor. Having in mind "'Bleeding Kansas' and her struggle for the freedom of mankind," Davis had "set his face toward the land of fair play and justice. . . ." On July 22, Davis told his story to Governor Henry J. Allen, admitting that he had fired into the mob of whites and claiming that he had killed four of the men in defense of his home and family. "I protested when one of my people was mobbed," Davis explained, and this exacerbated the town's already embittered race relations. A mob assembled with the intention not only of destroying Davis's property but also of hanging him. "They were coming with torches and oil and a rope." When they were but a short distance from his home, Davis opened fire with a revolver, dropping four men with fatal wounds. The mob retreated, giving Davis an opportunity to escape with his family. "We waded the river—back and forth to throw that mob off our trail. Sometimes the bloodhounds were within fifty feet of me. I knew of just two states that were truly dear," the fugitive continued, "Massachusetts, where I was educated [at Harvard]—and Kansas." In appealing to Governor Allen for protection, Davis explained that his extradition to Texas would precipitate renewed mob violence and would probably lead to his death as well. The governor, being sympathetic, suggested that Davis surrender to the county sheriff. In this way, a full hearing of the case would have to be held when the State of Texas sought extradition, and, the governor added, "all would be well." The doctor was grateful, but later that day he quietly departed the city. Reporters noted that Davis had expressed concern about his family, whom he said he had sent to Boston, "so he left Topeka in an automobile driven by a recently returned soldier without saying anything to anyone." Whatever were the other results of this visit, the doctor's tale of courage and resistance was an inspiration to the black people who read or heard about it. "Now," declared the Topeka *Plaindealer*, "let all the good . . . white people join with the blacks and make America a better and fit place in which to live. Now let it be known from now on henceforth and forever, that the colored people are not going to stand for insults and not resent them."[12]

It is at this point that the story of the Longview riot resembles a Hollywood film with two endings supplied for different audiences. Who was the Topeka Dr. Davis? His saga made exciting copy for the press, but was it authentic? No, it was not, as several discrepancies so vividly illustrate. The Longview Dr. Davis, for example, had been educated not at Harvard, but at Bishop College in Marshall, Texas, twenty-five miles east of Longview. After being awarded his M.D. degree from Howard University, he had received the offer of an internship at the Massachusetts General Hospital, which is associated with Harvard, but he declined it. In addition, the stories of the two Dr. Davises do not correspond. The Topeka Dr. Davis, for example, claimed that the immediate precipitating incident of the riot was the sudden appearance at his home of "six strong white men." They came, he said, "to whip my niece. They charged her with insolence toward her employer. She had already been beaten once. I drew a revolver and protected her." This appears, from all the available evidence, to have been a total fabrication. Also the Topeka Dr. Davis claims to have killed four white men, and this statement, too, is false. But the most convincing evidence is a recent affirmation by Dr. Davis's surviving family that the Topeka visitor was indeed an impostor. After escaping from Longview, the real Dr. Davis had traveled to Mexico, not to Kansas.[13]

In addition to the tale of the impostor, there was another postscript to the Longview riot, one that was tragic in its consequences. Only two days after interviewing Davis and Jones in Chicago, John Shilladay boarded a train for Austin, Texas. The governor and attorney general of Texas, it seems, had resolved to drive the NAACP out of the state, and they had begun by subpoenaing the books and papers of the Austin branch. The government contended that the NAACP was a "foreign corporation," not chartered to do business in Texas. But the actual complaint, as revealed by an assistant attorney general, was the belief of the whites that the advocacy of "racial equality" by organizations like the NAACP was not only "creating race trouble" but also fomenting violence by blacks against whites. Ever since the Longview riot, the Texas Rangers had been investigating the NAACP. Shortly before noon on August 22, Shilladay was walking back to his hotel after having met with some of Austin's black citizens. Suddenly, standing menacingly in his path, were six or eight men, including County Judge Dave J. Pickle and Constable Charles Hamby. "Why," Judge Pickle asked brusquely, "are you holding meetings and stirring up more trouble than Austin citizens can get rid of in ten years?" "You don't see my point of view," Shilladay replied. "I'll fix you so you can't see," Hamby grunted angrily, and he struck Shilladay in the eye with his fist. Then the other men joined in, beating Shilladay until the blood flowed freely down his face and he begged "for mercy." After pummeling Shilladay for several minutes the mob dragged him to the railroad station, forced him to purchase a ticket on the 12:20 to St. Louis, and gave him a final warning not to stop within the borders of the state. Letters and wires from the NAACP imploring the governor and local law enforcement officials to arrest the wrongdoers went unheeded, though not unanswered. From Governor W. P. Hobby came a telegram explaining that Shilladay had been "the only offender in connection with the matter," and he had been "punished." A deputy sheriff responded that Shilladay had merely encountered "red-blooded white men," who would not countenance having "Negro-loving white men" in Texas. And, finally, there was Judge Pickle, who stated that he would not "shirk responsibility" for the attack, but who added that he and his men were, of course, acting "unofficially."[14]

John Shilladay "never fully recovered spiritually from the experience" of the beating. This, at least, was the opinion of James Weldon Johnson, Shilladay's successor as executive secretary of the NAACP. "His face and body were badly bruised," and "he was broken in spirit. I don't think," Johnson noted, that "he was ever able to realize how such a thing could happen in the United States to an American, free, white, and twenty-one." He was like "a shell-shocked soldier," added Mary White Ovington, the NAACP's president. A year later, still dejected and shaken, Shilladay resigned his post with the organization.[15]

Neither Davis nor Jones ever returned to Longview. Their property and belongings having been confiscated and sold, they had little to go back to; and, of course, such a trip would have been foolhardy. In 1920, after being certified to practice medicine in Illinois, Davis transported his family from Racine, Wisconsin, to Chicago. Jones also settled in Chicago. The historian can only imagine the evenings that the two men spent together over the next several decades, talking with mixed emotions of the horror of the riot and of their courageous self-defense. The historian, too, can only imagine the sympathy that they must have had for John Shilladay, who, as Dr. Davis wrote sadly in June 1920, had suffered an "ill fated expedition into the heathen territory from which [we] came. . . ."[16]

Notes

1. James Weldon Johnson, *Along This Way: The Autobiography of James Weldon Johnson* (New York, 1968), 341.

2. See Robert K. Murray, *Red Scare: A Study in National Hysteria, 1919–1920* (Minneapolis, 1955), 3–17, 58–66; William M. Tuttle, Jr., *Race Riot: Chicago in the Red Summer of 1919* (New York, 1970), 3–31.

3. *The Liberator*, 2 July, 1919, 21.

4. "Interview with Prof. S. L. Jones and Dr. C.P. Davis, late of Longview, Texas, at Olivet Church,

Chicago, Illinois," August 18, 1919, in Arthur B. Spingarn Papers, Library of Congress; Arthur I. Waskow, *From Race Riot to Sit-In: 1919 and the 1960s* (Garden City, 1966), 16.

5. "Interview with Jones and Davis," Spingarn Papers.

6. *Chicago Defender*, February 17, August 11, September 15, October 6, 1917; *Chicago Broad-Ax*, June 15, 1918; Frederick G. Detweiler, *The Negro Press in the United States* (Chicago, 1922), 21; Emmett J. Scott (comp.), "Letters of Negro Migrants of 1916–1918," *Journal of Negro History* 4 (July 1919): 330; Department of Labor, Division of Negro Economics, *Negro Migration in 1916–1917* (Washington, DC, 1919), 30.

7. *Chicago Defender*, July 8, 1919.

8. "Interview with Jones and Davis," Spingarn Papers; and a paraphrasing of this interview which appeared as "The Riot at Longview, Texas," *The Crisis* 18 (October, 1919): 297–98. See also *Dallas Morning News*, July 12–15, 1919; San Antonio *Express*, July 12–17, 1919; *New York Times*, July 12, 14, 1919; Chicago *Herald and Examiner*, July 12–14, 1919; Shreveport *Times*, July 12, 13, 15, 17, 1919.

9. *Dallas Morning News*, July 13, 14, 1919.

10. Ibid., July 15, 1919; *New York Times*, July 14, 1919; Waskow, *Race Riot to Sit-In*, 18; Shreveport *Times*, July 27, 1919; NAACP Papers (in possession of the Middle Atlantic Youth Division of the NAACP, Washington, DC); P.A. Williams, Austin, Texas, to John R. Shillady, New York City, August 11, 1919; Williams to Mary White Ovington, New York City, August 16, 1919.

11. *Dallas Morning News*, July 15, 1919.

12. Topeka *Plaindealer*, July 25, 1919; Wichita *Protest*, July 25, 1919; Kansas City (Kansas) *Advocate*, July 25, 1919; Shreveport *Times*, July 23, 1919; Chicago *Herald and Examiner*, July 23, 1919.

13. Interview by the author with Mrs. Sarah Davis Elias, Baltimore, August 9, 1968; Rev. L. K. Williams, Chicago, to Francis W. Shepardson, Springfield, Illinois, April 21, 1920, Chicago Commission on Race Relations Papers; Dr. C. P. Davis, Chicago, to John R. Shillady, New York City, June 14, 1920, in NAACP Papers, Library of Congress (C-369); Walter F. White, New York City, to Davis, June 26, 1920; Topeka *Plaindealer*, July 25, 1919; Kansas City *Advocate*, July 25, 1919. The story of the four white fatalities was widespread, probably because of the publicity the imposter received; and this figure appeared in a governmental publication: US House of Representatives, 66th Cong., 2nd Sess., Committee on the Judiciary, *Hearings . . . on [Segregation and Anti-Lynching]* H.J. Res. 75; H.R. 259, 4123, 11873 (Washington, DC, 1920), 58. Another rumor was that eleven whites had been killed, and this rumor seems to have originated with Jones and the real Dr. Davis; see "The Riot at Longview, Texas," in *The Crisis*. Davis and his family had heard about the imposter and his visit to Topeka, but they never learned his true identity.

14. Charles Flint Kellogg, *NAACP: A History of the National Association for the Advancement of Colored People*, 1909–1920 (Baltimore, 1967), 230–40; New York *Age*, August 30, September 6, 13, 1919; Mary White Ovington, *When the Walls Came Tumbling Down* (New York, 1970), 172–75; *New York Times*, August 23–15, 1919.

15. Johnson, *Along This Way*, 342–43; Ovington, *When the Walls Came Tumbling Down*, 175; Kellogg, *NAACP*, 240–41.

16. Interview with Mrs. Elias; Davis to Shilladay, June 14, 1920, NAACP Papers (C-369); Williams to Shepardson, April 21, 1920, Chicago Commission on Race Relations Papers.

5

A "Good Job" in the Early Hours of the Morning

Monte Akers

Even though the Freestone County sheriff, Horace Mayo, earlier in the day arrested two white men for the murder of a young white woman, whites in the county assumed that blacks were responsible, and the youthful black man they targeted was McKinley "Snap" Curry. Curry learned of their suspicions, and attempted to escape from the mob of hundreds of men. Ultimately, near the home of Homer Miller, he was captured.

The Miller family took "Snap" Curry to Wortham, six miles from Millerville. There he was locked in the vault of the Wortham Bank at around 6:00 or 7:00 p.m. Sheriff Mayo was contacted in Kirven.[1]

When Mayo and Deputy Childs arrived, they found a mob milling about in the street. After parking the car in an alley behind the bank, Mayo and Childs entered the bank through the front door while the mob watched. Inside, the vault was opened and before the mob was any wiser, the two lawmen had slipped their prisoner through a rear window and into their waiting automobile.[2]

Mayo was afraid Curry would be lynched if he remained in Freestone County, so the sheriff sped south, toward Mexia, planning to turn west and drive to Waco. News of their flight was telephoned ahead, however, and cars were parked across the road to stop them.

When Mayo saw the roadblock, he backtracked, turned east, and headed for Fairfield. He arrived at the county seat without further incident, and locked Curry in a cell on the second floor of the jailhouse.[3]

Darkness had set in, but Curry was in jail only a few moments before a

Originally published in Monte Akers' *Flames After Midnight: Murder, Vengeance, and the Desolation of a Texas Community* (Austin: University of Texas Press, 1999), 57–68, 187–89. Reprinted with permission.

mob began to form outside. As men streamed in from Kirven, Wortham, and elsewhere, the size of the crowd swelled to more than five hundred.

Mayo had three deputies with him. Their identities are not recorded, but Jay Childs, Ed Foreman, and Luke Marberry are likely candidates. Mayo's wife and three daughters were also present, in their home in the first-floor living quarters of the jail. The *Kirven Commercial Record* reported that Curry made a statement while he was still in Wortham, implicating two other blacks, John Cornish and Mose Jones, who were immediately arrested and taken to Fairfield. The *Houston Chronicle* said that Curry made the statement while he was in the Fairfield jail, and that Mayo ordered authorities in Kirven to bring the other two men to the county seat.

More likely, Cornish and Jones were picked up and brought to the jail before the mob had a chance to form. Mayo wrote a week later that all three were simply "landed in jail" before the mob gathered.[4] At some point, fifteen dollars was found in the pocket of one of the three men, probably Curry.[5]

J. C. Whatley, who was in the mob, said, "Well, they carried that nigger on, and he implemented [*sic*] these others, see, and they went and got 'em down in jail in Fairfield, and a bunch of us went down there to get 'em and the sheriff said 'no'."[6]

Johnny Cornish was mistakenly identified by the Associated Press as J. H. Varney, and several newspapers across the country repeated the error.[7] Cornish was a 19-year-old farmhand who, until recently, had lived with his mother, Nettie, outside of Kirven near the site of Eula Ausley's murder.[8] The proximity of his former home to the crime scene may have been a factor in his becoming a suspect. A few weeks earlier, he had married, and he and his new bride were living in Kirven.[9]

Bertha Williams, who had known Johnny since he was a baby, said he worked occasionally for Otis King, Eula's uncle, chopping cotton or moving cattle, but was not a steady hired hand of the Kings. Johnny's family remembered him as a loner who never had many friends, and who spent a lot of time by himself in the woods or fishing. Oddly, one of the few close friends he did have was a white physician, Dr. William Sneed, who lived in Fairfield.[10]

Johnny was the oldest of six children. Their mother, Nettie, was black, but all her children were listed in the census records as mulatto.[11]

Their father was a white man named Bud Thompson. Thompson had not lived with Nettie and their children, but he had taken care of the family and had openly acknowledged the relationship.[12] According to the recollections of natives, Thompson had been a businessman and a respected member of the community, which is some testament to the relaxed nature of race relations around Kirven prior to May 1922.[13]

Thompson had passed away a year or two previously, however, and the family was relegated to living in a tent near Hinds Lake. Quite recently they had begun moving to Fairfield, where Nettie had family, and were still in the process of doing so on May 5, driving back and forth between Kirven and Fairfield in a wagon.[14]

Mose Jones, at 46, was the oldest of the three arrested men. Like Cornish, he worked part-time for Otis King. His wife, Louise, was twenty years younger than he, and the couple shared their home with Mose's parents, seventy-five-year old Lige Jones and sixty-three-year-old Melissa Jones.

Mose and Louise had three children, the oldest a six-year-old daughter named Nattie. The names of the other children were a stinging irony in light of what was about to happen. Otis Jones was five. Kirven Jones was three.[15]

Sometime between 10:00 p.m. and midnight, a committee of the mob approached the jail and asked the sheriff's permission to interview the prisoners. Mayo agreed.[16]

Supposedly, Curry confessed to the committee in the jail, although no written version is known to exist, and if he confessed at all, he may have done so an hour or more later. Whether the confession occurred in the jail or not at all, newspapers provided several particulars of Curry's alleged statement.

The *Kirven Commercial Record* reported Curry's words in the following way:

> . . . he made a full and frank confession of the crime, stating that he and the other two negroes under arrest had planned the same several days before. He stated that another lady was to have been served in the same manner. According to the statement of Curry, who said that he knew he was to be killed at once and that he believed he deserved death, he joined the other two negroes at the lonely spot where a creek crossed the road traveled by the girl on her way to and from school. When the girl came up, riding horseback, Curry seized the horse's bridle while the other two negroes dragged her from the saddle. He stated that the girl was so strong it took the utmost efforts of the three of them to carry her the several hundred yards to where the body was found. Miss King screamed a number of times while being carried to the thicket, according to Curry. Arriving at the bank of a small running branch covered with dense growth of small timber, Curry said that both of the other negroes committed a criminal assault upon the young girl, after which Cornish stabbed her 25 times with a pocket knife. Both Jones and Cornish then beat her head and face into the ground with a large club found nearby, according to Curry's statement, and that Cornish also mutilated the body with a stick in a most horrible manner. After the crime was committed, Curry said the negroes separated and that he at once returned to his home.[17]

The *Dallas Times Herald* reported on May 6 that Curry said the trio planned to assault not one, but two other women from the Kirven vicinity at the same time, and that Jones alone beat Eula's head into the ground, after Cornish stabbed her twenty-five times. On May 7, the same paper declared Eula was first dragged into the woods and assaulted, or raped, after which one of the three blacks searched the creek for a hole deep enough to drown her. Spared such a death by a shortage of water, she was killed by stabbing and having her throat slashed, after which "her head and face were beaten and stamped to pulp to prevent recognition." Another account said the men cut out Eula's tongue so she would not tell on them, after which they realized she could still write, so they killed her.[18]

The *Austin Statesman* said the three men had planned the crime since January.

The committee came out of Curry's cell and told Mayo they "had decided to wait until two more negroes suspected of being implicated in the matter were caught and examined before any further action against the three prisoners was taken."[19] They left the jail and reported their finding to the rest of the mob.

Whether Curry actually confessed or not, and if he did, whether he did so in the detail reported, the mob was certain of the guilt of the trio, and spent little time debating the legal and philosophical considerations of its next step.

As Mayo later wrote, "I was again requested to parley with the crowd, and when I opened the door, was seized and held while men rushed the jail and took all three negroes. Resistance to the determined citizens would have been folly as well as suicide on the part of myself and three deputies. The men had formed and carried out their preparations too calmly and thoroughly to brook opposition, and I feel certain they would have torn the jail down stone by stone if it had been necessary to take the negroes."[20]

J. C. Whitley, who was outside the jail with the rest of the mob, said, "When Mayo opened the door the second time, the old ex-sheriff just knocked the hell out of him and knocked him out."[21] He did not identify the ex-sheriff, but Mayo's three daughters, who were in the jail, were certain that their father was not knocked unconscious, or even hit.

The three girls remembered the mob taking the prisoners, and said that they were not loud or boisterous. Instead, the mob moved with silent, deadly purpose, speaking, if at all, in vesper voices.

"Daddy told us to go and stay in our rooms," Lura Bess recalled, "and don't get out and don't turn our lights on or anything, and just be real quiet because there were some men coming to take some of the prisoners upstairs, and they had an outside entrance to the thing there, and he just said to stay in there, and, 'I'm going to be in here with you, so don't be afraid.'"

The entrance to which she referred was outside the first-floor living quarters, but inside the front door. A stairway ascended directly to the jail at a right angle from the outside entrance, while another door—locked—stood between the family and the entryway.

"We never heard a thing," Lura Bess continued, "and we were scared to death. They took those men out of their cells and down the stairs, and we never even heard them go. . . . It was just the slickest thing you ever saw. You wouldn't have known a thing was happening. . . . There wasn't any yelling or screaming. It was just as silent as could be, and we didn't, we were right there, and we couldn't hear them coming down the steps, even. They didn't make any noise or anything."

Then, contemplating, she added, "I don't know why it never made a mark on us kids that we didn't get over, but it made a mark on my daddy, one he never could get over."[22]

The three terrified prisoners were placed in two automobiles, Curry in one and Cornish and Jones in another. Members of "the committee" crowded in around them, and others in the mob dashed to their own cars.[23] Soon a funeral-like caravan of at least 165 vehicles was winding along the dirt back road between Fairfield and Kirven.[24] Along the way, the cars crossed concrete bridges built years before by Mayo.

According to the Kirven newspaper, Curry was in the back seat of one of the lead cars, where he was "between two members of the committee who had questioned him without much success in the jail, and he made a full and frank confession of the crime. . . ." One can imagine him sitting between two furious members of the mob, immobile, enduring scathing verbal abuse and promises of terrible punishment, any hope of survival gone.

It was past midnight when the cavalcade filed into Kirven, which, despite the excitement of the day, was dark and asleep. According to a report in the *Houston Chronicle*, though, "As the procession advanced to the town square, windows were thrown open, lights appeared, and a few minutes later, practically every man, woman and child gathered around the little square."[25]

The place where the procession stopped was often described in newspapers as the town square, or even as the courthouse square, but the site was neither. The place was a large vacant lot located immediately south of the downtown business district, between the Methodist and Baptist churches, the same place where V. B. Starnes had pitched his revival tent and Eula Ausley had accepted Christ into her heart two months earlier.[26]

Some of the cars following the leading vehicles parked on the north side of the open lot, across from the Methodist church. Some may have left their engines idling and their headlights on. The rest pulled into whatever parking spaces the drivers could find, and their occupants hurried to join the circle forming in the lot. The members of the mob, together with the populace of Kirven that had turned out, brought the number in the crowd to somewhere between five hundred and one thousand people.[27] While the crowd gathered, the King brothers held council. The Kirven newspaper said that "at the request of one of the uncles of the dead girl, the crowd discussed the matter quietly," but such democratic deliberation was cursory at best. The members of the mob knew their purpose, and "soon probably fifty men began carrying wood and other inflammable material."[28]

The source of the wood was reported later to have been the T. & B. V. Railroad. The local railroad section chief, Cap Spurgeon, was said to have generously donated a stack of cross ties, as a kind of civic contribution from local industry, to the project.[29] If so, however, the cross ties were not the initial fuel supply.

John Green—Hallie King's father and John T.'s father-in-law—had ten cords of firewood piled against the side of his drug store, immediately next door to the vacant lot, and he contributed the logs freely. The wood had been cut on Green's land outside of town by an elderly black man and his wife who could not have dreamed how the fruit of their labor would be utilized.[30]

The hideous intention of the mob was apparent, but some of the participants were not content with the punishment about to be inflicted. "Out from the cars the blacks were dragged to the ground. A curtain of men screened them from the onlookers. A knife flashed . . . , and the negroes lay upon the ground, horribly mutilated."[31]

J.C. Whatley, who was present, but did not claim any credit, described the act of the mob more simply: "They castrated one or two of them, or something like that."[32] Another contemporary said, "They cut off everything the negroes had."[33] Another commentator was artfully euphemistic, reporting that "no organ of the negroes was allowed to remain protruding."[34]

More likely, only Curry was unsexed. The men in the mob, particularly Grandfather King, had reservations about the guilt of Jones and Cornish. Also, anecdotal information, which follows, suggests the latter two victims were unharmed, even spirited, prior to being put on the fire.

A sulky riding plow, often referred to in newspaper accounts as a cultivator, and locally as a breaking or turning plow, was either in the vacant lot or nearby, and was dragged into the center of the lot. The farming implement was relatively small, but heavy, designed to be pulled by a mule, with cast-iron wheels, a single large blade, and a metal seat.[35]

According to one newspaper report of the event, "an old plow was obtained from somewhere—kerosene and crude oil appeared as if by magic. From the cowering trio, the mob dragged 'Snap' Curry, the only one of the three who had confessed. With a rope he was strapped to the seat of the plow. He was apparently unafraid, although he must have suffered horribly from the mutilation."[36]

At approximately this time, the preachers from Kirven's two churches, the Methodist minister and Dr. Andrew of the Baptist Church, "came forward and prayed for the salvation of the blacks' souls."[37]

J. C. Whatley said he opened Dr. Whiteside's drug store, and was serving cold drinks to members of the crowd while everyone else was doing the dirty work.[38] Perhaps he was. Mobbing and lynching could be thirsty work, and Dr. Whiteside may have sanctioned the serving of refreshments. On the other hand, it seems unlikely that members of the mob would suddenly decide to leave the excitement and take a break for a cold soda pop. Whatley may have told the story in order to distance himself from as much guilt as possible, but without taking himself out of the picture, or he may have served drinks later, before the crowd dispersed, and conveniently changed the timing of his activities.

Wood was stacked around the plow and doused with gasoline, kerosene, and oil. A match was applied, and flames leaped up and crawled toward the doomed man. The crowd was silent, staring.

Someone asked Curry if the other two men were guilty, and he replied loudly enough for all to hear, "Burn those other Negroes too. They are just as guilty as me."[39] Another version of his statement was, "You can't do no more to me than you're doing, but nothing you do will make me suffer as much as she [Eula] did."[40]

One newspaper claimed that "a lick of flame ignited the oil-soaked clothes of the black" but he "continued to answer questions from the crowd by giving more details of the crime, his answers checking exactly with his previous statements."[41]

A less credulity-straining version of Curry's last words was printed in several papers. Apparently, he began to sing. The song was an old hymn, "Lord I Am Coming."[42]

Not every citizen of Kirven was on the scene. B. J. Ausley, Eula's nephew, was certain his mother's parents, the Hudsons, would not have come out of the house. "Mrs. Hudson was one of those old types who never did anything but sit and look at the Good Book," he said. "They wouldn't have participated."[43]

Walter Whatley forbade his youngest daughter, eleven-year-old Ruby Kate, to leave the house, and the Beavers, Whit and Emma, locked their doors and stayed at home. For years thereafter they remembered "hearing the screams."[44]

Other parents made a point of calling their children out to witness what was about to happen. James Claude Goolsby, a barber and part owner of the town's confectionery, called his young son, Jim, out of the house to watch. He thought witnessing the punishment would be "a good lesson" for the boy. Instead, what the boy saw haunted him for the rest of his life.[45]

Still other parents had responsibilities to tend to, and were too busy or distracted to keep track of their offspring. One such couple consisted of a man who attempted to lend calm to the event and a woman with two infants to care for. Their older sons, aged twelve and ten, were asleep on a pallet in their parents' bedroom—they had been too frightened by the events of the day to stay in their own bedroom—when their next-door neighbor pounded on the bedroom window and shouted, "Wake up. They're bringing the Negroes back. They're going to burn them out here."[46]

The parents and boys got out of bed quickly. The father, a religious man, had already attempted to calm the emotion-charged environment during the day. After the report of the arrest of the three men, he had hoped tensions would subside. Now they had reached a towering new zenith. He rushed out as soon as he was dressed after hearing the neighbor's report, but found he could do nothing except talk to the members of the mob and pray for the three men's souls.

The two brothers threw on their clothes and went outside after their father. The boys' mother stayed at home to care for her two babies, the youngest of whom was only six months old.

The boys saw the crowd gathered in the vacant lot, and went to the steps of the Methodist church to watch. The event was under way when the brothers arrived. Curry was already burning. The younger of the two boys said the mob was in a circle with a center about the size of a typical living room, and that the people stood in rows ten to twenty persons deep. He could not see Curry, but said he assumed "the Negro wasn't in much of an upright position anyway."

Both brothers remembered the members of the mob being serious and intent upon their work. "It was quite a good-sized crowd," the younger one said. "There wasn't a lot of noise. It was a fairly silent crowd for that many people." The older brother agreed, saying, "The crowd wasn't particularly loud."[47]

Neither of the boys mentioned what Curry was saying, if anything. He may have been silenced before they arrived on the scene, but one report stated that "as the flames mounted about Curry's body, his chant rose higher and higher until he could be heard throughout the downtown part of town."[48]

Curry lost consciousness in ten minutes and died.[49] The smell of burning flesh filled the air. The wind took on a taste.

"A few moments later, the bonds were burned through and he dropped, face first into the flames."[50]

The crowd hesitated at this point. Neither Cornish nor Jones had confessed, despite "third degree methods" having been administered to them.[51] They were still denying their guilt, and displayed a degree of confidence.

Cornish was heard to ask Jones while Curry was burning, "Will we get that too?" "No," Jones replied, "what have we done?"[52]

"A slight delay occurred as the leaders debated the fate of Jones and Cornish, who reiterated their innocence," the Kirven newspaper reported. John King, "the gray haired old grandfather, a patriarch in appearance," supposedly came forward at this moment, "and a most affecting scene took place. In a shaking voice the old man questioned the two remaining negroes and told the crowd he was convinced they were guilty."[53]

Later revelations, as well as Cornish and Jones's steadfast denials of guilt, make this detail seem unlikely.

More likely is that "it was decided that Curry's confession was proof enough" and Jones was brought forward. A traditional version of his death was that the fire was too hot at this point to tie or chain him to the plow, so a rope soaked in water was tied to his wrists and members of the crowd proceeded to drag him back and forth through the flames until he died.[54]

Sitting in a lawn chair in front of his trailer house in Kirven on May 5, 1987, two hundred yards from the scene of the burning, J. C. Whatley scoffed at this anecdote.

The day of his interview was a pleasant spring day in a quiet place, significantly different from the turmoil sixty-five years earlier. The meadowlark was still calling, and a silver needle of a jet was pulling a white thread of vapor beneath the sun. Whatley was drinking iced tea and holding court.

"They was all tied to the plow, soaked with gasoline and set afire all together," he declared. "I wouldn't know how many gallons of gasoline they used, see," he stated, "but I stood right there in the front door of that drug store and stared just as straight and level as I'm looking at your car right here, and that's the way they died."

Pausing a moment, he repeated a claim he made twice that day, and that he had probably made numerous times over the years. "Yeah, well, I saw it. I was there, but I never went across the street to it, see, and I never threw a damned stick of wood on them."[55]

By his own admission, however, Whatley was in the drug store serving drinks most of the time, or at least he was across the street, and there were a lot of people between him and the fire. His is the only account that suggests all three were burned together. Every newspaper said they were burned one at a time, and the youngest of the two brothers who were watching said, "When one man burned up, they pitched another on the fire, and when that one burned they threw the third one in the fire."[56]

What may have happened is that Whatley did not see the three bodies until after all were dead, and had been raked together on the pyre for final cremation, and he assumed all three were burned simultaneously.

Another traditional anecdote was that members of the mob stood around the fire, and if one of the victims tried to crawl out, they kicked him and hit him and drove him back into the flames. The older of the two brothers who watched the men being burned said, "One would wriggle out every once in a while and get thrown back in."[57]

More specifically, Mose Jones was said to have made a dash out of the flames immediately after being thrown in, despite being secured with a rope, only to run directly into Otis King. The namesake of Mose Jones's infant son was armed with a radius rod from a Model T Ford, and he swung the heavy piece of iron like a club, smashing his former hired hand in the face and knocking one of the doomed man's eyes from its socket.

Jones supposedly reached up and wiped the eyeball from his cheek, stared at the carnage on the back of his hand with his remaining eye, and was jerked backward into the flames by the members of the crowd who were holding the rope.[58]

Jones died in about six minutes,[59] and the mob turned to Cornish. The details of his death are better substantiated, and even more bizarre. As he was brought into the light from the fire, several Kirven men recognized him. Foreman Carter, who knew both Johnny and the boy's white father, Bud Thompson, and who heard the story from his stepfather, Jenkins Carter, described what happened next.

> Some of the guys, some of the Whites, said, "That's Bud Thompson's boy, get him out of there, that's Bud Thompson's boy." So they got him out, but he had such a nasty mouth . . . you see, your mouth can get you in a lot of trouble. Well, he didn't know no better. He was raised that way. His mother had a filthy mouth, and he used four letter words all the time, and he cussed at the guys, and so they said, "Throw him back in there. Hell, put him back in." They got him out, but he had such a nasty mouth, they said put him back in.[60]

Roped, bound, having seen the agony of his companions, but too stubborn to be docile, Cornish tossed away his last chance for redemption. His death might be viewed as a microcosm of early-twentieth-century southern racism. A black man with the right connections would be protected, even when associated with heinous crime, but only so long as he respected the codes, acted docile, and "kept his place." Johnny Cornish did not. He reacted angrily, and bravely. Your mouth, as Foreman Carter observed, can get you in a lot of trouble.

He was pulled into the fire, pulled back, pulled forward. Then he fell quickly to the ground, "clasped his arms around the plow," thrust his face into the flames, and inhaled deeply, meeting death in the quickest manner available.[61]

"After the third negro had been burned to a crisp, all three bodies were piled together and a mass of fuel and oil flung over them. This was ignited, the flames soaring 25 or 30 feet in the air." More wood and fuel was piled on them, and the bodies were cremated.[62]

Daylight was breaking, gray as crematorium ash, and the crowd began to disperse. According to the younger of the two brothers, they had been here nearly two hours, and, according to the *Kirven Commercial Record*, "after forty-eight hours of sleeplessness and without paying much attention to meals, the citizens of three counties who had worked unceasingly in the effort to solve the most dastardly crime in the history of Freestone County returned to their homes believing that the three negroes had met the fate they deserved, and that they alone were guilty of the crime."[63]

The *Houston Chronicle* carried a similar summary: "The blackest entry in Texas' history of crime had been chalked down on the records against the negro trio—and the general feeling here was that the mob of 600 did a 'good job' in the early hours of the morning."[64]

The shameful entries in Texas' history, the horror, and the cruel irony were over . . . for about a day.

Notes

1. *Dallas Times Herald*, May 6, 1922; *Houston Chronicle*, May 7, 1922; *Kirven Commercial Record*, May 7, 1922.
2. *Dallas Times Herald*, May 6, 1922; *Fairfield Recorder*, May 19, 1922.
3. *Dallas Times Herald*, May 6, 1922; *Houston Chronicle*, May 7, 1922; *Kirven Commercial Record*, May 7, 1922.
4. *Teague Chronicle*, May 19, 1922.
5. This critical piece of information was not revealed in any Texas newspaper, nor in any non-Texas African American paper, but in the *New York Call*, a predominantly socialist paper, on Sunday, May 7, 1922. The source of the information was stated to be Sheriff Horace Mayo.
6. Interview of J. C. Whatley, May 5, 1987.
7. *Austin Statesman*, May 6, 1922; *Houston Chronicle*, May 6, 1922; *St. Louis Argus*, May 12, 1922.
8. Fourteenth Census (1920), Freestone County, Precinct Six; interview conducted April 8, 1995.
9. Interview conducted November 19, 1995.
10. Ibid.
11. Fourteenth Census (1920), Freestone County, Precinct Six.
12. Interview of Foreman Carter, April 9, 1995; interview conducted November 19, 1995.
13. Interview of Foreman Carter, July 19, 1995.
14. Interview conducted November 19, 1995.
15. Fourteenth Census (1920), Freestone County, Precinct Six.
16. *Kirven Commercial Record*, May 7, 1922; *Fairfield Recorder*, May 19, 1922.
17. *Kirven Commercial Record*, May 7, 1922.
18. Foreman Carter interview.
19. *Fairfield Recorder*, May 19, 1922.

20. Ibid.

21. J. C. Whatley interview.

22. Interview of Lura Bess Mayo Sprague, December 3, 1994.

23. *Kirven Commercial Record*, May 7, 1922.

24. *Houston Chronicle*, May 7, 1922.

25. Ibid.

26. Foreman Carter interview; interview conducted April 8, 1995; interview conducted April 5, 1995.

27. The *Houston Chronicle* of May 7, 1922, said the crowd in Fairfield numbered eight hundred. Other papers, such as the *Kirven Commercial Record* of May 7, 1922, placed the number at five hundred. The *Chicago Defender* of May 13, 1922 said there were one thousand men, women, and children.

28. *Kirven Commercial Record*, May 7, 1922.

29. Interview of Harry Hughes, January 9, 1995.

30. *New York Call*, May 7, 1922; interview conducted January 8, 1995; J. C. Whatley interview.

31. *Houston Chronicle*, May 7, 1922.

32. J. C. Whatley interview.

33. Interview conducted November 3, 1986.

34. Although the *Brooklyn Citizen* for May 6, 1922, is quoted to this effect in Ralph Ginzburg's *100 Years of Lynching* (New York: Lancer Books, 1974), 162, that issue of the newspaper does not, in fact, contain the statement. The date may be incorrect, or Ginzburg may have applied literary license to a statement in the *Chicago Defender* of May 13, 1922, that "no independent organ of the body was left untouched," and attributed the statement to the wrong newspaper.

35. Photograph provided by B. J. Ausley; Harry Hughes interview; interview conducted January 9, 1995; J. C. Whatley interview.

36. *Houston Chronicle*, May 7, 1922.

37. Once again, Ginzburg cites the May 6, 1922, issue of the *Brooklyn Citizen* for this information, but that issue of the *Citizen* does not, in fact, mention the preachers. The *Chicago Defender* for May 13, however, does refer to the preachers conducting a ceremony, although that newspaper describes it in a mocking manner. A witness who knew the Methodist minister said that it would have been consistent with his personality and ministry to pray for the condemned men.

38. J. C. Whatley interview.

39. *Dallas Times Herald*, May 7, 1922; *Kirven Commercial Record*, May 7, 1922; *New York Call*, May 7, 1922; "Report of Dan Kelly"; *Brooklyn Citizen*, May 6, 1922, as quoted by Ginzburg in *100 Years of Lynching*, 162.

40. Interview of B. J. Ausley, April 9, 1995; interview conducted July 19, 1995.

41. *Kirven Commercial Record*, May 7, 1922.

42. Ibid.; *Brooklyn Citizen*, May 6, 1922; *Houston Chronicle*, May 7, 1922; *New York Call*, May 7, 1922; *Fairfield Recorder*, May 12, 1922; *Teague Chronicle*, May 12, 1922.

43. B. J. Ausley interview.

44. J. C. Whatley interview; interview of Willie Mae Keeling Beaver, October 24, 1986; interview conducted October 28, 1986.

45. Harry Hughes interview.

46. Interviews conducted January 9, 1995, and April 5, 1995.

47. Ibid.

48. Again, Ginzburg cites the *Brooklyn Citizen* of May 6, 1922 for this statement, although it is not, in fact, in that newspaper article, nor is it in the *Chicago Defender*.

49. Ibid.

50. *Houston Chronicle*, May 7, 1922.

51. *Brooklyn Citizen*, May 6, 1922, as quoted by Ginzburg in *100 Years of Lynching*, 163.

52. "Report of Dan Kelly."

53. *Kirven Commercial Record*, May 7, 1922.

54. Interview conducted October 28, 1986. The "Report of Dan Kelly" partially substantiates this version, at least with respect to one of the three victims.

55. J. C. Whatley interview.

56. Interview conducted January 9, 1995.

57. Interview conducted April 5, 1995.

58. Harry Hughes interview.

59. *Brooklyn Citizen*, May 6, 1922, as quoted by Ginzburg in *100 Years of Lynching*, 163.

60. Interview of Foreman Carter, April 9, 1995.

61. "Report of Dan Kelly"; interview conducted October 28, 1986.

62. *Dallas Times Herald*, May 7, 1922; *Houston Chronicle*, May 7, 1922; *New York Call*, May 7, 1922.

63. *Kirven Commercial Record*, May 7, 1922.

64. *Houston Chronicle*, May 7, 1922.

6

The Sherman Courthouse Riot of 1930

Edward Hake Phillips

Three times since its founding as the seat of Grayson County in 1846, Sherman, Texas, has attracted nationwide attention. On "Black Friday," May 15, 1896, one of the worst tornadoes in Texas history struck Sherman, killing at least sixty-six persons but sparing the courthouse. In April 1905, a human "cyclone" visited courthouse square. This was Teddy Roosevelt, who drew the largest crowd in Sherman's history. In May 1930, the square again experienced great excitement, but the drawing card was only an obscure black man, George Hughes.[1]

On Saturday, May 3, in a farmhouse five miles southeast of Sherman, Hughes, forty-one years of age, a farm worker, allegedly assaulted his white employer's wife. Tracked down by a deputy sheriff, Hughes apparently fired twice at the officer's car, then surrendered, and was hustled to the county jail, an imposing structure located two blocks west of the courthouse.[2]

The wheels of justice turned rapidly. A confession was obtained from Hughes, he was indicted on Monday, and his trial was set for Friday, May 9, the earliest date possible under state law. It appeared to be "an open and shut" case that should have little effect on history. Sherman was a college town, known as "the Athens of Texas," and the county, perched at the extreme edge of the cotton kingdom, was scarcely "redneck" country. True, in 1901 a West Grayson posse had lynched a black man accused of murder, but in those days lynching was rampant throughout the South.[3] By 1930, lynchings were rare even in the Black Belt. The previous year, 1929, had seen the fewest lynchings since Reconstruction, and, though the ten lynchings were ten too many, they represented a great decline from the eighty-three in 1919. Ominously,

Originally published in the *East Texas Historical Journal* 25.2 (1987): 12–19. Reprinted with permission of the East Texas Historical Association.

however, in the two weeks preceding Hughes's assault, three separate lynchings had occurred in the South.[4]

Other violence filled the papers as the week began. Heavy rains and tornadoes pounded Texas, shattering the town of Frost.[5] The people of Grayson County were edgy, and on Sunday the sheriff, Arthur Vaughan, said he was "using every precaution against [the] possibility of mob violence."[6]

Tuesday night came the first hint of serious trouble. A gang, described as "a small group of boys in their late teens . . . with a bare sprinkling of men," appeared before the jail to demand the prisoner.[7] When the county attorney sought to assure the youths that the black man was not in the jail, they drenched the attorney with water from a hose. Some stones were thrown at the windows, and a telephone pole was brought up to force an entrance. The sheriff offered to let five representatives of the mob see for themselves that Hughes was not there, and a deputy escorted them through the building. This took much of the steam out of the mob, and the sheriff's wife soon put an end to the foolishness, phoning her husband that she heard the mob was trampling her flowers around the jail. "I feel like kicking some of those little rascals," she said. "They are ruining all my flowers."[8] And that was that.

Wednesday afternoon a smaller crowd appeared at the jail, again demanding Hughes, and again a delegation was given a tour of the "Bastille." The authorities were worried and requested Governor Dan Moody to send four Texas Rangers to guard against mob violence at the trial. Early Thursday morning four Rangers arrived, led by Capt. Frank Hamer, from Headquarters Company in Austin. Their presence seemed to have a quieting effect, and that morning Hughes was arraigned in court without incident. Elsewhere, however, agitators were fanning out into the county and urging farmers to be at the courthouse the next day.[9]

Friday, the crowds gathered early, filling the stairs and hallways of the fifty-four-year-old courthouse, while hundreds stood outside. The prisoner had arrived earlier and at 9:30 a.m. Judge R.M. Carter opened the trial; by 11:45 a jury was impaneled. Then an incident occurred that seemed to trigger the tragic riot. The victim of the assault arrived by ambulance and was carried on a stretcher through the crowd to the courtroom, where, according to one report, upon seeing Hughes, she let out a shriek.[10] The people made a rush for the courtroom, gaining partial entrance. One fellow got dangerously close to Hughes before the Rangers, drawing their guns, forced the crowd back into the hallway. A semblance of order was restored, and the trial proceeded, with Hughes pleading guilty. The first witness had begun his testimony when a new surge by the crowd caused Judge Carter to suspend the trial. Tear gas was used to dislodge the mob, but its acrid fumes forced clerks in the county offices to the windows for fresh air, and the poor victim of Hughes's alleged assault now became a victim of tear gas. The fire department was summoned to evacuate jurors, witnesses, and clerks by ladders from the second floor. For his protection Hughes was taken into the district clerk's office, which was a huge two-story vault of steel and concrete.[11]

About one o'clock the Rangers stood off another rush from the mob, but a report spread that the governor had sent Captain Hamer a message to save the prisoner if possible but not to shoot anybody. The report was later proved false, but the crowd believed it and acted accordingly.[12] Belatedly, Judge Carter agreed to a change of venue and sent an urgent request to the governor for state troops. At 2:20 p.m. troops at Dallas received orders to proceed to Sherman, where now a young woman with black eyes and clenched fist egged on the crowd. "Break the windows, fellows," she shouted, and she promptly hurled a rock through a courthouse window. Scores of men and boys followed her example. A reporter asked this hellion, "Do you think they'll ever get him?" "Get him?" she repeated scornfully, "H——L yes, we'll get him."[13]

Two youths were then seen moving to the southeast corner with a gasoline can. In a moment, a roar was heard from the tax collector's office, and the building was ablaze. The fire department attempted to get its men and hoses into action, but the hoses were cut almost as fast as they were laid. One big man with a huge knife went around methodically cutting each hose.[14] One old boy "shook in his tracks with excitement and screamed: 'Let 'er wilt like a cucumber in the sun! Let 'er burn till the last hobnail in the nigger's boots is melted.'"[15] In fifteen minutes the flames shot through the roof, and the building's fate was sealed.

The Rangers were the last to leave the building—except for Hughes, who remained in the vault, some said from choice, others because the vault could not be opened. Firefighting was not one of the Rangers' assignments, so after hanging around a few minutes, they headed for Dallas, stopping at Howe and McKinney to phone for instructions.[16] Meanwhile, Dallas guardsmen were heading in the opposite direction, and Governor Moody tried frantically to get more Rangers to the scene. Unable to contact Tom Hickman, captain of B Company, he managed to phone Sgt. Manuel "Lone Wolf' Gonzaullas in Dallas. "'Get up to Sherman just as fast as you can . . . and get in touch with Randolph Bryant, the U.S. District Attorney. . . . I understand they are going to storm the county jail and burn all the niggers in there. I don't want any of those prisoners molested or mistreated or hurt. I don't care what it costs you, you understand?'" [17]

Gonzaullas understood. He wasted no time in getting to Sherman. After phoning Bryant, he hid his white hat and mingled with the crowd to see what he was up against. He found bedlam. At the jail Bryant pulled no punches. He said he expected Gonzaullas to hold that jail, which contained

Federal prisoners, and the one-man Ranger force went into action. Putting on his white hat, strapping on two pistols, leaning a Thompson submachine gun beside him, and cradling an automatic sawed-off shotgun, the "Lone Ranger" took a position at the front entrance of the jail, ready for all comers. And they soon came, taunting him, hurling everything imaginable at him, even dynamite, but they kept a good distance from the formidable Ranger, especially after he reinforced his warnings with buckshot.[18]

Meanwhile the National Guard had begun to arrive. A few guardsmen from Denison were the first to reach the frightening scene. As they marched to the square, young boys followed them, kicking and tripping them and making their march miserable.[19] At 6:20 p.m. a sizable force of guardsmen under Col. Laurence McGee arrived by Interurban Railway from Dallas. After contacting local officials, McGee marched his troops to the square. Fearing the troops had come to rescue the prisoner, the mob became infuriated and assaulted the guardsmen. They tossed bricks, stones, two-by-fours, and especially pop bottles, which a young lady at a refreshment stand eagerly supplied. Several guardsmen were injured, at least one lost his rifle, and Capt. Albert Sidney Johnson, going to a soldier's aid, was struck in the face by a missile and was hurt badly. McGee ordered the troops to fall back to the jail, and their retreat was a tortuous one, missiles arching at their heads and the mob howling at their heels.[20]

The figure of "Lone Wolf" Gonzaullas guarding the jail was welcome to the guardsmen, who now took a stand. Attention shifted back to the courthouse, where the mob tried to break into the vault to find Hughes. Tools and dynamite proved ineffective, but someone produced an acetylene torch and soon the outer shell and concrete lining were breached. Next a charge of dynamite was exploded against a plate of the inner shell, and with a roar the plate was driven into the vault. When the smoke subsided, a man crawled into the hole and shouted, "Here he is." Hughes's body, showing no signs of life, was lifted out of the vault and was dropped down the ladder, striking the ground with a thud, as the crowd shrieked in glee or horror. The young, black-eyed woman showed particular satisfaction.[21]

The body was dragged through the crowd and hitched by a chain to a car, which soon began a gruesome journey to Sherman's main black residential section. By a hotel used by blacks near the Union Station, members of the mob hung the body to a tree and prepared kindling beneath it for the climactic ritual of lynching. Soon the body was roasting over the huge bonfire, while the crowd turned its attention to looting and burning an entire block of stores and dwellings.[22] To sensitive observers, it was a startling scene. "Sidewalks were covered with broken glass which, sparkling in the glare from torches, the flaming building, and the moon, cast grotesque shadows on the dangling figure of the Negro," wrote one.[23] Another noted the "brilliant Texas moon," which "added its rays to one of the most gruesome sights in the history of the state."[24]

Once again, the weary and nearly hose-less firemen responded and attempted to control the flames. One white man saved a whole block of the blacks' houses from the mob by falsely asserting that they all belonged to him.[25] The mob's enthusiasm cooled somewhat when they found some of the blacks ready to defend their property. A respected black doctor sat on his porch, shotgun in hand, ready to shoot the first looter or arsonist who violated his property.[26] Around 2 a.m., reinforcements having arrived, the guardsmen ventured from the jail and set about dispersing the mob in the black sector. Small knots of rowdies continued to cause trouble, but the worst was over. By dawn the city was in a state of exhaustion.[27]

Many blacks had fled the city and hid in brush thickets. Some hid in sewers, and a number were given refuge by sympathetic whites, especially employers.[28] In the morning, Rangers and militiamen rounded up many exiles, escorted them back to their homes, and assured them their lives and property would be protected.[29] As far as the blacks' business property was concerned, the promise came too late. Their hotel, drug store, movie house, restaurant, barbershop, and two undertaking parlors lay in ruins, a total loss, for insurance policies had fine print exempting damage by riots. It marked the end of black business in Sherman.[30]

Hughes's body, contorted by the heat and flames, still hung from the tree, as many Graysonites had their picture snapped beside it, until a guardsman cut the body down.[31] Since the undertaking establishments for blacks had been destroyed, a white undertaker had to be persuaded to bury the body. Without fanfare the body was taken to the county farm. There it was laid in an unmarked grave, where it rests today.[32]

It was a long while before Sherman returned to normal. First it was inundated by swarms of sightseers. Then rumors of new outbreaks caused Sherman's leaders to ask the governor for martial law, which was proclaimed at 10:30 p.m., May 10.[33] For the next two weeks "the Athens of Texas" seemed more like Sparta. Machine guns were mounted on the square and around the jail, while patrols guarded the black districts. The guardsmen had difficulty handling their weapons. One accidentally shot himself on the courthouse lawn, and two were shot while in their quarters in the Grayson Hotel when a pistol accidentally discharged.[34]

Sherman's blacks, frightened, dismayed, and angry, tried to pick up the pieces of their lives. Some whites expressed sympathy and offered help, but some posted notices warning all blacks to leave Sherman or have their homes destroyed. Several employers received warnings to fire their black employees.[35] Each day the Rangers brought more suspected rioters to the jail, which became nearly filled.[36] Governor Moody condemned the rioters, accusing them of murder, arson, and treason, and he assured the nation that those guilty would be subjected to the full penalty of the law. He deplored the unfavorable publicity the riot brought Texas. A journalist phoned him from England and asked, "Well, well, is this a common occurrence in Texas?"[37]

On May 20, fourteen suspected leaders of the mob were indicted.[38] The wheels of justice which had turned so swiftly for Hughes now slowed to a crawl. First, a change of venue was made to Dallas, where the trials were delayed until November. Then the judge ruled that no jury willing to convict could be found nearer than Austin, so the cases were moved there.[39] Not until June 1931 was the first man tried, but that trial made history, for the defendant was found guilty of arson and given two years imprisonment. The judgment was proclaimed as "the first conviction in Texas in a case growing out of mob violence against a Negro attacker of a white woman."[40] Having made this gesture, the authorities apparently lost interest. The other cases were postponed and then moved back north to neighboring Cooke County. In October, charges against all but three of the men were dismissed, and, though the county attorney promised action on the others, nothing more was done.[41]

On May 24, 1930, martial law ended in Sherman. The effects of the riot did not pass away so quickly.[42] Sherman's riot contributed to a mania for lynching that spread eastward to Honey Grove on May 16 and then northward to Chickasha, Oklahoma, on May 31. Fourteen more lynchings occurred before the year ended.[43] Not for years would Sherman's blacks recover, and though much interracial progress has been made in recent years, scars remain from that "terrifying day and terrifying night" in May 1930, when "King Mob" ran "amuck."[44]

Not all was lost. If the Rangers had lost a prisoner, they never lost another. Manuel Gonzaullas said, "You learn every time you get kicked."[45] Two months later, at Shamrock in a similar case, he and his Rangers demonstrated well what they had learned in Sherman, and, though their prisoner would die, it would be in Huntsville's electric chair, not in a charred courthouse.[46] Sherman also learned a lesson. A lynching was a terrible price to pay for gaining national attention. This city never paid that price again.

Notes

1. *New York Times*, May 16, 1896; April 6, 1905; May 10, 1930.

2. The main sources for the Hughes incident and subsequent events culminating in the courthouse riot are the May 1930 articles in the *Sherman Daily Democrat*, *Denison Herald*, *Dallas Times Herald*, *Austin American*, and *New York Times* and the fine study by Arthur F. Raper, *The Tragedy of Lynching* (Montclair, N.J.: 1969), 319–355. A good, more recent account is Dave Roberts, "The Day Lawlessness Prevailed," *Denison Herald*, September 12, 1976.

3. *Sherman Register*, August 20–21, 1901; *Whitesboro News*, August 21, 1901.

4. *New York Times*, November 10, 1931.

5. *Dallas Times Herald*, May 2 and 7, 1930.

6. *Dallas Times Herald*, May 4, 1930.

7. *Sherman Daily Democrat*, May 7, 1930.

8. *Denison Herald*, May 7, 1930.

9. *Sherman Daily Democrat*, May 7–8, 1930; Raper, *The Tragedy of Lynching*, 321.

10. There is considerable variation in the accounts of the events inside the courthouse as well as the events of the next twenty-four hours. This writer has had to choose which reports seem most reliable. Most reports agree that the arrival of Hughes's alleged victim set off the violence. *Austin American*, May 10, 1930; *Fort Worth Star Telegram*, May 10, 1930.

11. *Sherman Daily Democrat*, May 9, *Denison Herald*, May 9, *Austin American*, May 10, 1930.

12. *Dallas Times Herald*, May 11, 1930, and *Austin American*, May 15, 1930, which includes Frank Hamer's personal account. A military court of inquiry found that a *Denison Herald* reporter carelessly gave credence to the rumor and spread it as fact. *Austin American*, May 18, 1930.

13. *Denison Herald*, May 11, 1930.

14. *Denison Herald*, May 11, 1930; *Sherman Daily Democrat*, May 9, 1930; *Dallas Semi-Weekly Farm News*, May 13, 1930; "King Mob Runs Amuck in Texas," *Literary Digest*, May 24, 1930; Raper, *Tragedy of Lynching*, 324–325; and interviews of Clyde L. Hall and J. Cecil Taliaferro, January 16, 1973.

15. *Sherman Daily Democrat*, May 11, 1930.

16. Hamer's account is in *Austin American*, May 15, 1930, and H. Gordon Frost and John H. Jenkins, *"I'm Frank Hamer," The Life of a Texas Peace Officer* (Austin, 1968), 164, 167. See also Green Peyton, *For God and Texas: The Life of P.B. Hill* (New York, 1947), 134–136.

17. Capt. Manuel Gonzaullas, interview, December 15, 1972.

18. Col. Robert L. Cox, interview, December 12, 1972.

19. Col. Cox, interview, and Judge J.N. Dickson, interview, January 12, 1973.

20. "The Sherman Race Riot," *Report of the Adjutant General of the State of Texas, 1929–1930* (Austin, 1930), 54–55; Laurence E. McGee, Colonel to the Adjutant General, State of Texas, "Final Report re. Martial Law Duty, Sherman, Texas," May 27, 1930, Archives, Adjutant General's Department, Camp Mabry, Austin; *Dallas Semi-Weekly Farm News*, May 13, 1930; Raper, *The Tragedy of Lynching*, 325–326. Six guardsmen were injured. *Dallas Times Herald*, May 11, 1930.

21. *Sherman Daily Democrat* and *Denison Herald*, May 11, 1930; William Lazenby (eyewitness) to Edward H. Phillips, November 12, 1972; Judge W. Ralph Elliott, tape (Austin College), March 10, 1971.

22. *Austin American*, May 10, *Sherman Daily Democrat*, May 11, and *Dallas Semi-Weekly Farm News*, May 13, 1930; Raper, *The Tragedy of Lynching*, 326–327; "King Mob Runs Amuck in Texas," *Literary Digest*, May 24, 1930, 11.

23. *Dallas Times Herald*, May 10, 1930.

24. *Denison Herald*, May 11, 1930.

25. Raper, *The Tragedy of Lynching*, 328 and 332.

26. Judge W. Ralph Elliott, tape; Glennie O. Ham, interview by Willie Boddie, January 28, 1972.

27. Col. Robert L. Cox, interview; *Dallas Times Herald*, May 10, 1930.

28. Capt. Manuel Gonzaullas, interview; Clyde L. Hall, interview.

29. Capt. Manuel Gonzaullas, interview; *Denison Herald*, May 11, 1930.

30. Glennie O. Ham, interview; *Dallas Times Herald*, May 10, and *Sherman Daily Democrat*, May 11, 1930; Raper, *The Tragedy of Lynching*, 328.

31. This writer has seen several such photographs of the contorted body and numerous onlookers, and he has been told that one collector has a piece of Hughes's anatomy, cut from the corpse.

32. *Fort Worth Star Telegram*, May 12, 1930; "Record and Bill of Items," Dannel-Scott Funeral Home, Sherman. The undertaker listed as cause of death, "Suffocation in Vault at Court House," certified by the Justice of Peace, W.M. Blalock. Hughes's casket cost $17.35. See also *Denison Herald*, May 12, 1930.

33. *Sherman Daily Democrat*, May 11–12, *Denison Herald*, May 12, and *Dallas Semi-Weekly Farm News*, May 13, 1930.

34. *Fort Worth Star Telegram*, May 11, and *Sherman Daily Democrat*, May 12, 1930; "Shooting of Private John Heard, Troop A, 112th Cavalry, May 12, 1930," and "Report of Accidental Shooting of Sgt. E.J. Boyle and Pvt. Sam Bryant, March 14, 1930," Adjutant General's Department, "Sherman Strike, 1930" File, Camp Mabry.

35. *Sherman Daily Democrat* and *Denison Herald*, May 13, and *Fort Worth Star Telegram*, May 14, 1930.

36. Capt. Manuel Gonzaullas, interview. By Tuesday, thirty-nine suspects had been rounded up, one of them a woman. *Sherman Daily Democrat*, May 13, 1930. Sixty-eight persons were jailed during the period of martial law. Jail Record, May 10 to 22, 1930, "Sherman Strike, 1930" File.

37. *Sherman Daily Democrat* and *Austin American*, May 11, 1930; "NO. 5, Treason," *Time Magazine*, May 19, 1390.

38. *Sherman Daily Democrat*, May 23, 1930.

39. *Sherman Daily Democrat*, May 23, June 1, and November 17, 1930.

40. *Sherman Daily Democrat*, April 19, May 27–30, and June 1–6, 1931. Following his conviction on arson, the defendant, J.B. McCasland of Sherman, pleaded guilty to the charge of rioting. He was given two years sentence on each charge, to be served consecutively. Raper, in stating that there were two convictions in the Sherman Riot, gives the impression that two persons were convicted, but McCasland was the only one. Raper, *The Tragedy of Lynching*, 333.

41. *Sherman Daily Democrat*, November 2, 1931. On June 2, 1932, all charges against the remaining three defendants were dismissed and the case was closed. *Sherman Daily Democrat*, June 3, 1932, and Sixteenth District Court (Gainesville), *Criminal Minute Book, VII*, 2 (June 2, 1932).

42. Raper, *The Tragedy of Lynching*, 341–342.

43. Raper, *The Tragedy of Lynching*, 356–383, and *Sherman Daily Democrat*, May 16 and June 1, 1930.

44. Glennie O. Ham, interview; "King Mob Runs Amuck in Texas," 11; and *Dallas Times Herald*, May 10, 1930.

45. Capt. Manuel Gonzaullas, interview.

46. Raper, *The Tragedy of Lynching*, 450–451.

7

Violence in an "Arsenal of Democracy": The Beaumont Race Riot, 1943

James A. Burran

War forcibly alters a nation. The economic, political, and social structure is tested, perhaps shaken or crumbled. Not the least of the alterations produced by war has been a redirection in the role of black Americans. World War II proved no exception as the years of conflict fostered increased hope and frustration for blacks. Having been disproportionately represented on the unemployment rolls of the 1930s, they welcomed the defense buildup that began in 1940. But, they would soon discover, the fruits belonged to whites only. As blacks came to realize this they proved more reticent to engage wholly in the war effort, demonstrating a renewed awareness of the hypocrisy of American democratic principles through such activities as the March on Washington Movement. While controversy exists over whether the position of blacks in the war was conservative in nature or a time of genuine protest, the racial violence of 1943 suggests that changes were occurring. The race riots of that year, moreover, seriously threatened an American war effort for the first time and thus assumed new dimensions. Of the rash of racial conflagrations during the war years, that in Beaumont, Texas, was perhaps the last in which blacks and their property proved exclusively to be the victims.[1]

Beaumont is located on the banks of the Neches River just east of Houston. In 1940 Beaumont contained fifty-nine thousand citizens, with black residents forming 32 percent of the population. By mid-1943 the city had grown to an estimated eighty thousand persons, or an increase of twenty-one thousand inhabitants in three years, with blacks still representing fully one-third of the citizenry.[2]

Originally published in the *East Texas Historical Journal* 14.1 (1976): 39–51. Reprinted with permission of the East Texas Historical Association.

The city and its surrounding area was an "arsenal of democracy," teeming with war production. Pennsylvania Shipyards, Inc., a ship repair and construction business that handled mostly cargo ships and built the famous Liberty Ships, constituted by far the largest single war industry in Beaumont. The shipyard employed eighty-five hundred men at its location on the Neches River and held yearly government contracts in excess of $100 million. Oil refineries of major petroleum companies, concerns that produced bombs and other wartime goods, and several other shipyards dotted the area. In Orange, Texas, situated twenty-six miles east of Beaumont on the Louisiana border, lay the Consolidated Steel Shipyards, erected as part of the Maritime Commission's expansion project in 1940. It ultimately became larger than any other neighboring shipyard, with yearly government contracts totaling $240 million.[3]

With such a profusion of war industries employing black and white laborers, it should have been no surprise that by 1942 Beaumont began to seethe with racial discord. The maze of businesses, both large and small, caused overcrowding. Because Beaumont lacked adequate housing, many workers had to be transported to and from the city from outlying areas every day. In one instance, auto transport trucks were converted into makeshift buses to help ease the problem.[4]

Economic restriction was a second general cause of racial animosity in Beaumont during the war years. Wages reached an all-time high, jobs were plentiful—for whites at least—and in general a period of economic well-being existed. This boom condition was not confined to Beaumont, of course, but prevailed in every war center. But with restrictions on many domestic items, the public was unable to use its economic affluence in accordance with its wishes. Since consumer items were unavailable, most people were forced to be content with possession of a fat bank account and a prewar car with threadbare tires and an empty gasoline tank. Thus many became dissatisfied with the norms of a planned economy, and tempers grew short as the weight of wartime society began to be felt.

City transportation further aggravated problems. The Beaumont City Lines bus service had been quite adequate in 1940, but with the rapid growth of the city the system became overcrowded. And, since no cars or buses were being produced for domestic use, the company could not expand to meet new needs. Overcrowding caused a severe strain between blacks and whites, because when the buses were packed, blacks often stood in the aisles ahead of the dividing signs for the segregated sections required by city ordinance. Intolerant whites demanded that the law be obeyed to the letter, especially to avoid contact between black men and white women. This situation spawned the first burst of racial violence in the city, and served as a precursor to more widespread discord.

On June 30, 1942, three altercations between blacks and whites occurred aboard city buses within the black district. Each of these incidents involved the presence of black passengers in the white sections of the buses because of overflow from Jim Crow sections. Further racial difficulties aboard buses occurred on July 2, provoking the ire of whites and undoubtedly stimulating discord.[5]

On July 27 another confrontation developed aboard a city bus, this one between the driver and a black passenger, Charles J. Reco. The black man, a military policeman at home on leave, boarded the vehicle and took a seat next to the Jim Crow sign where his knees protruded into the white section. The driver ordered Reco to move but was roundly cursed. Taken aback, the driver sent word for the police to arrest Reco, and four officers arrived on the scene and forcibly removed him to a waiting squad car. During this incident, Reco continued to resist the policemen, and at one point reached for Officer Billy Brown's nightstick and revolver. At this Brown pulled his gun and, with Reco's hand on the barrel, shot the black man three times. Officer Ben B. White then shot Reco an additional time, and Officer Clyde Brown, despite a fractured hand suffered while removing Reco from the bus, managed to club the victim with his nightstick.[6]

Police transported Reco to the police station where he was charged with using abusive language. Subsequently, Reco recovered from his wounds at Fort Crockett near Galveston, but not before he brought the US government into the incident. Reco's superiors, astounded at what had occurred, duly related the details to the War Department, which in turn informed US Attorney General Francis Biddle. Without hesitation Biddle launched a scorching verbal barrage against the Beaumont Police Department and Ross Dickey, chief of police since mid-1942 and a former state patrolman. The federal district attorney in Beaumont began an investigation, and a grand jury convened to hear evidence on the incident.

But as in many other cases, the investigation came to nothing. The grand jury on August 19 exonerated the policemen of all responsibility in the incident, and the Attorney General's office quietly dropped the Reco case since there seemed to be "no prospect of conviction." Once again discrimination had emerged victorious while those who saw the actual course of race relations in Beaumont could only grimace helplessly.[7]

The remainder of 1942 and the early months of 1943 appeared relatively calm in Beaumont, as well as in the state and nation, as the country worked feverishly for victory. But while building itself into an arsenal of war, the nation concurrently produced a lethal atmosphere of strain and suspicion as society grew to fit the needs of the era. This tension developed in Beaumont as much as anywhere, while traditional discrimination and racial inequality during the winter of 1942 and spring of 1943 made the situation even more ominous.[8]

As the summer of 1943 approached, the nation had reached full production, and economic conditions were good when compared with those of the previous decade. However, wartime tensions, suspicions, and the instability of society culminated in a highly combustible racial atmosphere, which finally erupted in a full summer of racial bedlam, resulting in many deaths, untold injuries, and inestimable financial losses.

The first race riot of the long summer of 1943 had occurred in Mobile, Alabama. Pressure from the Fair Employment Practice Committee (FEPC) to upgrade jobs for blacks forced the Alabama Drydock and Shipbuilding Company to place several blacks alongside whites on the shipways in skilled positions. Violence resulted on May 25, but fortunately no deaths occurred. The shipyard then sent home all seven thousand black employees until the situation was rectified, keeping the twenty-two thousand white workers on the job. The result was segregation, as the FEPC permitted the shipyard to allow blacks exclusively to man four shipways while whites manned the rest. This proved a poor substitute for the original principles of the FEPC and understandably brought denunciation from the black community.[9]

On June 3, racial violence again occurred, this time in Los Angeles—the infamous "zoot-suit" riots. Here white servicemen and civilians victimized Mexican Americans in an outburst of racial discord caused largely by racist sensationalism from the local press. In the several days of rioting, injuries abounded as the downtown areas swarmed with crazed rioters. As in other similar incidents, most of the participants escaped punishment.[10]

During the turbulence at Los Angeles, Beaumont began seething with its own racial hatred. Curtis Thomas, a young black man, beat and raped an eighteen-year-old white telephone operator on the night of June 4. Thomas, who had been called for induction into the army, was clearly irrational as he explained to the victim his motive for the assault: "The army is going to get me, and if I do this, I'll get killed for this and I won't be going to the army." True to his prognostication, Thomas later that night found himself in the "negro ward" of Hotel Dieu hospital near death after police shot him several times as he attempted to escape from the scene, momentarily having lost the desire to die.[11]

About 3:00 a.m. on the morning of June 6, a potential lynch mob formed outside the hospital and began calling for Thomas. Fortunately, the angry crowd—numbering about fifty—lacked a leader or spokesman so that it never took decisive action, especially after Police Chief Dickey arrived and verbally accosted them. Reminding them that Thomas, who had been spirited away to the city jail, would undoubtedly die as a result of his wounds,

Dickey persuaded the mob to disperse. The fact that Thomas succumbed on June 8 precluded another lynching attempt, but the racial hatred of some whites became even more indignant since Thomas had died before he could be properly punished. This attitude proved predominant among the white employees of Pennsylvania Shipyards, who had formed the majority of the mob. Many of these individuals were not native Beaumonters, but had been attracted to the city by the lure of good jobs. Rootless, frustrated, and alienated, these citizens, as well as other whites, proved potentially dangerous.[12]

On the afternoon of June 15, 1943, the Beaumont police received a telephone call from a woman stating that she had been raped by a black man.[13] This sent officers scurrying to the scene to determine the identity of the alleged rapist and the condition of the victim. Roadblocks were thrown up in the vicinity and groups of policemen, sheriff's department officers, state troopers, and interested citizens began to scour the area in search of the black man. Other officers searched the woman's house for telltale fingerprints, but none were found. The authorities possessed only the woman's vague description of her assailant: he was of average build and features.

As word of this incident spread throughout the city, many Beaumonters must have fumed at the thought of the attack but apparently refused to be driven to violence by rumors. In the Pennsylvania Shipyards, however, a different mood existed. Employees exchanged information about the incident, and rumor begat rumor as night shift employees began to enter the yards for work and tell of what had happened in more tainted detail. Quickly the shipyard employees became excited and restive as they recounted the Curtis Thomas affair and now the violation of a young mother.

About nine o'clock on the night of June 15, over two thousand shipyard workers dropped their tools and marched out of the yards. The walkout appeared to be spontaneous, with almost all white workers taking part. The mob crossed the bridge separating the shipyard island from the rest of the city and continued downtown toward the city hall, police station, and Jefferson County Courthouse, all situated only a few blocks apart. Along the way the crowd swelled to perhaps three thousand as interested bystanders joined.[14]

When the mob reached the police station it had driven itself into a wild frenzy. A lack of organization and leadership fortunately prevailed, and they simply milled about the city jail section of the police station, demanding that the rapist be handed over to be lynched. Chief of Police Dickey, fearing mass destruction, brought the alleged victim to the scene in an effort to pacify the throng, but her pleas went unheeded.

As the mob grew increasingly hostile, some continued to the courthouse, where they demanded that Sheriff W. W. Richardson escort them through the county jail to make sure the alleged rapist was not present. Richardson consented, but why the group wanted a tour is unclear, since no one could have recognized the criminal had he been there. Satisfied that the black was not present, the throng moved back to the police station to rejoin the main body, which soon burst out of control. Even though leadership was lacking, the mob spontaneously reacted to the situation in a fashion characteristic of other race riots.[15]

About midnight on June 15, the mob, which may have numbered over four thousand, began rioting through the nearby black districts of the city. This rioting continued widespread and uncontrolled until about daylight on the morning of June 16. During these hours confusion reigned as the rioters swarmed over most of the downtown area, causing death and destruction.

As in most other race riots, the violence in Beaumont began and continued spontaneously. No ringleaders guided the crowd. Because it was disorganized, the riot proved less destructive than it might have been. The mob, numbering probably between three thousand and four thousand when it assembled at the police station, certainly could have become larger once the actual rioting began and as interested citizens swelled the ranks. With a mob of perhaps five thousand the chances for a widespread holocaust appeared strong, but the lack of leadership contributed to the relative brevity of the riot and limited destruction by the rioters.

The lack of leadership and disorganization also affected the overall pattern of turbulence in Beaumont. The black districts of the city encompassed much of downtown, but there were two general areas where blacks were concentrated. One lay in the downtown district, and the other in the northern sector of the city. Since the two sections lay some distance apart, an "organized" mob probably would have attacked one at a time, or by splitting the crowd, might have attacked both districts simultaneously. But for lack of leadership, the attack lost its full force. The mob, once it resolved to riot, broke up into small bands and roamed the downtown area all night. Each band, usually consisting of from five to twenty-five members, carried out its own plan of destruction. Very rarely did these bodies join into a large throng to cause particularly devastating ruination.

Before leaving the police station around midnight, the mob took as its first victim an unfortunate black man who attempted to drive past the scene in his car. Some of the throng pulled him from the vehicle, pummeled him, then overturned his auto and set it ablaze. The aggregation then broke up and either rampaged through the downtown area or journeyed to the northern sector of the city, largely a black residential district.

Downtown, the mob generally spent its time setting fire to buildings and autos, while beating every black encountered. Some buildings burned to the ground, among them the city's three black funeral homes, a jewelry store that undoubtedly was looted, and a pharmacy. Against this onslaught, most black inhabitants retreated to the inner areas of the black district where the rioters dared not venture.[16]

In the city's northern black district, as downtown, pandemonium prevailed. The rioters, in small groups, roamed the area in total darkness, leading to several cases of mistaken identity—at least four whites were shot. Property destruction here became more widespread than downtown. Several autos met a fiery demise, as did many buildings, leading the fire chief to later opine that the fire department spent most of the period from midnight to daybreak battling blazes in the northern district. Sixteen major fires were reported in the area, together with numerous smaller blazes. Looting occurred as well, and autos could be seen speeding through the city filled with assorted stolen goods.[17]

One black man had a clear view of the destruction as looters swept through the Dew Drop Inn on Gladys Street. P. G. Thomas, the restaurant owner, remained inside when rioters arrived shortly after midnight to break down the front door and sack the building. From a service window, Thomas observed in horror as they systematically destroyed the interior of the structure. Nearby, Perrodin's Radio and Sound Service, Bendy's Cafe, and the Canton Cafe received similar treatment.[18]

Personal violence ran rampant along with the destruction and looting. A black shot a white man as he walked home from work. A white youth, undoubtedly taking part in the rioting, suffered a bullet in the back as he stood alongside an auto. Many blacks had their teeth knocked out and jaws smashed by a group of hammer-wielding whites. Their fate resembled that of countless other blacks whom rioters encountered.

One of the most concentrated areas of personal violence occurred at the bus depot on Park Street. Fifty-two black draftees who had been in Houston for their physical examinations waited in the station for a bus to their homes in Port Arthur. About midnight a mob of three- to four-hundred rioters appeared: "Here they are, a whole bunch of them. Let's get them." As a result, most of the black inductees received injuries, many of which proved serious. Irvin Collins received numerous blows from iron pipes and proved a target for armed rioters. He finally crawled under a nearby house where he remained until the next day. Roy Ford, another draftee, climbed on top of the depot to escape serious injury and witnessed a panoramic view of the holocaust. Alex Mouton received several blows while still inside the building. He ran out, only to be clubbed mercilessly by whites. He suffered a serious heart injury in the affray, and subsequently died on October 4.[19]

Other serious injuries occurred throughout the town. John Johnson, a black employee of the American Ice Company, had just entered his car after working past midnight when a group of whites shot-gunned him in the abdomen. He died on the operating table.

In the fringes of the riot area, Ellis C. Brown, a white carpenter, was found dead with a crushed skull. There were no witnesses, but police speculated that a group of blacks was responsible. This is not to suggest that blacks acted as aggressively as whites during the riot. Most blacks remained on the defensive, but a few undoubtedly used the situation to vent their frustrations on whites through retaliatory action.[20]

Blacks suffered many casualties and witnessed much destruction during the riot. Rioters reportedly broke into over two hundred homes, many of which they set on fire. Probably at least three hundred or four hundred blacks received injuries, and some were hospitalized. Hospital records do not accurately reflect the number of injuries, however, since most blacks felt apprehensive about entering the hospital for fear of further beating or arrest for rioting. Besides those injured, about twenty-five hundred blacks fled the city by foot or auto, some never to return. Many of those who left included black shipyard workers.[21]

During the period of death and destruction, the law enforcement contingents engaged in chaotic activity. At the outset of the violence Chief Dickey called the entire regular force to duty and mobilized the 150-member police auxiliary. The sheriff activated his department, and city officials called up four companies of the 18th Battalion of the Texas State Guard, which consisted of Beaumont residents commanded by Maj. Fred C. Stone, a local architect.

Unfortunately, during the height of rioting, these relatively scant forces had to battle the holocaust alone since most units called in later from outlying areas did not arrive until the violence had subsided. Accordingly, Dickey placed most of the force on hand in the riot-torn sections of the city where it attempted to curb the violence. This effort proved fruitless, although peace officers endeavored to incarcerate suspected rioters. Most of those who found themselves confronted by suspicious officials, however, either argued their way out of arrest or silently disappeared into the darkness.[22]

This accounted for the meager tally of arrests made during the riot—only 206. What made the figure even more surprising, however, was that the total enforcement contingent could not have numbered less than four hundred. Part of the explanation lay in the lack of detention facilities. By summarily arresting individuals who appeared to be rioters, lawmen quickly filled to capacity the city and county jails. A makeshift remedy was finally found, and officers herded subsequent prisoners into a large building on the county fairgrounds. Other reasons for the relatively small number arrested included the laxity of enforcement and general confusion. Despite these conditions, officers did confiscate 156 pistols, 56 shotguns, 44 rifles, 86 knives, 43 clubs, 11 brass knuckles, a huge quantity of ammunition, and other "miscellaneous weapons including hammers, pipes, sashweights, etc."[23]

Most of the arrests and confiscations took place without the help of the four companies of the Texas State Guard, since this body of erstwhile soldiers spent the bulk of the night organizing for action. After moving from the courthouse, where its weapons lay, to Beaumont High School, where it stood for hours, the battalion moved a third time, to the lawn of City Hall. Pup tents and barbed wire sprang up, and a Salvation Anny canteen appeared to feed the warriors.

Most of the guardsmen, including the 18th Battalion and the other forces that later arrived, spent their time patrolling the streets for would-be rioters. The guardsmen did capture and jail some persons, but patrolling stricken areas of the city remained the major responsibility of the men during their activation, which lasted until June 20.[24]

At the first sign of violence on June 15, the city administration had contacted the state government in Austin. Unfortunately, Governor Coke R. Stevenson was on his way to Washington, and the lieutenant governor, John Lee Smith, was in the Midwest. In place of the top executives stood A. M. Aikin Jr., the president pro tempore of the Texas Senate. Aikin had occupied the acting governor's office only one day when the riot erupted.

Aikin understandably hesitated to take action, but shortly after the riot began authorized the deployment of an additional one thousand six hundred Texas State Guardsmen from nearby cities, as well as Department of Public Safety men and other police units. None of these contingents arrived during the actual rioting, but they helped control an additional outbreak about midday of the 16th.

The major violence had subsided about daybreak, with the riot simply exhausting itself rather than being brought under control by outside forces. But at the courthouse about two hundred men, mostly shipyard workers, gathered about noon on the 16th to demand of Sheriff Richardson the whereabouts of the alleged rapist whose actions had precipitated the violence. Richardson, however, proved to be at wit's end.[25] He appeared on the front steps of the building with a submachine gun crooked under one arm, and notified the throng that he was "damn tired of all this." The sheriff then ordered the crowd to disperse and "go back to building ships like you should be doing." The unruly mob began jeering at Richardson, who then shouted that he would take them "all on one at a time. And let me tell you, I'm going to keep law and order in this county."[26]

Rebuffed, the mob dispersed. In a few minutes, however, most of these men congregated again and headed for the downtown black district, apparently bent on causing trouble. They subsequently met a barricade manned by Texas Rangers, who told them to disband. When they did not, the officers sprayed the throng with tear gas, an action that effectively ended the rioting in Beaumont. The violence had claimed three lives; several hundred persons received injuries; untold property was destroyed.[27]

At 5:55 p.m. on June 16 Acting Governor Aikin declared martial law in Beaumont. Communications had continued between the city administration and Aikin since the affray erupted, and by the afternoon of June 16 they had determined that in order to avoid further violence in a critical war production center quick enactment of martial law would be necessary. Aikin accordingly issued the long overdue order, placing control of the city in the hands of Lt. Col. Sidney C. Mason of the Adjutant General's Department. The acting governor assured Mason that martial law would be maintained in the city as long as it was deemed necessary.[28]

By nightfall on the June 16, about two thousand four hundred law enforcement personnel occupied the city, consisting of one thousand eight hundred Texas State Guardsmen, as well as city policemen, the police auxiliary, Texas Rangers, state policemen, and sheriff's department officials. The city looked like a military camp. The all-important defense plants lay paralyzed, with work at Pennsylvania Shipyards stopping on the night of the riot and not reaching full production again for a week. Agitation continued in the yards, and possibly violence could have recurred had it not been for the presence of the troops.[29]

The riot temporarily affected the daily routine of wartime life. On June 16 city officials cancelled "Juneteenth" (a June 19 holiday that commemorates the emancipation of blacks in Texas) since they feared it might spark another conflagration. Chief of Police Dickey ordered all city buses off the streets, and also diverted Greyhound buses around the city. Military authorities placed the city off-limits to service personnel, possibly to avoid racial violence such as occurred in Los Angeles only a fortnight before.

Many restaurants, hotels, laundries, and other businesses remained closed for a week; mail service was also severely curtailed since most Beaumont mail carriers were black. On the 16th, city officials closed all liquor stores in the area, and guardsmen patrolled these places to insure against looting. Additionally, all city swimming pools, parks, and downtown stores closed to keep people off the streets. In short, most functions of the city either closed or operated on a severely restricted basis so that no large bodies of people could amass until the highly combustible atmosphere cleared somewhat.[30]

The rioting affected not only Beaumont but also surrounding towns. The Consolidated Steel Shipyards in Orange temporarily dismissed all black employees beginning on June 16 but retained the whites to avert further violence. The City of Orange placed its state guard contingent on alert. The large rubber plant in Port Neches sent its one thousand two hundred black employees home. Similar precautions were taken in Port Arthur, Baytown, and other nearby cities. In response to rumors that floated in from Beaumont, the city administration in nearby Houston placed a full page statement in the *Houston Post* on June 18, imploring citizens to "stop circulating rumors which create tenseness and interfere with war production and attend to your own business." Obviously the tensions, resentments, and general instability of wartime society existed not only in Beaumont but also throughout southeast Texas and in much of wartime America.[31]

Local authorities naturally concerned themselves with the reasons for the riot. The general assertion that sabotage inspired Beaumont's racial turbulence became the standard argument: the city, a critical production area, had spawned a riot which pitted American against American and crippled vital war production, thereby stirring fears that Axis influence had incited the recent violence.

The editor of the local *Beaumont Enterprise* concluded:

> By committing lawless acts and halting work in vital war industries, they [the rioters] played right into the hands of the enemy. Some of the men who said they had quit work "to protect their families" may have been the unconscious tools of enemy agents.
>
> There is a strong suspicion that enemy agents are trying to create racial friction here, that they have been engaged in this kind of subversive work for months. Evidently their work is bearing fruit.[32]

This view lacked credence, however, as proved in an inquiry by the Federal Bureau of Investigation. FBI agents arrived on the 16th and remained in the city for the next several days. They naturally pursued the possibility of enemy influence, and to that end collected numerous depositions and considerable evidence. While the agents made no public report of their findings, the press disclosed that, according to "unquotable" but presumably reliable sources, the FBI found no sign of enemy activity in relation to the riot. The blame for the outbreak was thus placed upon the local citizenry, with emphasis on the shipyard workers.[33]

While the FBI investigation continued, an inquiry by the state simultaneously occurred. Lt. Col. Royal G. Phillips of the Department of Public Safety arrived in the city on June 17 and began hearing the 206 prisoners who had been incarcerated in connection with the riot. This military tribunal commenced its investigation on June 17 and worked almost without pause until all had been heard on the afternoon of June 20. Of the total, officials held only twenty-nine men for further action, the remainder being released largely for lack of evidence. Of those retained, the majority were charged with such offenses as loitering, drunkenness, and carrying firearms. These crimes carried a penalty of twenty-five dollars plus court costs, so that participation in the riot, regardless of what had happened to the black community, essentially carried a fine of thirty dollars and twenty cents.

On June 22 Phillips officially ended his inquiry and pronounced the case closed as far as the State of Texas was concerned. Of several thousand rioters, only 206 had been brought to court, and only a fraction of that number faced conviction. None received serious penalties. No effort was made to discover the murderers of Ellis C. Brown, John Johnson, or Alex Mouton. Moreover, the fact that no arson charges were levied seemed consistent with the fashion in which the administration of nation, state, and city handled the entire affair. That the guilty parties remained undiscovered seemed to produce no remorse from those charged with investigating the affray since ending the riot was more important at the time than seeking justice.[34]

Ironically, a day after the rioting ended, the results were released of a physical examination performed on the woman who reported being raped by a black man on June 15. The examination, directed by Dr. Barker D. Chunn, a reputable Beaumont physician, disclosed that the woman had in fact not been raped. Moreover, Chunn determined that sexual relations had been absent during the twenty-four hour period surrounding the alleged assault.[35]

During the period of speculation and investigation Beaumont remained quiet. June 19 passed serenely, although officials had been apprehensive about the maintenance of peace in the city because of the cancelled Juneteenth celebration and a city recall election that resulted in the removal of the current city administration—and eventually led to the resignation of Chief of Police Ross Dickey, whom the voters blamed for the riot. The lack of renewed violence on that day proved to be an indicant that the state officials had been watching for, and on June 20 Acting Governor Aikin lifted martial law. The troops in the city were deactivated, and control of the stricken area returned to city officials.[36]

If the riot had been a traumatic experience for the city, its effects on Beaumont proved to be negligible. By the end of July, the war production of the area had returned to normal, still with segregation and discrimination against blacks. Pennsylvania Shipyards undoubtedly listed fewer blacks on its employment rolls, but otherwise conditions remained the same. Racial agitation was minimized throughout the city, but this was due to fear of another riot rather than improved relations between blacks and whites. Subsequent police chiefs and city administrations ignored the race problem as had been done in the past, and over the years the gradual improvement of conditions for blacks has occurred in spite of the white majority.

While Beaumont smoldered in the aftermath of violence, a much larger affray occurred as a continuation of the summer of domestic rioting. The Detroit race riot began on June 20, caused largely by rumor and long-standing social and economic ill will between whites and blacks. Several days of rioting witnessed not only white aggression but black retaliation, in large part against white-owned property, a trend that foreshadowed a new pattern of racial rioting that would unfold in the 1960s. The violence resulted in millions of dollars worth of destruction, thousands of injuries, and deaths of thirty-four persons, most of whom were black.[37]

The final chapter in the long summer of 1943 was written in Harlem on August 1–2. Trouble had simmered there for years, since the riot of 1935. Blacks, who felt alienated in what seemed to be a white man's world, vented their frustrations upon white-owned property in the ghetto for two days following an altercation that involved a black woman and a white policeman. This pattern clearly served as a precursor for future domestic racial violence. Fiorello LaGuardia, New York's popular mayor, skillfully deployed officials—many of whom were black—throughout the area to stop the violence while he remained on the scene to direct affairs. He successfully curtailed what could have become a much larger affray. Nonetheless, five persons died, injuries occurred to at least three hundred others, and rioters destroyed at least $5 million in property.[38]

Of the five race riots in 1943, the incident in Beaumont provided a clear example of white intolerance toward gradual black advancement. While subsequent riots showed blacks becoming more militant and whites more defensive, the affray in Beaumont retained the characteristics of white aggression sparked by conservative reaction. The rumor of interracial rape, a familiar southern theme, precipitated the violence. Lower class whites, seeking to maintain social distinctions between themselves and blacks, spontaneously began to riot, and the black community proved the obvious target. Generally helpless victims of white prejudice, only a few blacks were militant enough to offer resistance. The enforcement bodies were ineffective, perhaps intentionally so, and the violence ran its full course with no interruption. Taken together, these characteristics marked the Beaumont riot as perhaps the last in which whites mercilessly murdered and pillaged without encountering substantial black retaliation.

Seen in this light, the Beaumont riot illustrated the unrest and impending change in race relations. Subsequent violence showed a redirection in the life of black Americans, further underscored by judicial decisions, presidential leadership for civil rights, new scientific views on race, and the emergence of the Third World. The Beaumont riot was one of the last setbacks to the racial upheaval of later years, yet another forlorn attempt to stave off the twentieth century in the South.

Notes

1. Richard M. Dalfiume, "The 'Forgotten Years' of the Negro Revolution," *Journal of American History*, LV (June, 1968): 91; Harvard Sitkoff, "Racial Militancy and Interracial Violence in the Second

World War," *Journal of American History,* LVIII (December, 1971): 662-63; Lee Finkle, "The Conservative Aims of Militant Rhetoric: Black Protest During World War II," *Journal of American History,* LX (December, 1973): 692.

2. US Department of Commerce, Bureau of the Census, *Seventeenth Census of the United States, 1950: Population,* II, 43-100; Morrison and Fourmy Directory Co., *Beaumont City Directory, 1943* (Dallas, 1943), 10.

3. Morrison and Fourmy, *Beaumont City Directory,* 10-12; Frederic C. Lane, *Ships for Victory, A History of Shipbuilding Under the U. S. Maritime Commission in World War II* (Baltimore, 1951), 34–35; *Beaumont Enterprise,* November 7, 1943, 1.

4. Catherine McMaster to James A. Burran, interview, December 20, 1972, Beaumont, Texas.

5. *Beaumont Enterprise,* July 1, 1942, 1; July 3, 1942, 1.

6. *Beaumont Enterprise,* July 28, 1942, 1, 3; August 15, 1942, 2; Walter White, "Behind the Harlem Riot," *The New Republic,* August 16, 1943, 220–22; *Houston Informer,* August 1, 1942, 3.

7. *Beaumont Enterprise,* August 20, 1942, 16; November 28, 1943, 1; Walter White, "Behind the Harlem Riot," 220–22.

8. Richard Polenberg, *War and Society, The United States, 1941–1945* (Philadelphia, 1972), 109–14, 131–40.

9. Committee on Fair Employment Practice, *Field Investigation Report,* R. G. 228, Central Files, National Archives, Washington.

10. Richard Hofstadter and Michael Wallace, *American Violence, A Documentary History* (New York, 1970), 336; Carey McWiliams, "The Zoot Suit Riots," *The New Republic,* June 21, 1943, 818–20; *Pittsburgh Courier,* June 19, 1943, 8.

11. *Beaumont Journal,* June 5, 1943, 1; June 25, 1943,1; *Beaumont Enterprise,* June 6, 1943, 1, 7.

12. *Beaumont Enterprise,* June 7, 1943, 1, 2; *Beaumont Journal,* June 7, 1943; *Chicago Defender,* June 19, 1943, 5.

13. The identity of this woman has yet to be discovered, despite repeated inquiries. According to newspaper sources, the woman's family moved to Beaumont from Galveston in April or May 1943, and prior to that resided in Port Arthur. *Beaumont Enterprise,* June 16, 1943.

14. *Beaumont Enterprise,* June 16, 1943, 1.

15. Ibid., June 16, 1943, 1; June 17, 1943, 1; Willie E. Bauer to James A. Burran, interview, December 20, 1972, Beaumont, Texas; Clyde C. Rush to James A. Burran, interview, December 19, 1972, Beaumont, Texas; *Pittsburgh Courier,* June 26, 1943, 1; *Chicago Defender,* June 26, 1943, 1.

16. *Beaumont Journal,* June 16, 1943, 1; *Beaumont Enterprise* , June 17, 1943, 1; *Houston Informer,* June 19, 1943, 1, 8; June 26, 1943, 1.

17. *Dallas Morning News,* June 17, 1943, 1; *Chicago Defender,* June 26, 1943, 1; *Beaumont Journal,* June 16, 1943, 1; *Pittsburgh Courier,* June 26, 1943, 1.

18. P. G. Thomas to James A. Burran, March 1, 1973; *Houston Informer,* June 26, 1943, 1.

19. *Houston Informer,* June 26, 1943, 8; *Beaumont Enterprise,* October 6, 1943, 4.

20. *Beaumont Enterprise,* June 17, 1943, 1.

21. Ibid.

22. Ibid., June 22, 1943, 12; Clyde C . Rush to James A. Burran, interview.

23. *Houston Post,* June 17, 1943, 1; *Beaumont Enterprise,* June 22, 1943, 12; The low number of riot arrests in comparison with the number of enforcement officials on hand is not peculiar to the Beaumont incident. This trend proved common to many racial affrays, such as the East St. Louis riot of 1917, in which a total of fifty-two policemen and several hundred guardsmen managed to arrest only about two hundred persons. The Chicago riot of 1919 exhibited the same trend, because with three thousand policemen and three regiments of militia only 229 persons found themselves incarcerated. Elliott M. Rudwick, *Race Riot at East St. Louis, July 2, 1917* (Carbondale, 1964), 89–96; The Chicago Commission on Race Relations, *The Negro in Chicago, A Study of Race Relations and a Race Riot* (Chicago, 1922), 35–41.

24. Henry C. Anderson to James A. Burran, interview, December 20, 1972, Beaumont, Texas; Gilbert T. Adams, Sr., to James A. Burran, interview, December 20, 1972, Beaumont, Texas.

25. *Beaumont Enterprise,* June 16, 1943, 1; *The State Observer,* June 21, 1943, 5; *Dallas Morning News,* June 17, 1943, 1, 9.

26. *Pittsburgh Courier,* June 26, 1943, 1.

27. Ibid.

28. *Beaumont Enterprise,* June 17, 1943, 1.

29. Ibid., June 18, 1943, 1.

30. Ibid., June 17, 1943, 1; *Beaumont Journal,* June 16, 1943, 1.

31. *Beaumont Enterprise,* June 17, 1943, 1; *Houston Post,* June 18, 1943, 2.

32. Editorial, *Beaumont Enterprise,* June 17, 1943, 6.

33. *Pittsburgh Courier,* June 26, 1941, 1; *Beaumont Enterprise,* July 8, 1943, 1.

34. *Beaumont Enterprise,* June 18, 1943, 1; June 19, 1943, 1; June 20, 1943, 1; June 22, 1943, 1; July 10, 1943, 1; *Beaumont Journal,* June 19, 1943, 1; The author was unable to examine the report of the military court of inquiry filed by Lt. Col. Royal G. Phillips because, according to Department of Public Safety officials, it has disappeared.

35. Clyde C. Rush to James A. Burran, interview; *New York PM,* June 18, 1943, 4; John Dollard, in Chapter VII of *Caste and Class in a Southern Town* (New York, 1937), suggests that fabricated rape stories by white women are in many cases results of hysterical and masochistic tendencies, together with covert sexual attraction toward black men.

36. *Beaumont Enterprise,* June 20, 1943, 1; June 22, 1943, 12; July 7, 1943, 12.

37. Joseph Boskin, ed., *Urban Racial Violence in the Twentieth Century* (Beverly Hills, 1969), 40; Alfred McClung Lee and Norman D. Humphrey, *Race Riot* (New York, 1969), 27–48; Harvard Sitkoff, "The Detroit Race Riot of 1943," *Michigan History,* LUI (Fall, 1969), 183–206; Thurgood Marshall, "The Gestapo in Detroit," *The Crisis* (August, 1943): 232–33, 246.

38. *Beaumont Enterprise,* August 3, 1943, 1; Lee and Humphrey, *Race Riot,* 98–100.

8

Houston and the TSU Riot

Bernard Friedberg

The author's depiction of the TSU Riot is readable, and a good synthesis of the event. Since the article was published a number of years ago (1969), when the use of the word Negro was generally acceptable, this editor has changed use of that word to either black or African American, depending on the circumstances. Also, do not accept the fact that, as the author asserted, "Houston blacks have no past." *We all have a past, Houston African Americans do, and that is why we study history.*

This is not a sociological study of African Americans in Houston, Texas, but primarily an account, based on fact but somewhat editorial in nature, of one event in the long history of a city. This event, however, is indicative of the reality of life for black people in the area and reflects the entire range of racial problems in Houston.

Houston was founded more than 130 years ago, but its real development did not start until it became a port city in 1914, and its real population growth has been spread over the last twenty-five years. Its impressive skyline, looming over the plain, is only fifteen years old. Houston is a 132-year-old child and, at the same time, a case study in contradictions.

The city likes to be considered part of the Southwest, not the South, thus indicating a more liberal-western orientation. Yet more blacks live in Houston (two hundred and seventy-five thousand) than in any city in the South, including Atlanta.

The citizens of Houston can appropriate, through a bond issue, $31 million to construct an air-conditioned domed stadium, yet they seem unable to

Originally published in *Life Styles in the Black Ghetto*, eds. William McCord, John Howard, Bernard Friedberg, and Edwin Harwood (New York: W. W. Norton, 1969), 36–51. Used by permission of W. W. Norton Company, Inc.

construct a zoning law that would aid in urban renewal and the elimination of some of the worst slum areas in the nation.

Houstonians elected a black woman in 1961 to the school board, one of the most conservative groups in a conservative area, but defeated the same woman when she ran for re-election in 1967.

The same city that welcomed Harry Belafonte as an entertainer in 1964 greeted Belafonte and Dr. Martin Luther King Jr. with stink bombs in 1967.

Houston, like the Texas of fact and legend, has more of many things than any other area. It has massive oil and space industrial complexes and high unemployment; it has more millionaires living in mansions and more poverty-level families living in hovels. But primarily it is a twenty-first-century city with a nineteenth-century approach to the problems of society. For example, the school board sponsored a bond election in 1967 providing for the air conditioning of all new schools but ignored the fact that the new schools were being built in areas not accessible to African American students.

It might be helpful to visualize what it is like to be black in Houston. This description is not meant to indicate that all nonwhites in Houston are subject to the same continual discouragement and disillusionment, only that the following is somewhat typical for the majority.

A good composite example might be something like this. He is a high school graduate, the son of an unemployed former farmer. His house is not air conditioned, although Houston is the most air-conditioned city in the world. He has to draw water from the fire hydrant up the street for his morning shave although Houstonians use more water on their lawns than anywhere else in the country. He has to take the bus to work (not air conditioned, although suburban buses are). To get to the bus stop he has to walk on a dirt road although Houston has more miles of paved streets and freeways than any other city except Los Angeles. He rides the bus fifteen miles across town, although Houston has more two-car families than any other American city. He works all day pumping gas although the city has a teacher shortage. He goes home at night and watches television, and the next morning repeats the same schedule.

Admittedly this is an extreme look at conditions for African Americans in Houston, but the civil rights movement flourished only briefly there, and everyone, especially those benefiting from the status quo, has since gone back to the old homily, "We don't have any problems here."

On a relative scale, this homily has some truth to it. For example, the US Department of Labor has reported that "a family of four could live more cheaply in Houston than in any of 20 other large cities in the country."[1] Further, unemployment does not scar the community quite as deeply as in Watts or in Oakland. In December 1966, for example, city officials estimated the unemployment rate at 1.7 percent for Houston as a whole and at 7 percent for the black population. It should also be noted that somewhat over half of Houston's blacks were born in the Deep South (excluding Houston) or in some small Texas community. Not unnaturally, people who emerge from such an environment find Houston to be a comparatively open and comfortable place to live; indeed, some local African American folk songs describe the city as "heavenly Houston."

Yet a closer look at some of the objective facts leads to a more somber portrayal of the black situation in Houston:

Economically, the 1960 census reported that 22 percent of Houston's population had an income under $3,000 a year. White families earned a median income of $5,902 while blacks had an annual median of $3,426.[2] In a more recent study, done in 1965, the Houston antipoverty program sampled ten geographical areas which included 196,603 African Americans. The study indicated that 53 percent of blacks had family incomes of $4,000 a year or less, as compared to 36 percent of whites and 11 percent of Mexican Americans who also lived in these "impoverished" sections.[3] Moreover, most objective observers agreed that the antipoverty had come to a massive halt in Houston by 1968. Due to internal feuds, a significant proportion of the Houston antipoverty staff resigned. Following the lead of Earl Allen (former director of the Community Action Program), they founded HOPE—an activist group that sought to raise the ghetto by its economic bootstraps. The organization soon incurred the wrath of the white establishment.

Educationally, African Americans lagged drastically behind whites. White adults in Houston had completed a median of 11.3 years of schooling while blacks had finished only 8.9 years.[4] A conservative majority of the school board, adhering to a notion of "neighborhood schools," managed to insure almost total racial segregation in the schools. The board even resorted to such measures as busing black children several miles past white schools to deposit them in ghetto schools. Whites, meanwhile, were bussed in the opposite direction. At Texas Southern University, a predominantly black school, approximately 50 percent of graduates failed to pass national achievement tests that would have allowed them to become teachers.

Housing in Houston presented an anomaly. A few high income African Americans own homes costing from $40,000 to $125,000 in the gilded ghettos of "Sugar Hill" and Timbercrest. Nonetheless, most blacks have to live in substandard housing, often without plumbing or water. In 1960 the census described 47.49 percent of Houston housing as unsound, and blacks occupied most of these premises.[5]

Unlike all other major cities in America, Houston has no zoning ordinance. This constitutes a bonanza for the financial community, since they can place a plant, supermarket, or night club anywhere they wish. For African Americans, the lack of zoning brings some benefits since a few people can, for example, commute more easily to their industrial jobs than in a city such as Chicago. Yet, the very lack of zoning carries with it major penalties for the poor. As one instance, Houston's haphazard planning disqualifies it from participating in the Model Cities program.

The TSU Incident

One could proceed at length with more statistics, but other chapters in *Life Styles in the Black Ghetto* present detailed accounts of the plight of blacks and the state of the human-rights movement. They also give the reasons—poor housing, inferior education, lack of employment opportunities, police insensitivity—and they quote extensively from personal interviews indicating that the black community is ready to explode and indeed has exploded in most cities. Most of this material was prepared before the report of the President's Commission on Civil Disorders was written. The Commission's report makes even more abundantly clear the accuracy of the assessment of black attitudes that have reached a survival or genocide stalemate. This account of one particular event in the broad spectrum of events daily crushing the minorities in this country does not differ substantially from accounts in other chapters of *Life Styles in the Black Ghetto.*

However, it seems this account of a less than full-scale riot illustrates a slightly different dimension of the problem—that of public suppression of communication, elimination of African American leadership through subtle payoffs, and the lack of attention by the national civil rights movement to an area crying for recognition and, in fact, no different from Oakland, Watts, and all the other areas that have erupted. This particular event, like many others, received national publicity and could have been the motivating force behind a movement for reform. It was not and could not be, for reasons that will be enumerated.

During the late evening hours of May 16 and the early morning hours of May 17, 1967, the campus of Texas Southern University, in the heart of Houston's black ghetto, was the scene of a major racial incident that resulted in the death of one police officer, the wounding of at least two other officers and at least two students, minor injuries to several other students, extensive damage to school and personal property, the arrest of 488 persons, and the destruction of the already tenuous bridges between white and black people in Houston.

This incident was the culmination of (but not necessarily caused by) six months of energetic organizational activity by a number of individual students and nonstudents on the predominantly African American campus and of two months of almost continuous demonstrations on a variety of issues ranging from the location of a garbage dump to a demand for the closing of a main street running through the university campus.

Mass-media coverage of the events of May 16–17 was extensive, as might be expected. Radio, television, and newspaper copy ran into tens of thousands of words, and there were thousands of feet of news film. There was no doubt of the importance of this particular news on a local, regional, and national scale, and it necessitated telling, indirectly, the Houston race-relations story. This story had never been told with veracity; therefore, the average citizen was unable to interpret these events except through the emotional outpouring of the moment, which tended to place the entire episode in the category of a national disaster.

As much as any other event in the history of Houston's race problems, the Texas Southern University incident is indicative of the total disregard, the denigration, and the ignorance of the plight of the black man in the city. A summary of civil rights agitation in the city from September 1966 through May 17, 1967, will illustrate the atmosphere in which such events can take place.

At the beginning of the fall school term at TSU, a group known as the Friends of the Student Nonviolent Coordinating Committee, about twenty strong, began meeting on the school campus. For several months their activity consisted only of sporadic speechmaking and the distribution of handbills promoting the organization and attempting to recruit new members. These organizational efforts were only moderately successful and by March 1967 the movement was struggling to maintain its identity. However, at this point the university administration gave the SNCC group an unsuspected boost by denying them a meeting place on campus and simultaneously relieving the group's faculty advisor of teaching duties, which brought immediate protests from the students still active in the organization. Campus meetings were held, speeches were made on the steps of the school auditorium, and demonstrations were staged in the school cafeteria. These events served to excite interest in heretofore uncommitted students, and membership in the SNCC began to rise rapidly. The administration soon granted official recognition to the group, but the banishment had nevertheless served as a springboard for rapid growth and produced area-wide publicity.

On April 4 the situation on the campus reached a new climax. The administration, which had been acting cautiously, cracked down when three SNCC leaders allegedly threatened the lives of police officers during several campus rallies. The three were arrested and placed under $25,000 bond in the Harris County jail. The campus was aroused by this precipitous action and a protest march was immediately organized. Nearly four hundred students marched peacefully from the campus to the courthouse, where a sidewalk vigil was maintained for nearly twenty-four hours. The three men were tried on April 7, pled guilty to a lesser charge, and were released when bail was lowered to $1,000.

Community attention remained focused on the university campus at this time, however, because of the appearance of Stokely Carmichael, then national chairman of SNCC. His arrival in Houston had not been planned to coincide with, or even closely follow, the courthouse demonstration, but this nevertheless appeared to be the reason for his visit. Carmichael spoke on April 13 and 14 at the University of Houston and TSU and drew large audiences at both schools. His presentations were moderate, and no incidents occurred during or immediately following his appearance.

Early in May, TSU students began to congregate almost nightly on campus and on at least two occasions threw rocks and bottles at passing cars, causing some damage and injuring several persons. Thereupon the police closed the campus to all traffic and ringed the area with police emergency units.

The week of May 8 brought a series of daily demonstrations at two widely separated points in the city. One was held at a garbage dump in which a black child had recently drowned, and the other at a newly integrated junior high school in a blue-collar neighborhood. On May 17 approximately sixty arrests were made at these two sites; the demonstrators were jailed but released the same day.

At about 10:30 P.M. on the 16th, following a day of persistent rumors about the shooting of a black child by a white man, a student was arrested on the TSU campus. The arrest was made by two plainclothes policemen who were on campus as a general precautionary measure. Events developed swiftly. Students began throwing rocks and bottles, and a shot was fired, apparently from the men's dormitory, wounding one of the plainclothesmen and bringing a call for additional police assistance. Police reinforcements arrived and a period of general sniping followed, some of it between policemen themselves. Students in the dormitory rebuffed several attempts by recognized black leaders to negotiate a truce, and after a two-hour period when no shots were fired, a group of unidentified students rolled barrels into the main street on the campus and set them afire. This action seemed to tip the scale and the police began to advance on the dormitory with the intention of clearing it out.

Shots, again apparently from the dormitory, were answered by three thousand rounds of pistol and automatic-rifle fire from the police. In the exchange one policeman was fatally wounded. The police then charged the building, forced their way in, and began removing students, 488 of whom were arrested, booked, and fingerprinted. Most were released the next day but five were held under $10,000 bond each on a charge of inciting to riot. The police subsequently searched the dormitory, destroying a great deal of personal property and ripping out ceilings and walls in a vain search for the weapons used to fire on them. This was Houston's riot, and thus far it was mostly a police affair.

The reason for this detailed account of a single incident, rather minor in the overall picture of the last three years, is its indication of the vast underlying problems facing the black community and the total attitude of whites toward blacks in Houston. This incident negates the necessity for a long history of the African American in Houston, where he came from, his wants and desires, for, in actuality, Houston blacks have no past—only a present and possibly a future.

The TSU affair revealed a total lack of public understanding of the state of race relations in the community (largely the fault of local media), the steps civil authority will take to preserve the status quo, the insensitivity of the police, and the lack of black leadership long ago bought off by the white establishment.

Let us take each of these charges and examine them.

The Role of the News Media

That the TSU incident, and those preceding it, took the general public by such surprise is an indication of the dearth of news coverage in the area of race relations. There had simply been no in-depth coverage of racial stories or of the mass movements and organizations that had been prominent in most of the recent developments on the national scene. No attempt had been made to report the programs or purposes, when such have existed, of the established civil rights groups such as the NAACP and the Urban League, let alone the more militant SNCC, CORE, and Black Muslims. The ordinary newspaper-reading, television-watching citizen of Houston was, therefore, at a loss to interpret news of these organizations because he had been presented with only a palatable summary of their activities and has thus remained ill informed. The average Houstonian cannot recognize the names of leaders of these groups, cannot define any aspects of their programs, and has no knowledge of their methods (the term "black power" has never been adequately explained to him). In fact, the average Houston citizen, expressing a lack of understanding not necessarily of his own making, is perfectly willing to lump all civil rights organizations together under the general heading of "Communist agitation."

A little background information that might have provided citizens with a basis for interpreting the violence of recent years has not been presented in the local media. Material on the general deprivation of a large portion of the country's population, the problem of poverty, job discrimination, housing bias, and the denial of equal educational opportunities has been wholly lacking. Although such information was readily available to the Houston media through national news services and the various governmental agencies concerned with these problems, it was either not sought or not used.

On the other hand, the media have focused on press releases from the office of the mayor of Houston that describe the progress being made through the city's efforts, citing apparently successful programs in almost all areas of the city dealing with problems affecting intergroup relations in the community. This emphasis has created a smoke screen behind which the public has settled into a false sense of security, not realizing the depth of the problems or the shallowness of the stopgap solutions being fostered by the city. Further, this overemphasis on positive programing has created a widening gap between the expectations of the minority community and its hope for more effective measures in solving problems and the realities of the situation, which indicate painfully slow progress.

The creation of this euphoria resulted in the disproportionately shocking impact of a single event on the citizenry. People reacted uniformly, decrying the situation and expressing total dismay that it could happen in their community.

The reporting of incidents that occurred prior to the major disturbance at TSU was not only sketchy but also unbalanced, and served mainly to implant the false idea in the public mind that the problems being protested were new (created by agitators) and of little significance. The realistic and symbolic importance of these protests was not explained or even commented on in the local media, and again background coverage was absent. For example, the demonstrations at the junior high school received some notice in the media but at no time was mention made of the repeated fights between white and black residents and their children or the seemingly arbitrary disciplinary measures meted out to black students involved in a disturbance at the school and the absence of equally harsh discipline for white students embroiled in the same disturbance. Similarly, little notice was given to the precipitating factor in the demonstrations at the dumpsite, namely, the drowning of a black child in one of the water-filled holes in the dump. Neither was any conclusion drawn from the fact that a remarkably similar demonstration by whites at a compost-plant site in a fashionable section of the city resulted in no arrests and the closing of the plant.

There was no advance notice of Stokely Carmichael's visit to the local campus, and the rock-throwing incidents were shoved under the rug because apparently, in the judgment of the media, the citizens of Houston were not capable of understanding the situation. It is no wonder then that Houstonians were caught by surprise by the violent events at TSU. They had falsely been led to believe that good race relations existed in their city.

The first reporting of the TSU events, recognizing the fluidity of the situation, was as accurate as could be expected and responsible to a fair degree. The stories used the following day were a good deal less objective. Radio, television, and newspaper coverage was radically unbalanced in that it failed to recognize the possibility of anything other than student guilt for the incident or that a large percentage of the student body was not involved in any way. Outside agitators and nonstudents were attacked by the press, whose anger showed in an overreaction to the disturbance (showing a lack of knowledge of basic causes) and an immediate attempt to place blame on someone. Sharp focus was placed on the death of the police officer, including stories about his wife and family, but little mention was made of the injured students or of the fact that one wounded student received no medical attention for twelve hours.

The mayor and the police chief became the only spokesmen to whom the media listened. The mayor's words tended to be defensive and self-justifying, producing the unmistakable impression of student and TSU administrative guilt brightly contrasted with police and city government innocence. Student activists and spokesmen, school administrators, and persons simply caught up in the general disorder were not approached for comment by local media, and it was left for the national networks to follow this aspect of the story.

These shortcomings in the Houston media are possibly peculiar to the area but more likely are expressions of the faults of the communications media in general. There is an obvious need for skilled reporting, complete candor, and careful objectivity in reporting racial stories. Room for error is great because of the extremely emotional subject matter; therefore, editing and headline writing must be done with unusual care. More high-management supervision at the news-desk level is needed. However, the overriding need is for an educational program aimed directly at the media to sensitize them to the problems of the minority communities, a kind of human-relations education, to provide them with the insight and knowledge necessary to make intelligent and perceptive news reporting possible in the race-relations field. Obviously, no amount of information would have totally prepared the public for the TSU problems, but total surprise could have been avoided by an objective and informative appraisal, months or years ago, of the underlying causes of the complex social problems of our times. The mass media must take the responsibility for informing the citizens of the community.

Perhaps too much emphasis is placed here on the media; however, the importance of establishing the climate in a community cannot be overemphasized. Community opinion, both positive and negative, has been a major contributing factor in the creation of riot situations and their prevention.

Reactions of White Houstonians

The white climate of opinion in Houston has been clearly outlined in a public-opinion poll conducted by political scientist Victor Emmanuel.[6] In 1967 Emmanuel selected a probability sample (accurately reflecting geographical and income groups in the city) from the voting-registration list of Houston. Considering only the 320 "Anglos" in the study, one finds that, on the basis of their reported voting behavior, about 74 percent could be classified as "conservative," 13 percent as "independent," and 13 percent as "liberal." Thus, despite the influx of northerners into such operations as the Manned Space Craft Center, Houston has remained an essentially conservative city.

This basic conservatism naturally reflected itself in attitudes toward African Americans and rioting. Only 22 percent of white Houstonians believed that poverty contributed to rioting (in direct contrast to the beliefs of black Houstonians). Twenty percent believed that Communists were the basic cause of riots, when, in fact, it would be extremely difficult to find a single Communist of any variety in Houston's civil rights movement.

When asked what steps should be taken in response to riots, white Houstonians flatly affirmed their belief in violent repression: 77 percent wanted to "call in the army," "shoot the rioters," or use some other kind of force. Only 16 percent could think of other measures, and the remaining 7 percent just did not know what to do.

Nearly half of white Houstonians (47 percent) had either hazy notions or no ideas at all about what long-range solutions might alleviate the conditions underlying riots. The elimination of slums, for example, occurred to only 7 percent as a possible solution. A much higher proportion (25 percent) preferred to enhance the authority, power, and numbers of the police as the solution.

Reactions of Civil Authorities

In such an atmosphere, one could hardly expect civil authorities, particularly those who held elective office, to respond in an enlightened manner to civic disturbances.

The insensitivity of civil authority—in Houston, the mayor's office—has long contributed to the establishment and maintenance of the status quo and has in essence prevented the development of local black leadership that would better serve the interests of the general community. Speaking more specifically, the mayor of Houston has long maintained that his communication with black leaders was all that was necessary to prevent civil disorders; he could always call on his friends to get the facts and to set the black community straight. This may have been true five years ago but the mayor has failed to keep himself abreast of events in the civil rights field and, blinded by the lack of general civil rights agitation in Houston, has assumed his theory to be correct. In fact, no one person or group can today speak for the black citizens of Houston or any other city. All the communication in the world will not prevent an explosion, and communication with the traditional black leadership can only anger the more militant younger generation and precipitate the incendiary actions that traditional leaders are trying desperately to avoid.

Only recently has Houston, under the direction of the mayor, taken any action to convince black people that the city cares about them. A department of city government has been established, staffed by two men, which serves as a complaint-processing mechanism to placate the militant blacks. This office also serves as a hedge for the mayor when someone asks what he is doing about community tensions, the problems of the slums, police brutality, or any other problem that concerns race relations. This smoke screen has been effective thus far, but very real actions must be taken by the city before tensions will be eased, and they will only be taken when city government, including the Houston school board, which wields tremendous power, becomes truly sensitive to minority-group problems, especially poverty and education. Many private citizens and special-interest groups are attempting to educate city government, but the road is difficult and the conservative attitude in Texas will not be breached easily.

Houston is not unique in that accredited and potential African American leadership is eventually bought off by subtle or overt means. Students leading demonstrations suddenly appear as highly paid members of the poverty program. Ministers influencing large congregations to more militancy are soon seen heading federally financed education projects. The black middle class in Houston looks on, sometimes in dismay but more often as if these problems were not their concern. This lack of developed, trusted leadership has resulted in an ineffective poverty program when the program could have been a step toward effective community action, the bettering of life for a large number of minority citizens, and a portion of credibility to Houston's claim of progressive activity. This long-standing system of paying off minority leadership has resulted in a vacuum easily filled by "outside agitators" and extremists, who are more likely to destroy the status quo than any other element of society.

The Role of the Police

Another major factor in racial unrest in Houston is the attitude and makeup of the police force and the image projected by the chief of police, who was especially appointed by the present mayor. Unlike Atlanta, Houston's major competitor for leadership in the South, the Houston police had adopted none of the recommendations of the Kerner Commission report and had often made apparent their disdain for the advancements being made elsewhere in police-community relations. The chief, Herman Short, a good, hard-headed policeman, has no room in his department for a study of the underlying causes of racial unrest, and he makes no secret of this attitude. His desire to keep order transcends the equal enforcement of the law and even the normal measures used to quell civil disturbances. For instance, during the TSU incident his order to charge and clean out the dormitory was given without any regard for those students who were not taking part in the disturbance. No bullhorns were used to inform the dormitory residents of the impending attack and no tear gas was used at any time. Instead, there was a barrage of rifle and pistol fire that could have killed scores of students.

As in most other major cities, Houston needs policemen who are thoroughly trained in human relations as well as combat techniques. The department is underpaid and understaffed, but this is no excuse for being undertrained.[7]

It is doubtful that conditions in Houston are any more or less degrading for the African American than they are in other areas, but the contrast between what could be accomplished by the community in Houston and what is being accomplished in the elimination of the causes of riots and disturbances is truly frightening. The gap between the haves and have-nots is widening almost as fast as the population and skyline are growing. The problem is that blacks and other minorities in Houston have begun to see the gap. They are beginning to want what white Houston has now. They will develop their own leadership, and that new leadership will find it easy to point out these discrepancies. There is still time in Houston to prevent the serious rioting that has occurred in most American cities, but it is the eleventh hour.

Notes

1. *Houston Post*, February 19, 1967.
2. Episcopal Society for Cultural and Racial Unity, "Nowhere to Go," c. 1962 Houston, 3.
3. Houston-Harris County Economic Opportunity Organization, "Dimensions of Poverty," Houston, 1965, 13.
4. Episcopal Society, "Nowhere to Go," 2.
5. Derived from 1960 census data for the City of Houston.
6. Victor Emmanuel, "Houston Citizens' Survey," unpublished study, University of Houston, 1967.
7. Belatedly, in 1968, Houston police officers were given a short course in human relations.

9

Loyal Garner Arrest

HOWARD SWINDLE

Troy Lee Starling was the first, killed on a tarpaper night beside a deserted East Texas highway. A blue steel muzzle was pointed close to the back of his neck. One clean shot, with enough velocity to pierce the engine block of a car, tore through Starling's neck, blowing a gaping exit hole in his Adam's apple. The .357 magnum was issued by the Texas Department of Public Safety; the man who pulled the trigger was a state trooper.

Four months later, on Christmas night, 1987, Loyal Garner Jr. was bludgeoned with a blackjack, then dragged out of the sight of witnesses into an isolated room. When his friends next saw him, his eyes were locked open in an eerie, sightless freeze frame. Propped against a cement wall, he slid like cold syrup along the wall and onto the floor. A pathologist later would characterize the injuries to Garner's head as similar to those of a person who had gone through a car windshield at one hundred miles an hour. Garner was last seen conscious in the company of three police officers.

Spring hadn't fully settled in East Texas when Kenneth "Hambone" Simpson died. There had been no more dignity in the man's death than in that of a road-killed armadillo left beside the highway. Ambulance attendants found Simpson's body hog-tied on the cement floor of a jail cell, his hands cuffed behind his back and his ankles bound together with disposable plastic cuffs. He wore no shirt; his pants had been pulled below his buttocks. A pool of blood beside his left shoulder had dried onto the cement floor. Rigor mortis had set in, posing no small problem for the attendants, whose job it was to remove Simpson's contorted body from the cell onto a gurney. Eleven officers admitted being in the eight-foot-square cell during

Originally published in Howard Swindle's *Deliberate Indifference: A Story of Racial Injustice and Murder* (New York: Viking Penguin, 1993), 1–18. Reprinted with permission.

five frenzied minutes of violence. All of them swore that Simpson had been alive when they left.

In eight months that straddled 1987 and 1988, Starling, Garner, and Simpson died within one hundred miles of each other in a triangular slice of wondrous pine thickets known as Deep East Texas. Nothing suggests that any of them ever had occasion to meet. Starling operated a forklift, Garner drove a truck, and Simpson was a sidewalk scammer, a nickel-and-dimer whose enterprises included gambling, drugs, and other people's property.

Indeed, the three men shared more in death than in life. Each met death under the color of law. Each fell into police custody for misdemeanor offenses that shouldn't have overly challenged the peace and dignity of local society—speeding, drunk driving, stealing a ballpoint pen. None of the victims was armed—no gun, no knife, not even the ubiquitous "shiny object" that officers inevitably claim to have mistaken for a weapon before electing to exercise lethal force.

Starling and Garner were black. The last faces they saw in life were those of white police officers. Simpson also was black. Eight of his eleven assailants were white officers, troopers, and deputies.

The similarities in death didn't end there. Among some members of the tiny communities in which the black men died, reaction was frighteningly similar: "Just another dead nigger."

For decades, long before the nation was outraged by the videotaped brutality of white Los Angeles police officers beating an unarmed and helpless black man, black life had been cheap in rural Texas—particularly if a black had the audacity, or ignorance, to step out of his "place."

By 1964, it was inevitable that Washington would mandate that blacks and whites would sit beside each other in public schools and in restaurants. But in 1987, more than twenty-five years after the Civil Rights Act of 1964, a black's place in most of Deep East Texas doesn't yet mean a badge, an elected office, or an integrated church. As if the seventy-foot-tall pines were an impenetrable social barrier, Deep East Texas lies stagnant in a civil rights time warp, more forties and fifties than eighties and nineties.

Texas, not Alabama or Mississippi, leads the nation in the number of federal civil rights investigations annually. And within Texas, the majority of those officers investigated for beating, torturing, and shooting defendants practice their professions in small towns east of Interstate 35, the major artery that splits the state in half. Ironically, it is within this same piece of geography, broadly known as East Texas, that history and culture has situated the bulk of the state's black population. Not surprising, black residents of these farming and sawmill towns become victims in disproportionately high numbers of some of the toughest, most abusive cops in the nation.

In the deepest enclave of East Texas, the criminal-justice system is dominated by white cops, white grand juries, white jurors, and white judges. At best, the system tolerates black defendants. At worst, black defendants don't make it past the white cops even to be heard by the white grand juries: justice is administered swiftly and surely by a good ol' boy beside the road or in a booking room or jail cell.

Vollie Grace, a black contractor, deacon of his church, and father of four, was born and reared on a family farm just outside of Hemphill, Texas. He didn't set out to be a civil rights activist. He didn't *want* to be an activist. But when Loyal Garner Jr. was beaten unconscious in the Sabine County Jail in Hemphill, just a rock's throw from the Louisiana state line, Vollie Grace felt like he would suffocate on his silence. Garner died two days later without regaining consciousness. Not only was there no official explanation from law enforcement about the cause of his death, there was not even an acknowledgment of his death.

Grace forced an explanation from law enforcement, a group that for two hundred years in Sabine County has been exclusively white and which, its current sheriff vows, will continue to be exclusively white as long as he's alive and wearing a badge. When the acknowledgment of Garner's death did come, it was passive. Loyal Garner Jr., a valued, hardworking family man, had walked without threat or coercion into the one-story stucco jail, under his own power. The next morning he was rolled out on a gurney, his eyes locked in a half-open, surrealistic daze. Somehow, he "just got dead." A passive act, like "Well, he just took ill."

Troy Starling's and Kenneth Simpson's deaths never made it past grand juries. The white trooper who killed Starling was cleared without charges even before forensic lab tests were available. The tests proved that the officer's story of self-defense was scientifically implausible—about as likely, a forensic pathologist said, as "lightning striking the room while we're speaking." When the final vote came around, the grand jury's two black members abstained in disgust.

The eleven officers who last saw Simpson alive before he was found hogtied and suffocated in his cell were neither disciplined nor indicted by the grand jury. A year later, one of the officers sauntered up to a writer and asked why he hadn't been interviewed about the circumstances of Simpson's death. "I know what happened," he sneered, moving his face close to the writer's. "The nigger killed hisself."

The death of Loyal Garner Jr., perhaps no more heinous in circumstance than Starling's or Simpson's, was the only one of the three to be prosecuted in the criminal justice system responsible for law and order in Deep East Texas.

Justice for Garner wouldn't come easily. That it came at all, considering the legacy of human abuse in East Texas, was stunning enough to command two minutes of network news time and front-page headlines in *The New York Times*. Moreover, justice came reluctantly, and only when the good-ol'-boy system was dissected, magnified, and exposed. Garner's day in court came only after another jurisdiction fought to wrest responsibility from the tiny town that had tried so desperately to bury the evidence along with its sordid history of civil rights abuses. When the town realized it no longer could shield its officers from the glare of outside scrutiny, its residents rallied even more stubbornly behind the lawmen, pulling in ranks tightly and refusing to talk to outsiders. The people who lived in Hemphill called it community pride; outsiders called it paranoia. Whatever its genesis, the result was an impenetrable silence.

Beyond all else, Hemphill seemed to determine, its deliberate indifference should remain concealed within the familiar thickets of longleaf pines.

Texas Highway 87 is a scenic and incongruous stretch of two-lane blacktop, conceived as much for tourism as for commerce. From its origin near Galveston, it runs flat and straight for sixty picturesque miles along the lip of the Gulf of Mexico. Only a few thousand yards short of Louisiana, the highway veers hard left, ducks beneath the steady congestion of Interstate 10, and heads quietly due north for country that makes the Texas Department of Tourism proud. Texas 87 assumes a new personality with each northward mile, heading first up subtle inclines, then rolling gently and, by the time it skirts the pine-laden Big Thicket, bogging down logging trucks with its deceptively steep grades.

Fifty miles north of the Gulf Coast, Texas 87 already is well into Deep East Texas, the state's easternmost colony of counties, clustered along the Sabine River, the natural boundary that keeps Texas from running into Louisiana. On either side of the highway, seventy-foot longleaf pines grow so densely that they choke sunshine in midday. Even on nights with full moons, Deep East Texas is darker than coal tar in a cellar.

About an hour after dusk on Christmas Day, 1987, a chilly, sporadic drizzle was threatening to turn into genuine rain along Texas 87. Loyal Garner Jr. was less than two miles north of Hemphill, the county seat of Sabine County, when he saw the flashing red and blue lights in his rearview mirror. "Damn!" Garner muttered to the two friends beside him in the cab of the pickup truck. "I wonder if I didn't hook up those taillights?"

Moments later, as he stood beside the deserted highway, rain trickling from his brows into his eyes, Garner was looking up at one of the biggest cops he had ever seen.

It was part Good Samaritanism, part pride, and part his usual inability to say no that had prompted Loyal Garner Jr. to pry himself from the controlled Christmas chaos that he knew as head of a household that included three daughters and three sons—six loud, stair-stepped kids from three to thirteen, each separated by exactly two years.

The holiday frenzy actually had begun in earnest on Christmas Eve at the Garner home, a modest but livable three-bedroom frame house set on concrete blocks. It sat in a half-acre clearing surrounded by pines just outside the city limits of Florien, Louisiana. The pines, and the Boise-Cascade plant that cut, pressed, and pasted them into plywood, were Florien's only reasons for being. No more than a flyspeck on the map, Florien (pronounced "flo-REEN" by locals) was barely even in Louisiana; it snuggled close to the Sabine River and the Toledo Bend Reservoir, which formed the state line between Sabine County, Texas, and Sabine Parish, Louisiana.

On Christmas Eve, by family custom, Corrine Garner took the three girls, Carmica, Kimberly, and Valerie, with her to Many, Louisiana, ten miles north, to buy groceries and to stop off at the Laundromat. Christmas, particularly *this* Christmas, was no time to discuss it, Corrine knew, but a washer and a dryer were necessities for a family with six kids who seemed to create dirty clothes the way rain created mud. Buying a washer and a dryer always had been a priority, even with Loyal; but food and clothing always seemed to move them down the list. The phone had been a priority, too, but it sat idle in the living room. Loyal and Corrine had been forced to choose between paying the phone bill and sandbagging a little extra for the kids' Christmas, and the phone bill hadn't made the cut. The phone had been disconnected.

Garner kept the boys, Loyal Lynndell, Marlon, and Corey, at home, enlisting—or more accurately, *tolerating*—their help in applying the final touches to his black Ford Explorer pickup truck, a spotless nine-year-old relic he had rejuvenated with a wholesale overhaul. Only days earlier, Corrine, in mock seriousness, had drawn the line when rain had forced her husband to retreat to the kitchen, dragging with him his greasy carburetor and intake manifold, which he had plopped down on newspapers spread on the table. He grinned under the threat, the way he always did. "It ain't no use worrying, Corrine. No grease going to get on your table. I already cleaned them in gasoline."

When Corrine and the girls returned from Many in the afternoon, she set Carmica, Kimberly, and Valerie to folding clothes and straightening up the house while she got an early start on Christmas dinner. Christmas morning was for the kids, she always said, and she didn't want to be trapped in the kitchen cooking while they were playing with their booty from Santa. Christmas Eve she reserved for baking the pies and getting the vegetables ready. She also made the cornbread dressing and readied the turkey, needing only to pop them into the oven in the morning.

After dusk, Garner cajoled Corrine into a test ride in the Ford Explorer. He was like a kid at Christmas, Corrine mused, busily explaining mechanical intricacies that he knew she'd never understand. His ability to work with his hands, to fix or build just about anything, was one of the traits she most admired in him in the fourteen years they'd been married. His reputation as a "shade-tree mechanic," in fact, had meant a little extra money from fixing cars for friends. So, dutifully, Corrine nodded and smiled as her husband rambled on about timing chains, valves, and whatchamacallits.

Before heading home, the couple stopped off at Mr. Albert's. Florien was "dry," and while you could buy everything from a pump-action shotgun to French fries at John's Country Store, you couldn't buy Budweiser or Jim Beam. Alcohol meant a ten-mile trip up US 177 to Many. Mr. Albert, an elderly black man, operated under the entrepreneurial philosophy of supply and demand, or, more specifically, find a void and fill it. Mr. Albert was a bootlegger. Garner emerged from Mr. Albert's tiny lean-to house with a single can of Budweiser, which he swigged before they pulled up in their own muddy red driveway.

Thoughts of new toys had a grip on the two youngest Garners, five-year-old Marlon and three-year-old Corey, who successfully fought off sleep until midnight. Stern warnings from their father meant little on Christmas Eve, and the boys knew they were safe in pushing the limits. "We'll just have to get up a little earlier in the morning and get that bike put together before they wake up," Garner told Corrine, yawning and heading for the bedroom.

The bicycle, assembled and ready near the tree early Christmas morning, was a hit with the oldest boy, seven-year-old Loyal Lynndell—but no more than Corey's dump truck, which, his father explained, was just like the one he drove every day working for the Sabine Parish road crew. They were on the floor together, Garner and Corey, pushing the truck around the coffee table and behind the space heater, dodging the torn Christmas wrapping that littered the floor.

After Christmas dinner, around eleven thirty, Gerome Garner, one of Loyal's ten brothers, showed up on the front porch. Corrine, busy directing kitchen cleaning, saw Gerome offer her husband a beer, but duties took her away from the window, and she never saw whether he drank it. And she only casually noticed that Johnnie Maxie also appeared from down the road—to borrow a wrench to fix his down-and-out Ford Granada, Loyal told her after Maxie had gone.

Corrine didn't own a watch, but she later would estimate that Johnnie Maxie returned sometime between one and two in the afternoon, carrying the wrench and wearing a forlorn look on his ample face. Johnnie's younger brother, Alton, was with him in their mother's car. The wrench hadn't provided the solution to the Granadas' woes; Johnnie Maxie needed a timing chain for the engine.

"Corrine, I'm going to follow Johnnie and Alton on to their mother's and drop off her car," Loyal said. "Then I'm taking them over to Newton to pick up Johnnie's other car. He wants me to redo his engine. Shouldn't be gone more than two or three hours, I 'magine."

Newton was maybe fifty miles southwest of Florien, across the Sabine River on the Texas side. Garner walked out the front door wearing black boots, a freshly pressed striped shirt his wife had washed only the night before, and the new pair of jeans she had given him for Christmas.

The innocuous, over-the-shoulder conversation would be the last Corrine Garner ever had with her husband. When she next saw him, she would barely recognize him.

"Junior" Garner had known Johnnie and Alton Maxie all their lives, had gone to school with them and had socialized with their family. Like all the blacks and most of the whites around Florien, the Maxies were players in hardscrabble economics, always searching the system of too few good jobs for ways to make ends meet. Recently, the Maxies had signed on as roughnecks for a small oil drilling company in western Louisiana. The money was better than average, but the drilling rig was miles out in the pines. Alton, shorter and leaner, rode to work with his big brother. They had to have transportation to have a job.

Once he had collected them at their mother's house in his pickup truck, Garner suggested a change of plan.

"Corrine's brother up in Many does some mechanic work. He might know somebody who has a timing chain today. There's a bunch of ol' wrecking yards up in Zwolle. It's worth a try." Besides, Garner figured, the trip would be a good break-in for the Explorer's tight, reworked engine.

The three friends meandered leisurely up US 171, first to Many, where they just missed Corrine's brother, then on to Zwolle, where they tried a series of junkyards without finding one open. Garner was disappointed; he would have bet good money that one of the proprietors would have come out on Christmas to make a cash deal.

Jerry Lane Cartinez was open. He had owned the liquor store south of Zwolle only since Thanksgiving, and since the state of Louisiana didn't have any objections about selling booze on Christmas, he figured he needed the business.

At some point between five and seven that afternoon, three black men walked into his store. Cartinez recognized Alton Maxie, the smallest of the three. The proprietor and his customers chitchatted, first about the drizzly weather, then about the men's trip to Texas to pick up a car. Cartinez rang up their purchases—a six-pack of Budweiser, a half-pint of Bacardi rum, and a half-pint of Crown Royal bourbon.

"I got this," Johnnie said, pulling his belt up over his belly with his left hand and dipping his right hand into his pocket for a small wad of bills. "You been running me around all day on this car. I owe you."

As an afterthought, the third man, the solidly built, muscular one who was driving the black pickup, put a dollar on the counter for a raffle ticket. Holder of the winning ticket, Cartinez explained, won a fifth of bourbon. The fact that the man generally drank only beer didn't dissuade him from entering the raffle. On the back of the card, he wrote his name: "Loyal Garner Jr., Florien, La."

Within thirty minutes, the black Ford pickup had passed from Louisiana over the Pendleton Bridge, a two-and-a-half-mile concrete span over the Sabine River, and into Sabine County, Texas, en route to Newton.

Cartinez would see Garner's name in the newspaper and hear it on television in the next few days. The name struck a vaguely familiar chord. The liquor store owner shuffled through his raffle tickets until he found Garner's. That Garner had been in his store on Christmas making idle talk chilled him. He'd remember to tell his wife when he got home. He'd never known anybody who'd ended up in the news—not like that.

"Well, Junior, just *try* a swig of this Crown Royal. It's smooth stuff."

Johnnie knew Garner drank only beer, but he extended the half-pint of whiskey over Alton's chest anyway and motioned the small bottle toward the driver.

Garner looked dubiously at his friend, then took only enough from the bottle to confirm what he already suspected. "Damn, that stuff makes me sick. Don't like it. Just gimme one of them Buds."

Johnnie leaned into the floorboard and came up with a red, white, and blue can almost hidden by his huge fist. Alton took it and handed it to Garner. Both brothers say the driver nursed the single Budweiser until shortly before they were stopped beside Texas 87 outside Hemphill.

"It's got to be a taillight," Garner said again as the officer approached his door. The police officer who approached Garner's window was a bear of a man, six-foot-one, 270 pounds, with a belly that plunged heavily over his belt, concealing its buckle. From Johnnie Maxie's vantage point on the passenger side of the pickup, the full frame of the driver's window was filled with the officer's chest, forcing Garner to lean back in the driver's seat, cock his head toward the window, and peer up at his accuser. As Garner was told to step out of the truck and walk to the back, a second officer—smaller, wiry, and angular—appeared at the right rear of the Ford pickup, eyeing the Maxie brothers in the cab.

"Go on and get in the backseat of the patrol unit," he said to them, as he opened the passenger door, his eyes fixed on Johnnie.

The big one continued to talk to Garner. Then Garner joined his passengers in the backseat of the patrol car. The officers removed Garner's hunting rifle from the cab of the pickup and locked its doors.

As the big one pulled the Ford patrol car into gear and steered around the pickup truck on the shoulder of the road, Garner asked apparently his only question: "What about my pickup?"

"It'll be all right for a little while," came the answer from the front seat.

Garner was thirty-four years old and had never been arrested in his life. He was clearly perplexed, and looked toward the Maxies for explanation. Alton, sitting cramped in the middle, sensed Garner's silent question, shrugged, and rolled his eyes. Alton and Johnnie had been arrested before, but never for anything except for drunk driving. This arrest, the Maxies sensed, was strange, and nothing at all like the other times. Neither of the cops had told them what law they supposedly violated. They hadn't read them the Miranda warning. And even though the cops had to have noticed the beer and liquor on the floorboard of the pickup—Johnnie had made no effort to push it under the seat—the big one hadn't asked Garner to perform any field sobriety tests: no walking heel-to-toe, reciting the alphabet, or standing on one foot with his eyes closed. There was no mention of Breathalyzer or blood tests. There wasn't even mention of a faulty taillight.

Even more curious, Alton Maxie thought, the officers ordered them into the backseat of a patrol car that had no protective mesh screen without frisking them for weapons or even handcuffing them. Alton's mind was beginning to reel with paranoia; something, he sensed, was horribly wrong. *What the hell's going on here?*

The little one shattered Alton's thoughts. "Any of you boys got a gun or a knife back there?" It was a casual question, as if he were merely making small talk. Quickly, Johnnie Maxie dug into his left front pocket and surrendered a small fold-out pocket knife.

The ten-minute drive to the Sabine County Jail in Hemphill was ominously quiet. The three blacks huddled in the backseat asked no questions; the two white cops in front volunteered nothing.

After the men had been escorted through the sally port and down the cellblock hallway, Alton could stand the uncertainty no longer. "Uh . . . so what are you charging us with?" he asked timidly. The officers didn't acknowledge his question, and continued transposing information from the men's driver's licenses onto five-by-seven-inch jail cards.

Hell, they wouldn't be filling out those cards if they weren't going to put us in jail, Alton thought, and repeated his question, this time louder.

"You boys just sit down there and be quiet," one of the cops said. Periodically, one or the other of the officers would ask a perfunctory question. The three black men exchanged puzzled glances.

The third time Alton asked, his voice carried a definite edge, more of fear than of anger. "Look, if y'all are going to lock us up, don't you have to at least tell us what we're supposed to have done? I mean, this ain't right, you know?"

The little one looked up at Alton from his paperwork. "You come on and go with me." The instruction froze the room. The officer opened a metal cell door and led the smallest of the three black men out of sight and into the bowels of the jail.

As if Alton's departure were a cue, Garner obligingly stood up. Balancing himself on one foot, he sought to clarify an obvious misunderstanding. "Look at this," he said, balancing himself like a little boy on a train rail. "If you think I'm drunk, well, just look. . . ."

"Sit down."

"Well, okay—but I'd take one of them breath tests if you want to give me one."

After Garner and Johnnie Maxie had been booked, the two officers escorted them down the hall to the detox cell, where Alton already had been deposited. As the two new charges entered the cell, the cops motioned to Alton, who followed them back down the hall to the book-in room.

Moments later, Alton, escorted by both officers, was returned to the detox cell. As the metal door echoed shut, the three men looked silently around the tomblike room. Except for a toilet and a raised cement slab with no mattress, the cell was simply floor, walls, and ceiling. Opening onto the hallway was a heavy metal door with a glass-and-mesh screen at about eye level and a rectangular "bean hole" through which food could be passed.

The prisoners' conversation was tentative at first. "Ain't we supposed to be able to call somebody and tell them where we're at?" Garner asked of no one in particular. "Man, I know Corrine's gonna be wondering. I mean, it's Christmas and all. . . ."

Rapidly, the grousing became more vocal, the tone angrier. "Man, this is bullshit!" Alton screamed, making no attempt to conceal his mood.

"God damn it, this ain't right. Gimme the damn phone. I want to make a call. *Anybody* hear me?"

Their screams echoed and fell on silence. In frustration, Alton and Garner hit and kicked the metal door, over and over again. They kicked and slammed at the door until they were exhausted; they screamed until they were hoarse; then they kicked again.

Next door in B cell, Angus Bozeman had been incarcerated with Keith Miller and Trent Taylor for a month by the time the three black strangers were brought in. Between theft and criminal mischief, in fact, the red-haired and wiry nineteen-year-old had been in some jail or other for most of the last two years. B cell was his most recent home. Sitting on the edge of his bunk, Bozeman was tired of the commotion next door. He resented the intrusion. "You bastards next door better shut up," he yelled. "Some of us got to live here. We ain't getting out tomorrow. So shut the fuck up."

"Look, man, this ain't your deal. We ain't drunk and we got a right to a phone call. Mind your own goddamn business."

The argument through the concrete wall between captive neighbors quieted down when Bozeman heard the familiar footsteps of Lawton Crain, the jailer, in the passageway. In his month in the Sabine County Jail, Bozeman had learned to identify his captors not only by their voices, but by their footsteps. He knew he was right when he heard Crain's same old toothless threat directed next door at detox:

"If you boys don't shut up and get away from that door, I'm gonna come in there and stomp your ass."

"What you gonna do? Bring four or five with you?"

Within minutes, Bozeman heard the locks unlatch on the metal security door at the end of the hall. He leaned forward on his bunk, straining to hear, like a startled deer. He heard Thomas Ladner and Bo Hyden, the same pair he'd seen earlier through the bean hole escorting the three black prisoners down the hallway.

"Shit," Bozeman whispered to Taylor across the cell, "is about to hit the fan."

The voice was unmistakable and clear. It belonged to Ladner. "Who in hell is raising hell back there?"

The answer came from Crain: "Them niggers you brung in a while ago."

There were two sets of footsteps, and the voices were closer. Bozeman suspected they stopped outside the door to detox. He heard the voice he knew as Ladner's yelling down the hall to the jailer with the automatic controls. "Open detox!"

Metal clanged on metal. A door creaked on its hinges.

The swinging door startled Alton Maxie and Loyal Garner, both of whom were sitting on the concrete ledge just inside the cell. Across the cell, his back leaning against the wall, Johnnie Maxie straightened.

The little officer, his right hand on the butt of his holstered pistol, stood half in, half out of the doorway. The big one, a black, leather-covered, lead-weighted slapjack in his right hand, was staring down on Alton and Garner. It was Ladner, the huge one, who spoke. "Which one of you's beating on the motherfucking door?"

Garner was speaking even as he rose from the ledge. "I was. I just want to call my wife–"

The sound echoed next door in B cell, dropping Bozeman's eyes to floor.

Three times, staccato—*blap, blap, blap*—the sound of metal on skin and bone, like a bird hit by a car grille.

Immediately after the blows, Angus Bozeman heard a metal object—it sounded to him like a metal Zippo lighter—hit the floor and careen like a hockey puck down the long hallway outside detox. Locked in B cell, he had no way of seeing that the metal object wasn't a lighter but the lead insert from Ladner's blackjack. The last of the three blows to Garner's head had split the stitching that held the lead inside its leather sheath.

Barely inside detox, Alton Maxie looked up helplessly from the concrete ledge as Ladner, his beefy arm still grasping Garner's neck from behind, pushed, shoved, and carried the dazed prisoner to the open cell door. Even before the blows had rained down on Garner, Alton instinctively had tried to stand. "Sit down," commanded Bo Hyden, his hand still on the grip of his holstered pistol, and Alton knew better than to try again.

After Ladner had wrestled Garner into the hallway, and as Hyden began closing the metal door, the smaller deputy made ominous eye contact with Alton. "See, boy," he said, "it didn't take no four or five of us."

Bozeman heard the sound of scuffling as the door to detox slammed shut. Before the footsteps faded with distance down the hallway, Bozeman recognized two distinctive sets. A third set of footsteps, he thought, sounded different, like a combination of walking and dragging.

"They got one of 'em out," Bozeman whispered. "Aw, shit."

Alton and Johnnie Maxie were pacing nervously at the rear of the detox cell ten minutes later when Ladner and Hyden returned with their prisoner. Garner, his chin dangling on his chest and his feet only half touching the floor, was suspended between the two officers like wet pants on a clothesline. The front and side of his shirt were bloody.

Together, the two uniformed men backed Garner toward the wall, then swung and pitched their load like a bag of oats onto the concrete ledge. Garner's back slid a few inches down the wall until the weight of his tilted head pulled his torso onto the ledge.

Relieved of their load, the officers motioned to Alton. "Come on, let's go."

The trip lasted only twenty-five feet or so, but it was the longest in Alton's life. His heart pounded and his mind raced. When the officers opened the door to the processing room, Alton's eyes fell first on the metal armchair on rollers standing conspicuously in the middle of the room, then to the floor. Splotches of blood the size of a kitten's paws were littered around the chair. His mind flashed back to the cell and the sight of his bloodied friend.

Alton didn't know how he got in the chair, but Police Chief Thomas Ladner had assumed a position over his right shoulder by the file cabinets. The chief's eyes never left Alton. In his right hand, the burly officer held a black nightstick about eighteen inches long, which he tapped methodically into the opened palm of his left hand. Deputy Sheriff Bo Hyden was in the prisoner's face.

"Do you want some?"

"No sir."

"I want to know. Do you want some?"

"No sir, I don't. *No sir.*"

"Well, why are you back there raising so much hell?"

Alton braced himself in the chair, anticipating the worst. He heard his words come out apologetically. "Well, we just wanted to call somebody, you know, and let 'em know where we were."

"Let me tell you what's gonna happen. You're gonna go back there in that cell and keep your damn mouth shut. You understand that?"

"Yes sir, I do. *I do.*"

As the door to detox clanged shut behind him, a relieved Alton still was shaking so badly he wasn't certain he could stand. When he looked down on Garner slumped half-prone on the bloodstained concrete, Alton knew he was about to be sick.

The blood covering Garner's shirt, Alton saw, had seeped from a deep gash in his head. The man's forehead and hairline were littered with random, marble-sized knots, as if he had dozed off in a hailstorm. In one place well into Garner's hairline, a circular swatch of hair bigger than a half-dollar was missing, as if it had been ripped out by its roots. But even more unnerving were Garner's eyes. They were locked open in an eerie stare at the beige cement wall across the cell. The only indication of life from Garner's body—and it periodically would jolt the Maxie brothers with renewed horror—was an unpredictable wheeze for air.

It was Garner's stuporous stare that sent Johnnie, by far the biggest man in the cell, retreating to the back of the concrete cage, as far away from his best friend as he could get.

At some point in the waning hours of Christmas, Chief Thomas Lander appeared at the door to detox with Trent Taylor, Angus Bozeman's cellmate in B cell and a trusty in the Sabine County Jail. At twenty-one, the clean-cut, docile Taylor looked like a fraternity boy, maybe pre-med or computers. Only a look at his rap sheet lent justification to Taylor's current plight: he was an overachiever at breaking into other people's businesses and had been hauled off the street six times for burglary and theft. In the month he had been imprisoned in Hemphill, the soft-spoken, obliging Taylor had inherited the job of trusty, sweeping and mopping the cellblocks and washing clothes. In return, he enjoyed more freedom than the other prisoners within the confines of the bars. Occasionally, as it had happened this night, Taylor was rewarded with a cup of coffee in the kitchen.

"Grab a set of those clothes for one of those guys in detox," Ladner had told him in the jail's utility room, "and clean up anything you see needs cleaning."

When Ladner opened detox, Taylor saw the results of the sounds he had heard earlier from his cell. An unconscious black man was lying on the concrete ledge. The man's shirt hadn't absorbed all the blood from his head wounds; a twelve-inch-wide reservoir of blood had collected beside him.

The chief directed his instructions to the two other black men standing nervously at the rear of the cell. "Get him up and change his clothes."

The Maxie brothers fidgeted under the order before the smaller one finally answered. "Uh, maybe we just ought to leave him be. He's not doing too good. He hasn't moved a bit and he hasn't said nothing. You know, I think he needs to see a doctor."

Ladner eyed the two men, then redirected the order to Taylor. "Go ahead. Get those clean clothes on him."

"I just can't do it. I mean . . . well, I just can't touch him, you know?" The chief apparently underwent a change of mind. Before he shut the door, the bigger black man asked the trusty if he had a pinch of Skoal. The smaller one asked him for a cigarette. The trusty had neither.

Outside in the runaround adjacent to the cellblock, Taylor busied himself cleaning. Retrieving a mop, he cleaned up blood outside detox. He found more blood at the other end of the hall, outside the inmate processing room, and mopped that up too.

Taylor stowed the mop and bucket and headed for the dispatcher-jailer's office, directly across from the processing room. Crain was sitting at the desk. A blackjack was lying nearby. Taylor picked it up, looking at it curiously. It was medieval, black leather, about a foot long and skinny, maybe an inch wide, with a looped handhold on one end. The opposite end, the "business end," spread into a two-inch circle. Taylor noticed that the stitching around the circular part of the leather was unraveled. Then he elevated the skinny end, and a deceptively heavy and rounded chunk of lead fell out into the palm of his other hand.

Crain noticed the young trusty's preoccupation with the blackjack and grinned. "They don't make 'em like they used to."

Alton Maxie was on his knees peering through the bean hole, the rectangular hole about waist-high in the cell door, when he saw Chief Deputy Billy Ray Horton walk past detox. Horton, considerably older than the other two officers, wasn't a face Alton had seen before. Alton was losing his battle with panic. For what seemed an eternity, he and his brother had paced aimlessly at the rear of the cell, watching helplessly as their friend lay comatose and bleeding on the hard ledge. Now as he saw the new face in the uniform, Alton gambled.

"Uh . . . sir . . . could I come out and talk with you a minute?"

Soon the door rattled open and the older officer escorted him to the processing room in front of the jail. The prisoner searched the area with his eyes: Ladner and Hyden were gone; the rolling armchair had been returned to its position against the desk; there was no blood on the floor.

Playing out his gamble, the young black man studied his captor's face as he began talking, starting his tale innocuously with the uneventful arrest. Chief Deputy Horton, his face impassive, listened without saying anything. Gradually, the inmate related how the other officers had beaten Garner. Strategically, Alton structured his monologue to end with his two most important points: Garner, he emphasized, was in bad shape and needed a doctor; and could he *please* use the phone to tell someone their whereabouts?

Horton reached across the desk to the black phone and pulled it close. But before Alton was allowed to call his mother in Florien, the graying deputy established what Alton clearly understood to be guidelines. "It would be best," he intoned, "if you just tell her where you are and that she can't do anything about it until morning."

After Alton dialed his mother's number, Horton pulled the base of the phone away from him, leaving him with only the receiver. The inmate knew he had to follow the script; the deputy poised his index finger on the carriage of the phone just above the disconnect button, and listened intently.

10

The Jasper Lynching

JOYCE E. KING

Jasper is extremely small, a typical East Texas bedroom community. Home to nearly eight thousand people, it is the county seat, a proud distinction for any Texas town. Ask some residents and they'll tell you the city of Jasper is historically, as well as geographically, too near the likes of Vidor, Texas, a defiant Klan stronghold about fifty-five miles away. Folks who don't belong in Vidor, particularly black folks, steer clear of it. Listen to a few others and Jasper is a bastion of racial equality, a prosperous and fair place to raise kids, to set a good example.

Enlightened people who live within Jasper's city limits point to its obvious differences—their mayor, R. C. Horn, is black; prominent leaders of both races get along and work well together; and the census shows that the town itself is roughly made up of equal parts: though it fluctuates, Jasper is approximately 45 percent African-American and about 48 percent Anglo, with most of the remaining percentage Hispanic.

It is a pretty place, strikingly clean, and contemporary, but still connected to timeless traditions. Jasper has a rich history and attracts tourists annually for hugely profitable bass-fishing tournaments. A sprinkling of brand-name chain hotels, as well as quaint little lodging houses, lots of churches, tasty homemade food, and friendly people give Jasper a reputation for being a cut above most East Texas towns. It even has what proud residents jokingly call "the Mall," its huge twenty-four-hour Wal-Mart Supercenter, the biggest deal in town.

That the slow pace in Jasper does not hold much interest for its young people is something with which town leaders constantly struggle. There are five schools in the Jasper Independent School District, only one of them

Originally published in Joyce E. King's *Hate Crime: The Story of a Dragging in Jasper, Texas* (New York: Random House, 2002), 13–28. Used by permission of Knopf Doubleday Publishing Group—

a high school. Teens who graduate from the high school usually head for higher academic ground or better paying jobs at plants in larger Texas cities, like Beaumont or Port Arthur. A few others make the short commute to the southern end of the county to work at plants like the large paper mill in Evadale. Others make a decent living at oil refineries, mostly next door in Louisiana. Those who stay behind don't have many options, unless a relative owns a lumber mill. A lot of the other jobs pay only the minimum wage, or slightly better.

Routines reserved for weekdays—school, church events, and work—take place in a highly public fashion, in the open for all to participate in and judge. For the majority, the medium gait of life in Jasper is perfect—not too fast, not too slow. Residents take care of business and look out for each other. They do so without all the big-city hassles, without the rush and crush of traffic nightmares and rude citified behavior. Come six o'clock Friday night, things slow to a crawl; local streets empty as people rest and change their body clocks to reflect weekend time. By Saturday, many make the seventy-mile trek to Beaumont or twice that distance to faraway Houston, to break the monotony of Bud long necks, plate-sized chicken-fried steaks, and two- and three-star movies at the Twin Cinema. Given that there is little to do in Jasper on the weekend, others routinely grab Burger King specials or pack up their own food for picnic get-togethers at nearby Martin Dies Jr. State Park. Dozens more hitch up the boat or Jet Skis and head for Steinhagen Lake, Toledo Bend, or Sam Rayburn Reservoir, a beautiful body of water named after the native son who proudly served as one of the nation's most colorful speakers of the House of Representatives and who is widely remembered for his dogged insistence that his colleagues vote for the Civil Rights Act of 1964. Others, shunning big-city lights and nearby tourist attractions, love the quiet serenity and beauty of Jasper.

Like any small town, Jasper has its share of hotheads and lawbreakers, but for the most part, decent citizens want good, clean fun. Without any large nightclubs, a favorite Jasper pastime is an old-fashioned, blue-light house party with good music and close friends. Attendees can drink as much as they want in the privacy of someone's home and avoid the weekend crackdown on public alcohol consumption. Texas peace officers are rare but firm upholders of the state's hard-to-enforce open-container law: don't get caught driving while taking a swig. Residents make sure, day or night, that whatever they are drinking behind the wheel in a brown paper bag is a Coke or cream soda.

Yet, liquor is plentiful on the outskirts of Jasper, a dry community located within a very wet county of more than thirty thousand people. Many don't think it's a problem to serve alcohol at a private, invitation-only house party, even if they do live in a dry town. Some residents have even been known to bootleg—make their own barrel whiskey—an illegal activity that does not sit well with law-abiding neighbors. Jasper's pristine location in the Deep South Bible Belt provokes more than a few upright Christians to morally chastise their neighbors. One anonymous citizen posed the provocative question, "If Jasper's really a dry town and folks can't buy liquor here, why are there so many alcoholics?"

On Saturday night, June 6, 1998, Jimmie Mays had the perfect reason to have one of those old-fashioned parties at his house. Besides his son's birthday, it was his twentieth wedding anniversary. James Byrd Jr., a forty-nine-year-old unemployed former vacuum salesman, was among the guests who showed up at the large gray and white trailer home. Byrd was popular in Jasper, well known for his charisma and beautiful singing voice. In and out of minor legal scrapes since high school, Byrd was often described by family and friends as a man who never hurt anyone but himself. The divorced father of three was proud of his deserved reputation as a lover of life but equally ashamed of a very real drinking problem that sometimes left him lonely and alone.

Besides Byrd, more than forty people turned out to eat good food, drink good whiskey, sing, dance, and play cards and dominoes. At the end of a long week, many in the crowd were simply glad to be among friends and grateful that someone was in the mood to host a Saturday night house party. George "Billy" Mahathay was right in the thick of things.

Handsome, unmistakably a ladies' man, with curly jet-black hair and almond-colored eyes, Mahathay was something of a local fixture around town. The burly, friendly-looking owner of Billy's BBQ couldn't help but notice a slight difference in his boyhood friend. "Byrd's not his usual self," Mahathay would later testify, "quiet, not singing and dancing like he normally does."

Everyone at the lively get-together laughed, talked, drank, and toasted Mays and his wife. The weather was a tad warm, but pleasantly bearable. By tough Texas standards, the Mays' house party was a great success, a savory musical gumbo of blues, soul, hip-hop, jazz—a little something for everyone. Byrd half-enjoyed the music and wrestled with distant thoughts, maybe a personal dilemma. He seemed distracted but continued to drink and joke around. For whatever reason, Byrd did not belt out the tunes he was famous for.

Like a few others, Mahathay had had a bit too much to drink, but it was Saturday night and he was among friends. As the festive anniversary party came to a close, he chose a more sober friend, Samuel Williams, to give him a ride home. He smiled at the host and bid the Mays family goodnight.

The neat trailer emptied as the party ended. Williams and Mahathay left sometime between 1:30 and 1:45 a.m. on Sunday, June 7. It wasn't too far to

Mahathay's house, almost around the corner from Jimmie Mays, but Mahathay was glad for the ride.

Right near Martin Luther King Boulevard, the tipsy passenger noticed James Byrd Jr. on Bowie Street, near Mahathay's house. The men did not stop to give Byrd a ride; they believed he could make it on his own, as he had so many times before. Though Byrd owned an old car, one that had been out of commission a whole month, anyone who knew Byrd also knew that he was not afraid to walk anywhere in town. It was not uncommon for black people to walk in Jasper. Or white people, for that matter. Public transportation was almost nonexistent and there was no bus line or major taxi service. People paid small sums, if they had it, for neighbors and relatives to give them rides to necessary places. Or, they just walked.

When Billy Mahathay entered his residence, he was so sure Byrd could make it home that he never looked back. Byrd zigzagged down the road in a drunken stupor, taking step after wide step, a route he almost knew blindfolded, one that usually got him home in pitch-black darkness.

At about the same time the fun ended at the Mays' home, a private party also wrapped up across town at the Timbers Apartments, upstairs in number 214, a tiny rented space on West Gibson Street, the main drag in Jasper.

Twenty-one-year-old Keisha Adkins was there, along with her former boyfriend, twenty-three-year-old John William King, a handsome local with brown hair and brown eyes, and a justified reputation as the hotheaded boy next door who could turn abruptly nasty.

Earlier in the evening, Adkins had run into King at the local Wal-Mart. Out of jail only a few months, the persuasive talker extended an invitation to his apartment. Flattered by renewed attention from King, Adkins examined his five-foot-eight-inch frame and saw that King had put on a little weight. Still, he looked good to Adkins as she mulled over the tempting proposition.

At about 10:30 p.m., shy, soft-spoken Keisha Adkins, a pale brunette, firmly knocked on King's door. The Timbers was a plain apartment complex; the wood-planked stairs and a small landing were barely large enough for two people.

Adkins discovered that King was not alone. Jailhouse buddy Lawrence Russell Brewer, a thirty-one-year-old convict from Sulphur Springs, Texas, had arrived in town only days before and was staying with King. Adkins knew Brewer was new to Jasper, and she looked him over and noted his physical attributes: He was small in stature, about five feet six, 145 pounds, dark hair, and beady eyes. Remarkably muscular, he was a tough little man who looked as if he could take care of himself.

King and Brewer, a mutual admiration society of misfits, celebrated their victorious reunion, free men, at the same time, out in the world together. They started to drink cold Bud Lights and Coors Lights way before Adkins arrived. King playfully took off his shirt, another Saturday night ritual in June that in some neighborhoods went hand in hand with beer, white boys, and the pursuit of babes.

Not easily intimidated, Adkins studied King's drastically changed body—slightly potbellied and riddled with menacing tattoos. Adkins would later testify they did not offend her. The silly depiction of cartoon character Woody Woodpecker wearing a Klan robe was mildly humorous—if a person liked racist jokes. King's other tattoos were not so comical. One in particular, of a hanging black man, was neither a joke nor a cartoon. King did not openly discuss his radical views on race with Adkins, nor did he hide them. Tattooed arms, back, and torso spoke volumes. There was even a drawing of the Disney character Tinkerbell, located on King's genitals. It was the one tattoo King was ready to show Adkins privately.

While the ex-lovers renewed their relationship in the master bedroom, Brewer kept busy with loud music and the phone. He was on the lookout for King's current girlfriend. Brewer couldn't be happy that his role was relegated to watchdog, but that did not stop him from consuming more beer—beer the two convicted burglars had stolen earlier. Without money, there was not much else to do in Jasper on a Saturday night.

Kylie Greeney, King's very pregnant girlfriend, showed up at the front door. She banged on the door and forcefully demanded to be let in. While Adkins and King were together, just a few feet away, Brewer was left with strict orders not to let in the future mother of King's child. More afraid of King than of his girlfriend, Brewer faithfully guarded the front door. Upset and frustrated, Greeney finally gave up and stomped back down the steps and out of the complex.

Sometime after midnight, King's twenty-three-year-old roommate, Shawn Allen Berry, showed up. Berry, the only one of the three friends who held a regular job, had finished up work as manager of the Twin Cinema, locked the movie theater for the night, and returned to the one-bedroom apartment.

Highly regarded as someone who could hold his own in a fight, Berry always carried a sharp, straight blade. Though he was the shortest of the three friends—just five feet five, 160 pounds—Berry earned respect as a scrappy young man, one with dependable transportation, good looks, and a well-documented adventurous spirit. He was more personable than King or Brewer, and had adequate social skills and a number of hobbies, including bull riding. Berry lived for the end of each hard week. He couldn't wait to grab a cold beer to let off a little Saturday night steam. As usual, Shawn Berry was ready to roll.

Before June 6, King and Adkins had talked only by phone; they were excited to see one another. Oblivious to the painfully small apartment and extra companions, any potential discomfort or embarrassment wasn't apparent when they emerged from King's bedroom. Adkins hadn't seen her old boyfriend in two long years. King walked Adkins to her car. His impatient running buddies, eager to leave, brainstormed ideas on how to spend Saturday night in Jasper. Brewer wanted to try and find a girl who had earlier invited them to a party, where they might meet more girls. Berry, whose vehicle they rode around in, was restless, ready to go with the flow. But all did not go according to plan. Adkins was the only female the trio would get to see that Saturday night. Unfortunately for them, her presence at the Timbers Apartments helped to establish a crucial time line.

When all four walked out of King's apartment and concluded the quarantined party, Adkins believed the time was about 1:45 a.m., give or take a few minutes, on Sunday. Adkins got into her car and saw the three men climb into Berry's ashy-gray step-side pickup. She later testified as to the seat assignments, "Shawn is driving, Russell sits in the middle, and Bill is on the right side."

The three men drove away, and for a few minutes traveled just ahead of Adkins' car. She watched three animated heads bob and turn, fingers point and gesture. After Adkins turned off toward her home, forty-five miles away in Fred, the three partygoers loudly continued on down the road. Keisha Adkins rushed to get home before Brian, her common-law husband, pulled up from his graveyard shift.

Just as the three white boys drove off looking for entertainment in one part of Jasper, James Byrd Jr. left Jimmie Mays' anniversary party on the other side of town, in the black community. Four lives were set to collide.

James Byrd Jr. continued to stagger down Martin Luther King. He was drunk, but in the back of his mind, he believed he could make it to one of two places—his tiny, subsidized apartment on Pollard Street or his parents' home on nearby West Broad. Hopeful, but disoriented, he stumbled on.

Byrd, a lifelong resident, was easily recognized by many. People often spoke to him. Authorities picked him up. Total strangers liked to hear him sing. Although he took some wrong turns in life, Byrd was obsessed by a dream of fame and fortune with a new career that would allow him to perform.

Eighteen-year-old Steven Scott instantly identified Byrd on the side of the road, even slowed down. The lanky, well-mannered college student thought to offer Byrd a ride home, nearly did, but quickly changed his mind and followed "his conscience," which told him to drive on and leave Byrd alone. To the young man, it wasn't worth the trouble because Byrd appeared "very drunk," meandering all over the road. Momentarily remorseful, Scott drove right on by Byrd; he was the second acquaintance or friend to do so. After all, a lot of people in Jasper walked to get where they were going.

Scott was on his way home from a popular Beaumont nightclub. Determined to beat his mother's curfew, if only by a few minutes, and maybe get some rest before Sunday church service, Scott drove on. He did not want to use the few precious minutes he had left to "fool with Mr. Byrd." Scott's unshakable time line tallied with what Adkins later told authorities. She placed King, Brewer, and Berry in the pickup shortly before two o'clock in the morning. A few minutes later, Scott saw a fourth passenger in the truck, noting with surprise that Byrd was "riding on the back of a step-side truck," which zoomed right by him with three shadowy figures in the cab. His mother's front porch, right near a bright streetlight on Bowie, gave Scott a pretty decent view, "I saw three people inside the truck"—he was adamant—"and Mr. Byrd on the back."

The hyped-up friends rode around the whole of Jasper, a repetitious little adventure that only took a few minutes. They searched for the home of some girl who wanted them to drop by her party, but couldn't find it because Brewer had bungled or forgotten all the directions. King and Berry got mad. They were eager to chase blondes, brunettes, or redheads. It would not matter because the threesome didn't have any luck in the all but empty streets. Most folks were either headed home or already there. A red and white cooler, which contained beer, rested in the back of Berry's rickety 1982 Ford. They drank and rode. When they couldn't find any women, somebody got the idea that it might be fun to tie a chain around a wooden mailbox, uproot it, and drag it down the street. It was fun, for a while, but once the mailbox excitement played out and the beer in the cooler started to run low, they decided to take their fun to another level.

Moments later, the pranksters discovered a black man walking in the road, minding his own business. Their next diversion was about to begin. The unwitting victim believed someone would finally help him find the way home.

"Hey, you need a ride?" Berry called to Byrd, a man he knew by sight but not by name. No response. Berry tried again: "Do you want to go home or what?" Byrd was not so drunk he didn't recognize at least one friendly face, the one behind the wheel. "No, I'll hang out with you white boys for a while," he responded. Byrd, who served time for theft, and Berry had the same parole officer; their paths may have crossed before. James Byrd Jr. slowly climbed on the back of Shawn Berry's truck. He had no reason to fear. After all, everybody in Jasper knew everybody else.

Byrd quickly positioned himself farther up the truck's hard metal floor, back-to-back with King, Brewer, and Berry, who were all inside. The truck didn't have its tailgate on, so it was dangerous to sit too near the rear. An offer of beer was made and Byrd did not hesitate. The square picnic cooler was right near Byrd; he reached in, popped a top, and started to drink. Byrd was dog-tired and thirsty from a circular walk that had gotten him no closer to home.

The hospitality ended before Byrd could even consume the whole can of beer. Berry's simple offer to give a black man a ride home set King off. Livid, he turned to Berry, red-faced and suddenly more sober than drunk, and made an announcement: "That's some ho-ass shit, picking up a fucking nigger." Apparently unfazed by the tone or by the kind of racist language he heard all the time, Berry drove on, laughed it off, wound all the way down Martin Luther King Boulevard, picked up FM 776, a farm-to-market road, then turned on State Highway 63 and traveled east. A short time later, they pulled over at BJ's Grocery, a small mom-and-pop convenience store just off the highway. Though closed, it was at BJ's that events quickly escalated to the beginning of the end for James Byrd Jr. After the men relieved themselves out in the open, Byrd traded places with two men he did not know. Two avowed, die-hard racists, King and Brewer, posing as good colorblind Boy Scouts, volunteered their prime seats in the cab so a black man could sit up front.

Byrd, trusting and still inebriated, got in the cab with Berry while King and Brewer took their self-designated places, riding shotgun on the back of the truck, the fresh night air in their faces.

Byrd was mostly quiet. Still behind the wheel, Berry offered Byrd a smoke and headed for the off-road joyride that King suggested earlier. Deep into the Texas thicket was an old logging road, a trail few could find by light of sun or moon. Suddenly, Berry made a wild turn from the main road. Byrd's full attention was, at last, aroused. "Where we going?" he asked. Berry answered, "We're just riding."

Byrd almost instantly found himself in darker, thicker woods. Berry's truck bounced up and down, glided in and out of giant dirt pockets on the unmarked, out-of-the-way logging road, until, without warning, King banged hard on top of the truck and yelled to Berry, "Stop for a minute."

Berry obeyed, but before he could turn off the engine, King and Brewer excitedly jumped from the side and rear of the truck. The loud motor raced on as King and Brewer violently pulled at Byrd to tear him from the truck.

Byrd, disabled, a chronic arthritis sufferer, about five feet nine and 160 pounds, was trapped and suddenly in the battle of his life. He fought hard. For a tired, intoxicated man almost twice the age of his attackers, Byrd's defense was impressive. He kicked, screamed, hung on to the frame of the truck, yelled for help, all the while praying to figure out what he was up against. Not in complete control of his faculties, Byrd's motor skills were dull and awkward, but the fear fueled a passionate self-defense. He fought harder.

According to later testimony, Berry bolted from the truck, ran to the other side, and made some halfhearted attempt to stop the attack. King and Brewer continued the difficult task at hand—prying Byrd out of the truck in order to "scare the shit" out of him. The struggle intensified, got louder, faster, more furious. No one could believe all the energy it took to peel Byrd's hands from the frame of the pickup. He hung on for dear life. No one heard his pleas for help. Agitated by Byrd's raw audacity to fight, King stepped back and shouted, "Fuck it, let's kill this nigger."

The assailants finally managed to rip Byrd from the truck's cab. Once they did, it was relatively easy to pull him to the ground. While Byrd still asked God for help, begging for mercy, they began to beat and kick him as hard as possible. The earth absorbed missed blows, swallowed up evidence. Berry wet his pants. His waste trickled down designer blue jeans and past his polo boots, to the same ground where fresh drops of blood had fallen. A cheap Zippo cigarette lighter with the word "Possum" and "KKK" engraved on it flew out of its owner's pocket. A brand-new souvenir baseball cap with "San Francisco" emblazoned across the front was long gone from the victim's head. It was on the ground, joined by long-neck beer bottles, a partially empty pack of Marlboro Reds, cigarette butts, and a nut wrench with "Berry" scratched onto it. Pieces of a puzzle carelessly discarded, easy evidence for the state's prosecution.

Byrd was savagely beaten and kicked, maliciously hit about the body and head, too many blows to count. Brewer grabbed a can of black spray paint from the truck. Byrd still moved way too much. Brewer later admitted to pointing it right in Byrd's bruised face and spraying the black man with the black paint. King shouted, "Don't do that! Don't spray nobody in the face!" but Brewer asserted it was extra punishment and further humiliation for Byrd because he was mad that he hurt his foot kicking Byrd.

Seriously injured and unable to see, Byrd was stunned and helpless, flailing at anything he felt come near. Then, the hardest, hottest kick of all, straight to Byrd's head. He finally stopped fighting and dropped. He did not move again. He was blinded by the spray paint, flat on his back, out of breath, but still alive. His determined captors grabbed another item from the bed of the gray pickup—a used, rusty log chain.

Byrd's pants and underwear were pulled down to his ankles. Before they snatched loose his clothing, exposing Byrd in the most cruel physical way, King took a moment to explain to the others that the same thing was done in the old days to "niggers who messed with white women."

The log chain was unfolded and quickly looped around the ball on the hitch of the pickup, with each end strategically wrapped around Byrd's ankles. All three men jumped back into the truck's cab, prepared to drag a man while he was still alive. Though it was not too late to turn back, to stop, to call it off, not one of them did.

Before Byrd could reach his final destination, there was untold suffering, unimaginable pain. He felt every single weed, every endless speck of grass and dirt, every chasm, and every inch of asphalt.

The dragging started on the hemmed-in logging road. Not long after, Byrd's body slipped loose from the chain. They slammed on the brakes to recover their defenseless victim. Drunk with enthusiasm and frenzy, the driver backed up too far, too fast, possibly running over Byrd's extensively disfigured body, scraped, scratched, skinned alive. The body got tangled underneath the truck. Laughs echoed in the night, the driver accelerated forward, over Byrd once more. Someone jumped out. Seconds later, Byrd was re-chained and the dragging resumed.

Partly conscious, Byrd used his elbows and knees to try to keep his head up off the road. Meanwhile, from inside the cab of the truck, yells of fun pierced the night. "Look, that nigger's bouncing all over the place." Laughter reverberated as Byrd's body was dragged through rocks, loamy dirt, tree branches, and trash. The truck turned left onto an adjoining blacktop artery, Huff Creek Road, up out of the heavy bush, off of the no-name logging road, out into a more open space where people lived, went to church, and buried their dead. Byrd was alive but could not scream.

With what little strength he had left, Byrd made a valiant effort to keep his head above the hard concrete. The truck's driver sped on, driving his brand of racism and hatred smack dab into the middle of a black community, bold as you please.

Byrd's naked body was hurled from one side of the road to the other, then he hit a culvert that decapitated him. His brutal tormentors continued to drag Byrd's headless body. Parts were torn from his body like twigs from a branch. They fell by the side of the road, in a ditch, then near a decrepit wood-frame building, and all along the road. His head, partially attached to a separated shoulder, was about a mile from the ripped lower torso. The once human face had drag marks on it.

What was left of his body was released from the chain near a small black cemetery, holy ground where speechless ancestors witnessed the deed. His dismembered body sent a message to all: You could be next!

Daybreak was near. Sunday morning filled the area with parishioners who normally attended Rose Bloom Baptist Church, an ordinary, sweetly innocent country house of worship. Death's path of three miles was there for all to see. People, mostly black people, had to walk this way. They lived here, loved and died here, and had witnessed this kind of hatred before. To yet another generation, it seemed a revival of the activities of the White Citizens' Council, a Civil Rights-era committee of hood-free racists whose predecessors were brutal night riders with a preference for ropes and horses.

11

Bust Town

Nate Blakeslee

It's been two years since Tulia's tainted drug arrests first came to light. How much has changed there? Not nearly enough.

On the roadside billboards and church signs of the Panhandle, religion is sold chiefly as a form of encouragement, and when you get out on Interstate 27, it's easy to see why. Heading north from Lubbock, you soon find yourself in what is sometimes referred to as the Big Nothing: thousands of square miles of featureless High Plains dotted with little towns whose very names—Friendship, Happy, Progress, Pep—seem to be a defense against the ominous feeling of being a lone body, without cover or companionship, in a place that big and flat; a feeling of being conspicuously vertical, like a prairie dog caught too far from his hole with a red-tailed hawk circling overhead. Over the past two years, few communities in this area have needed uplift more than the people of Tulia, who have seen their town, and all its secrets, exposed to the glaring spotlight of the national news media.

When I first visited Tulia on assignment for the *Texas Observer*, in the spring of 2000, little had been written about the previous summer's now-famous drug busts. The story I came back with was a sort of perfect storm for drug-policy-reform advocates, neatly illustrating much that has gone wrong with the nation's domestic drug war. Sheriff Larry Stewart of Tulia, a ranching and farming town of five thousand roughly halfway between Lubbock and Amarillo, had used grant money from the governor's office to hire Tom Coleman, a gypsy cop with no experience in undercover work and, as it was later revealed, a checkered past. Coleman worked deep cover in Tulia for eighteen months with almost no supervision, during which time he reported making more than 130 drug buys, mostly small amounts of powdered cocaine, from forty-six dealers. Although the deliveries were small, an

Originally published in *Texas Monthly*, November 2002. Reprinted with permission.

unusually high percentage of them were alleged to have taken place near a school or a park, making them first-degree felonies.

Coleman's success seemed too good to be true, and it was. In not one single case did he wear a wire nor did anyone ever corroborate his claims with eyewitness or video evidence. When the arrests finally came, not one single suspect was found to be in possession of drugs. Perhaps most striking of all, thirty-nine of the suspects were black in a town with fewer than three hundred black residents. Few of the alleged dealers could afford to make bail. Several were known to be crack addicts, people who had neither the money nor the connections to acquire powdered cocaine. In a handful of the cases, Coleman botched the identification of his suspects so badly that the charges against them were quietly dismissed. None of that seemed to matter to the district attorney or to the juries that heard the first half a dozen cases, pronounced the defendants guilty, and handed down sentences of up to ninety years.

Defenders of civil liberties, particularly the William Moses Kunstler Fund for Racial Justice, in New York, and the American Civil Liberties Union of Texas, flogged the *Observer* story to everyone within range of a fax machine, and it gradually gained momentum; before long the *New York Times* re-reported it for page 1. Yet nothing concrete came of the publicity—almost none of the jailed defendants were released until they were paroled—and just as quickly the attention of the media and other interested parties dried up. Or it would have had it not been for a series of columns in the summer of 2002 by Bob Herbert of the *Times,* whose better-late-than-never outrage resuscitated the controversy. Suddenly, two years later, the black residents of Tulia are once again being asked to give interviews to the broadcast and print media, and so are the local authorities, particularly Stewart and District Attorney Terry McEachern, who have learned by now to let someone else answer the phone. And the wheels of state government have finally begun to turn: Shortly after Herbert's sixth column on the subject, Texas Attorney General John Cornyn—in a hotly contested campaign for a US Senate seat against, it should be noted, an African American—finally announced that he would support a state investigation into the Tulia arrests. (He had been begged to investigate for more than a year.)

It was a good time, I decided, to return to Tulia. So in September 2002, I made another trip up I-27 to check in on the people I had interviewed on my first visit and to see how the town had survived its newfound notoriety.

Since I last interviewed him, in May 2000, Joe Moore has had a lot of time to think about what happened in Tulia and why. Moore, who was accused of delivering about $400 worth of cocaine to Coleman, was the first to go before a jury, and his trial set the pattern for what was to follow. The state began its case one day at nine o'clock, presenting a baggie of cocaine as its sole piece of evidence and Coleman as its only witness. Moore's court-appointed lawyer called no witnesses. At noon the next day, he was sent away for ninety years.

If you ask Moore how this came to pass, he will begin with a short history of black Tulia. Much of that story—as the fifty-nine-year-old related it to me from a visitation booth in Abilene's Robertson Unit, where he is beginning his fourth year of incarceration—is about sheriffs and highway projects. When he first came to Tulia, in the fifties, the sheriff was a man named Darrell Smith. At that time, the black community was on the north side of town, and Smith used to drive through it almost every Friday and Saturday night. "His main thing was, he wanted us people to go to bed at twelve. He'd drive down there and if he didn't see any lights, he'd like to kick the door down." Moore laughed as he said this, showing the five teeth he has left in his giant head, one of them capped by the prison dentist in stainless steel. For all his toughness, Moore continued, Sheriff Smith was honest, and people respected him.

Later, when US 87 was extended into Tulia from the north, the highway department bought everyone out, and the black residents were encouraged—with promises of free running water—to relocate to the northwest side, west of the railroad tracks, in an area that came to be known as the Flats. John Gayler was the sheriff then, a fair man with a live-and-let-live philosophy. "As long as you didn't come across the tracks," Moore told me, "Gayler wasn't gonna mess with you."

Those were good days for Moore, who quit the backbreaking work of loading hay and opened a little juke joint stocked with bootleg beer bought in Nazareth, the nearest wet town. Not only blacks but also white businessmen and ranchers, in town for the cattle auction held every Monday, would stop in to drink and gamble, and Moore was selling one hundred cases of beer a week. "Nobody messed with me. My place was wide open," Moore said. He became known as the mayor of Sunset Addition, as whites called the neighborhood. Blacks just called him Bootie-Wootie.

In the late eighties a new highway—an expansion this time of I-27—was slated to be built, meaning anywhere from thirty to one hundred shacks in the Flats had to go. "They broke their deal with us," Moore said. Meanwhile, a new sheriff, Paul Scarborough, and his deputy, Larry Stewart, had taken office, and Moore says, they had a different view of his business. They began to arrest him, something Sheriff Gayler had rarely done (Stewart denies that this represented a change in policy). Moore went to prison for possession of cocaine in 1990. He did just three months, but while he was inside, his joint was pushed down. When he got out, Moore turned to raising hogs, leaving the hustling life behind. "That was my life: rattlesnakes, hogs, and calves," he said. Until Tom Coleman came to town.

Moore's chronology throws Tulia's fixation with drugs into a new light. Beginning with a few arrests in the mid-nineties, building momentum with a school drug-testing policy passed in 1996, and culminating in the big busts of 1999, the drug war in Tulia coincided roughly with the razing of the Flats and the black community's move across the tracks—essentially pushing black and white Tulia into the same space for the first time ever. Of course, the timing also corresponded with the arrival of crack in the tiny towns of the Panhandle but not with the arrival of drugs per se; Tulians black and white had always had access to them, though perhaps not in proportion to their counterparts in the bigger cities. So why now, and why black Tulia?

"Propaganda is a funny animal," said Gary O. Gardner, a farmer who lives in the nearby village of Vigo Park. Few reporters on the Tulia beat have filed their stories without a visit to Gardner's compound, where he holds court from a converted pool room piled high with transcripts, writs, and affidavits, along with the occasional box of ammo. If Moore is the mayor of black Tulia, then Gardner, who is white and hails from one of the area's original farming clans, is the mayor of rural Swisher County. Critical of the busts from early on, he has now made it his personal crusade to get Moore and the others out of prison. He blames politicians like McEachern for creating the atmosphere in which the busts could happen. "If you're gonna make your living off the backs of somebody that you want to convict, you have to make 'em the enemy," he said. "And in Tulia, everything is blamed on the black drug dealers."

That kind of sentiment, repeated in essence on newsstands and in living rooms across the country, has hit white Tulia hard. Almost every week a letter appears in the Lubbock or Amarillo paper from an aggrieved Tulian, protesting the treatment the good people of the town have received. "I feel we have been persecuted, but it doesn't really surprise us because we know what the media can do to a town," said Glenna Reynolds, one of the letter writers. Recent revelations have not dissuaded Reynolds, who doesn't fully support Coleman but does believe that most, if not all, of the defendants were guilty, possibly including Tonya White, who proved that she was in Oklahoma at the time of the alleged drug deal. "I just know her potential for being involved in drugs," Reynolds said. She did concede that at one point she thought some of the sentences were longer than they should have been—she does not now—and she hopes people are getting rehab in prison. More than anything, though, she's ready for it to be over. "I just wish they would allow us to heal and work our way through this thing," she said.

Thelma Mae Johnson, Joe Moore's longtime girlfriend and the leader, along with an Anglo minister named Alan Bean, of the local opposition to the busts, wants this to be over too—but only if it ends with everyone's release. She has little sympathy for those who feel the town has been vilified.

"When it comes to saying we've shamed our community by bringing the media here, I would say that when this bust came down and you paraded those people in front of the cameras and said, 'Look, it's the biggest drug bust in Texas!'—it would seem to me *that's* what put Tulia on the map."

What became of the other players in the sting? Officer Coleman—presented with an Outstanding Lawman of the Year award by Cornyn following the busts—has since been fired from two narcotics postings and has gone to ground in Waxahachie; his lawyer deflects the media inquiries that still regularly come, from Court TV to the London *Independent.* Thirteen of the defendants are still in prison and serving long sentences, despite the fact that the state legislature passed several reforms in 2001 in response to what one member termed the Tulia fiasco; a team of attorneys, led by Jeff Blackburn, of Amarillo, and Vanita Gupta, of the NAACP Legal Defense and Education Fund in Washington, DC, has taken up their cases. The governor's office has reorganized the grant program that funded the operation, putting agents like Coleman under the supervision of the Texas Department of Public Safety. An FBI investigation announced two years ago seems to have petered out. Local authorities, for their part, have refused to condemn McEachern and Stewart's handling of the cases or to call for the release of those still incarcerated. "The lesson in all of this is that there is no political benefit to ruling for these defendants, and the judges saw that clearly," one defense attorney said. "They asked themselves, 'Am I going to give up my career for these people?' And the answer was 'No.'" Or as one person in the black community put it, more succinctly, "There are a lot of good, honest people in this community. They just don't have any balls."

Paul Holloway found that out the hard way. An attorney in nearby Plainview, Holloway took on several of the cases in the original sting as a court-appointed attorney, and it was he who discovered much of Coleman's personal and professional history. The son of a well-known Texas Ranger, Coleman had, as deputy, skipped town on two different sheriff's offices over the past five years; in Cochran County, he also left $7,000 in unpaid bills. In interviews and documents collected by Holloway and other defense attorneys, former co-workers and associates of Coleman's in both towns referred to him as a pathological liar and a paranoid gun nut. Cochran County's sheriff filed charges against him in an effort to collect restitution and placed a letter in his official file warning future employers not to hire him in law enforcement. Deep cover in Tulia was apparently his last chance to make good. Sheriff Stewart discovered the Cochran County warrant about six months into Coleman's tenure but decided to continue the undercover operation anyway. (Stewart would not be interviewed for this story.)

Holloway packaged up what he thought he had found and presented it to District Judge Ed Self. He asked for money for expert witnesses, though he figured he wouldn't need them. "I thought that if somebody knew about Tom, it would all be stopped," Holloway said. Instead, Self sealed the information Holloway had spent weeks collecting and denied his request. "Do you know what this means, Judge?" Holloway asked to no avail.

"My kid is twelve years old," Holloway told me as we rolled through the wide, quiet streets of Plainview in his gold Mercedes, "and we just watched *To Kill a Mockingbird.* I told him the difference between me and Atticus Finch is this: at the end of the trial—this complete railroading of an innocent man—Atticus turned to his client immediately and said, 'Don't worry. We're going to appeal.'" But Holloway's grasp of reality would not allow him to do that in Tulia. "I took an oath as a lawyer not to disgrace this system, but I knew in my heart they would win no appeals. If this will be stopped, it will be when the prosecutor puts a stop to it."

That's not likely to happen any time soon. McEachern, who was pressured last summer to drop the two remaining cases from the sting, said he could not talk to me for this story either, citing pending appeals and a Department of Justice investigation, which, depending on whom you ask, is or is not still ongoing. "I wish I could tell you my side, because you'd hear a completely different story," he said. Asked if he still stood by Coleman after the dismissed cases, the troubling revelations about his past, and his disastrous record since leaving Tulia, McEachern did not answer directly. "I'll stand by what ninety-six jurors have found," he said. "I'll always stand by them."

And so far, the white citizens of Tulia have stood by him. the *New York Times* doesn't carry much weight in this town. If anything has put a dent in the picture McEachern painted for them of the drug problem here, it might have been another spectacular bust, one that barely made the papers but which everyone in town knew about shortly after it occurred. In June 2000, as the *Observer* story was going to press, a white teenager in Tulia told authorities that an older man had offered him cocaine in exchange for sex. The accusation became a jaw-dropper when the boy revealed the man's name: it was Charles Sturgess, one of the owners of the Tulia Livestock Auction. Tulia is built around that cattle auction, and Sturgess was one of the biggest wheels in town. Sheriff Stewart, who went to church with the Sturgess family and bought cows from Charles, asked the local Texas Ranger to conduct the investigation. The Ranger wired the boy and sent him back out to meet with Sturgess, who made the same proposition once again as they cruised slowly through a pasture that night in his truck. The Ranger swept in and arrested Sturgess, but the most important revelation was yet to come: a search of the truck yielded three and a half ounces of powdered cocaine.

In one single bust of a prominent white man—and a completely fortuitous one at that—many times more cocaine had been seized than in any single buy during Coleman's entire eighteen-month undercover operation.

That much cocaine is more than one person can use. How many kids did Sturgess give cocaine to? Tulia will never know the answer to that question. A few months after he bailed himself out of jail, Sturgess drove his truck out to a piece of deserted ranch property and shot himself dead.

Nobody told Joe Moore about Sturgess's death. When I gave him the news, he was amazed by every detail—except for the cocaine. Moore has lived in Tulia longer than most; he worked for Sturgess on occasion, just as he had for Sturgess' father. "I been around hustlin' and gamblin' all my life," he said. "I know what someone looks like when they've been using something." Moore also knew what a cop looked like, which is why, he said, he warned everyone he knew to stay away from Coleman when he came to town, and why he says he ran Coleman off his property when he came by to ask for dope.

Nonetheless, Moore will spend his sixtieth birthday, this January, in all likelihood where he has spent his last three—in prison in Abilene. His health has not been good. Prison doctors had him on the wrong medication for diabetes for months, and the concrete and steel is hard on his back and knees, which are battered from a lifetime of hard work. But he eagerly examines the updates his defenders send him every month and keeps a careful eye on his parole date. "I'm gonna make it," he told me. "I'm gonna make sure I make it."

12

The Beating of Billy Ray Johnson

Pamela Colloff

On a Saturday night in 2003, a mentally disabled black man from Linden was taken to a party filled with white kids half his age. A few hours later, he was dumped by the side of the road, bleeding and unconscious. But of all the crimes that were committed, none was worse than how the small East Texas town responded—and who were considered the victims.

Daybreak was still more than an hour away on the morning of September 28, 2003, when Cass County sheriff's deputy John Elder turned down Old Dump Road. Above the tree line, the sky was moonless and dark. Cass County is pressed deep into the northeastern corner of Texas, hard against the Arkansas and Louisiana state lines, and it is crisscrossed by back roads that meander into the woods, under pine awnings and over low-water crossings and past unincorporated communities not found on maps. Elder followed the blacktop as it tacked back and forth, and after roughly a mile, he spotted a silver pickup idling at a T in the road. Two young men who had called the sheriff's department were sitting inside. "He's over here," the driver called out, motioning for the deputy to follow him. Elder fell in behind the pickup as it headed to the left, down a county road that had few houses or mailboxes or signs of life.

They came to a stop after half a mile, and Elder could make out a figure on the ground, huddled in the fetal position. He was a short, slight black man, and he was wearing only a T-shirt and jeans despite the cool weather. Elder knelt down, and after fishing the man's identification out of his pocket, the deputy saw that he was Billy Ray Johnson. Around Linden, the county seat, Billy Ray was often seen hanging around the courthouse square or walking by the side of the road, and he was what people in town politely called "slow." Elder could see that he was alive but in bad shape. The

Originally published in *Texas Monthly*, February 2007. Reprinted with permission.

bottom half of his face was bruised and swollen, and his breathing sounded labored. His upper lip was cut, and blood had pooled on the ground under him. His entire body had been badly stung by fire ants. The deputy tried to wake him, but Billy Ray was unconscious.

Elder called for an ambulance and then inspected the pavement, searching for evidence of a hit-and-run. But he found no skid marks or broken glass, and so he turned to the two white men who had led him out there to ask them what they knew. Elder recognized the bigger, heavyset one with the crew cut as twenty-four-year-old Corey Hicks, who had served in the Navy and now worked at the sheriff's department, and Corey's friend, nineteen-year-old Wes Owens, who stood with his hands in his pockets and said little. "Now, how did y'all find him?" Elder asked.

Corey shrugged. "We were just riding around," he said, explaining that they had been at a party until early that Sunday morning. "We drove up on him and saw him laying there."

Elder nodded and didn't probe further. Billy Ray smelled of alcohol, and in the absence of any evidence of a hit-and-run, the deputy guessed that the forty-two-year-old had been out walking and had hit his head when he passed out. The two young men who had led him there were nothing if not helpful; when the paramedics arrived and loaded Billy Ray's limp body onto a gurney, they helped lift him into the back of the ambulance.

But by the following morning, Billy Ray had yet to regain consciousness. A CAT scan found that he had suffered a subarachnoid hemorrhage, a serious brain injury that can be caused by blunt force to the head. While he lay in a coma, word spread that he had last been seen Saturday night at a pasture party with some white boys half his age. Still, the sheriff's department did not grasp that it had a criminal investigation on its hands until Lt. Ray Copeland, the department's chief investigator, began receiving anonymous phone calls—three that week, all from what sounded to him like the same soft-spoken white man. "Y'all need to look into what happened to Billy Ray," the caller said, and hung up.

What the investigation unearthed was a story that no one in Linden wanted to believe: Billy Ray, who is mentally disabled, had been taken to a party, ridiculed, called racial slurs, knocked unconscious, and then dumped by the side of the road. Even the strangers who had come to his aid were not good Samaritans but two of the perpetrators. Had the town's white residents condemned what had happened to Billy Ray, the incident might have faded into memory; the crime pivoted on a single punch. Instead, they closed ranks, and juries in both criminal trials that followed declined to give the defendants more than a slap on the wrist. Now Morris Dees, one of the nation's preeminent civil rights lawyers, has taken up Billy Ray's case, and Linden—a place most Texans have never heard of—will likely become the focus of national attention when the wrongful-injury lawsuit goes to trial this spring. Whether a new jury will see things differently depends on how Linden perceives its own role in this drama, as a community that must redeem itself or as a town unfairly maligned by outsiders.

Billy Ray grew up less than two miles from where he had been found, in a sagging white trailer on Old Dump Road. He was raised by his widowed grandmother, Era Lockett Taylor—Miss Era, as she was called—after he was born with meningitis to mentally disabled parents. Billy Ray had five brothers, two of whom were also mentally disabled. (Relatives and neighbors raised all but the youngest son, Bonnie.) As a boy, Billy Ray was able to grasp simple concepts his mother had never mastered, like how to dial a phone number or pay for something in a store, but he couldn't learn to read or write, and he was often the butt of other kids' jokes; on the school bus, his cousins handed over their lunch money to his tormentors so he would be left alone. After he had to repeat the fifth grade, Miss Era pulled him out of school for good, and they lived in the woods apart from the world, for more than twenty years.

Miss Era discouraged anyone from bothering Billy Ray by keeping a 12-gauge shotgun propped beside the door. (A light pole on her property, which is pitted with lead shot, attests to her vigilance.) "No one messed with Billy Ray while Miss Era was alive," said his cousin Lenda Beachum. "We were all scared to death of her. If she said, 'Jump,' we asked her, 'How high?' Even as an adult, Billy Ray came into town only when Miss Era needed to pick something up at the store, and when she did, he would sit quietly in the passenger seat, gazing out the window. Everybody always thought he was a nothing and a nobody," said his cousin Lue Arthur Wilson. "I felt sorry for him being stuck out there all by himself. I used to stop by with my guitar and play music for him—he liked Lightnin' Hopkins and Jimmy Reed and Elmore James. I'd play until Miss Era would say, 'Billy Ray, ain't you tired of hearing that fuss?' And then I'd have to get going."

Billy Ray's transistor radio was his constant companion, and each day he sat on whichever side of Miss Era's trailer allowed him to pick up a stronger signal. He liked to slide on his sunglasses and listen to the R&B stations out of Shreveport and Tyler; at night, he picked up shows that were beamed in from faraway places like Nashville. Though life with Miss Era was tightly circumscribed, he had his own way of traveling beyond Old Dump Road. His grandmother's property was littered with the skeletons of half a dozen or so gutted, rusted-out cars, and he spent hours tinkering with them and taking his favorite ones out for test drives. Sitting behind the wheel, he would steer as if he were flying down the highway. He seemed not to care that the car he was driving had no transmission and was jacked up on concrete blocks in the middle of Miss Era's pasture.

Billy Ray lived with Miss Era until 1995, when she died of cancer, and he found himself, at 33, on his own. "She was all he knew," said his younger brother James. "He'd never been out in the world, never been with people his own age. He'd never had a drink until Miss Era died." Billy Ray stayed for two years in James's rent house and then moved in with his mother, who was living in a public housing project a few blocks from the courthouse square. Free to go where he pleased, he spent his days walking around town, nodding and smiling at strangers, but without Miss Era to look after him, sometimes he was at loose ends. A sandwich might be his only food for the day, or some peanut butter straight out of the jar. He bought a snappy new suit with one of his disability checks, but he didn't understand that it needed to be cleaned, and he wore it again and again until he looked like the homeless person that many people in Linden assumed him to be.

On the weekends, Billy Ray helped out at his cousin Lue's honky-tonk, the Bee Hive, a black club on one of Linden's back roads where patrons brought their own coolers and anyone was welcome to play the blues guitar. Billy Ray swept floors and picked up empty beer bottles and largely kept to himself, and yet customers enjoyed laughing at his expense. "People thought it was funny to make an ass out of him," Lue said. "They'd say, 'Come on, Billy Ray, you going to dance tonight?' And so he'd shuffle around for them. He couldn't dance, but he loved the attention." At the projects, Billy Ray was an even easier mark. "He was real popular once a month when he got his disability check," Lue said. "Women would sweet-talk him, crackheads would hit him up for loans. They'd say, 'Can I borrow some money and pay you back tomorrow?' Billy Ray didn't know no better. He was everybody's friend."

One afternoon in October, Lue took me to the house on Nelson Street where Billy Ray had been living with his mother in September 2003—a gray, dilapidated frame house where two days' worth of rain had turned the hard-packed dirt yard into a pool of mud. It was still home to Billy Ray's mother, Lizzie Mae Stephenson, who was slumped inside on a faded flower-print sofa, her body folded into its cushions. She was a small, frail woman in her seventies, and she did not seem to notice when we came in. The house was illuminated by a single bare bulb, and the rooms looked as if they had not been cleaned in years. Unwashed clothes were piled in heaps on the floor, and half-eaten plates of food rested on the kitchen counters. Roaches climbed the walls and skittered across the dining room table. Lizzie sat, staring at the wall, loudly humming a weird, gloomy tune. Her son James's girlfriend, Tina Thomas, had stopped by to check in and was trying to engage her in conversation, to which Lizzie at last responded with a few low, guttural sounds. She looked around the room, and when her eyes focused on me, a stranger, she looked frightened. She lifted herself off the couch and hurried into the bathroom, locking herself inside.

Lizzie, the family told me, had not been mentally disabled at birth. When she was an infant in Sulphur Springs—a little more than an hour's drive west of Linden—her parents, who were itinerant sharecroppers, had been coming back from church one Sunday when a group of white teenagers started throwing rocks at them. Lizzie was struck on the head, over her left eye, and the impact had cracked her skull open. She was forever changed, according to her sister Essie Lee Pryor; as a child, she was unable to do even menial work, and when the rest of the family picked cotton, she sat and watched. Even the children Lizzie went on to have who were not mentally disabled had never known a normal life. One son is currently in prison for aggravated assault; another was murdered in 1995. As I listened to Tina try to coax Lizzie out of the bathroom, I wondered how her life—and Billy Ray's—might have turned out if not for the cruel trajectory of one rock.

When Lizzie emerged, she sat down beside me, and I explained that I was working on an article about Billy Ray. At the mention of his name, she covered her face with her hands and began to cry out, "My son, my son, my son . . ."

The pasture party had already gotten under way that Saturday night when Wes Owens eased his pickup away from the bonfire and headed for the Country Store to buy some snuff. Wes was everything that Billy Ray was not. He was from an influential Linden family and had been a popular varsity football player in high school. But in a small town like Linden, which has 2,275 residents, even the most divergent lives are somehow connected, and when Billy Ray ambled into the Country Store that night, he and Wes stopped to shake hands. Their families had been acquainted for a long time; Billy Ray's father and two of his brothers used to work summers picking peas and hauling hay on Wes's grandfather's farm. The Owenses had given the Johnsons food and secondhand clothes over the years, and Wes had sometimes offered Billy Ray rides around town.

As they stood and talked that night, Billy Ray wore his usual lopsided grin. And then Wes—"the life of the party," according to friends, a guy who liked to be the center of attention—had an idea. He casually mentioned that he had invited some people to his father's place up the road, and he asked if Billy Ray wanted to join them.

Billy Ray shook his head. "I'm waiting on a ride," he said.

"I'll bring you back up here when your ride's supposed to be here," Wes offered. Though Wes had never invited him to a party before, Billy Ray was not in the habit of questioning things. He agreed and climbed into Wes's truck.

Wes drove less than a mile up the road to his father's property and turned into a wide grassy pasture where pickups were parked in a circle around a bonfire. According to court documents and police records, it was after midnight when they arrived, and about a dozen people were sitting on their tailgates drinking beer. When they looked to see who Wes had brought from town, they burst out laughing. One girl overheard twenty-year-old Colt Amox snicker, "Wes has a crazy nigger with him."

Wes would later say that he had never intended for Billy Ray to become the night's entertainment, but from the moment they arrived, the joke was on Billy Ray. Wes introduced him to his friends, making up nonsensical names for them as he went. Colt was "Bolt," while others were "C'mon," "We-pee," and "Casey Macaroni." Guileless, Billy Ray nodded and told each of them, "You can just call me Bill." Wes turned on some music and handed Billy Ray a beer, and soon he had Billy Ray dancing to Lil' Kim's "Magic Stick." Wes passed an imaginary stick back and forth to him while the group looked on and laughed. When the fire began to fade, Wes had him unload wood from the bed of his truck, and the errand became a game to see how much firewood he could pile on as he raced to and from the pickup. "Come on, Billy Ray, you can get more than that!" people shouted. Someone suggested that he reach into the fire and pull out one of the burning logs, and as Billy Ray bent down to comply, Wes stopped him. "Don't be stupid," he said.

The teasing had started to make some people uneasy, and before long, more than half the group decided to go home. Erica Hudson, a freshman at Tyler Junior College, told Wes as she was leaving, "It's not right."

Corey Hicks, who had recently gotten off work at the jail, drove up as the party was thinning out. He lived with Wes's sister, with whom he had two children. When Corey arrived, he turned to a heavy-lidded eighteen-year-old named Dallas Stone. "Why did Wes bring this stupid nigger out here?" he asked.

Dallas shrugged. "For a joke," he said.

Only six people remained at the party, including Billy Ray, and everyone was drinking heavily. As the night wore on, a pretty twenty-year-old student named Lacy Dorgan—the only woman left at the party—wandered off to throw up, and Wes followed her. The dome light inside her Mustang was on when she and Wes started having sex a few minutes later, and Corey watched them from a distance.

Bored and drunk, Corey, Colt, and Dallas nursed their beers while Billy Ray sat alone by the bonfire. Dallas would later claim that Corey said, "I wish someone would beat this nigger up." Corey was known for using incendiary language when it came to blacks, and several years earlier he had started a fight at a party with six black men in which he did not come out the victor. He couldn't beat up Billy Ray himself, he told Colt and Dallas, or he might lose his job, but he thought someone else should. After some goading, Colt agreed to do it, and the three friends all started to laugh. (Colt denies making this pledge.)

Until that point, rap music had been playing, but Colt switched it to country, which elicited complaints from Billy Ray. "If you don't like the music, you can go," Colt told him.

"You'd better leave, before the KKK comes and gets you," Dallas taunted him.

Billy Ray seemed to think they were joking, and he laughed along with them. "I'll go after I finish my beer," he said.

Dallas knocked the beer out of his hand. "You're finished now," he said.

Wes had dashed up, pulling on his pants as he ran from Lacy's Mustang, but it was too late. Colt, who had been a pitcher at Linden-Kildare High School, took a swing at Billy Ray, hitting him squarely in the face. He delivered a knockout punch. Billy Ray fell to the ground and stopped moving.

For nearly an hour the group debated what to do as Billy Ray lay a few feet away from them, unconscious. Wes thought they should call an ambulance, and both Dallas and Lacy offered to drive him to the hospital. But Corey overruled them and began barking orders. He did not want the police involved, he said, because his job was on the line. They were going to take Billy Ray to a back road and leave him there, he insisted, assuring the group that he would eventually wake up and walk home. At one point during the discussion, Wes grabbed Billy Ray and lifted him to his feet, trying to make him stand up on his own. When his legs would not support his weight, Wes let him go, and he fell backward, hitting his head on the ground. Finally they loaded him into the bed of Colt's truck, and Corey led the way while the others followed. Rather than driving a mile north to the hospital, he headed in the opposite direction, toward Old Dump Road. Wes thought Billy Ray might still have some family out there, but they decided against leaving him near a house for fear that someone might see them.

As Corey drove, he asked Lacy, who was riding with him, if she would sit closer. He and Wes's sister were having problems, he confided, and he had liked her for a long time.

"Why did this happen?" Lacy asked, changing the subject. "Why?"

"Because he's a fucking nigger," Corey said.

They turned off Old Dump Road, down County Road 1620, and unloaded him onto the road's shoulder. From there, Colt drove to the car wash in Linden, where he cleaned blood and vomit out of the bed of his pickup. Panicked, Dallas drove to a friend's house and woke him up to tell him what had happened; then he ran to the bathroom and got sick. Wes went to Corey's house, and they decided to drive back to check on Billy Ray. He was still breathing, but they could see he was bleeding from his mouth.

Almost two hours had passed since he had been knocked unconscious, and they wondered if he might be dying. Corey called the sheriff's department on Wes's cell phone. "There's a black man out here on the side of the road," he said. "He must have got drunk and fell out."

The investigation did not begin in earnest until that Thursday morning, four days after the attack, when Lieutenant Copeland sat Corey down to ask him a few questions after he finished his shift at the jail. When Copeland asked him to describe what had happened early Sunday morning, Corey recounted what he had already told Deputy Elder—he and Wes had been riding around when they came across Billy Ray—and he expressed concern for the stranger's welfare. "Do you know how he's doing?" he asked, adding that he had called the hospital a few times to check on Billy Ray's condition. (He did not tell Copeland that he had also visited the hospital with Wes and had made inquiries about Billy Ray at the front desk.) Their meeting ended with the investigator asking Corey to write a full report detailing what had occurred. Several hours later, Copeland received a call. "I need to talk to you about what we discussed this morning," Corey said, and asked if Copeland would come by his house.

Corey had heard from someone at the sheriff's department that he had been fingered as Billy Ray's assailant, and when Copeland arrived, he was quick to try to set the record straight. Waiting on the porch with him were Wes and Colt, who let him do the talking. Billy Ray had in fact been assaulted, Corey told Copeland, and it was his friend Colt—whom he pointed to—who had done it. As the investigator listened, Colt then narrated his version of events: how he had been sitting alone by the bonfire, waiting for his friends to return from town, when a black man had approached him on foot from out of nowhere. The man had been physically aggressive and had advanced toward him, demanding that he turn off the country music he was playing. Colt had repeatedly asked him to leave, and when the stranger moved toward him again, Colt had knocked him out with one punch. Frightened, he had single-handedly loaded the man into his pickup, driven him into the woods, and left him by the side of the road. When he was finally able to track down Corey and Wes, he showed them where he had left the man, Colt said, and his friends had notified the sheriff's department after he had gone home.

Colt's account started to unravel as soon as Linden police investigator David Martinez began to interview other people who had attended the party, particularly Lacy Dorgan. (After Colt gave his statement, the case was turned over to the police department, since the pasture where the crime had taken place was located within the city limits.) As a fuller picture emerged of what had happened that night. Martinez voiced the opinion that Linden might have a hate crime on its hands. That, an officer at the sheriff's department told me bitterly, "was like striking a match to dry brush." Police Chief Alton McWaters called in the FBI to investigate possible hate crimes and civil rights violations. The Associated Press picked up the story, and TV news trucks from Shreveport began rolling into town. The following week, the *Texarkana Gazette* ran the first of four damning editorials. ("We were vilified," one resident recalled.) Linden residents who braved the media did little to burnish the town's image when they tried to downplay the crime, talking about the "good boys" involved who had been remiss only in letting things get "out of hand" and who deserved "a slap on the wrist." Wilford Penny told the *Chicago Tribune* one month after stepping down as Linden's mayor that the incident had been "an unfortunate and senseless thing" but that "the black boy was somewhere he shouldn't have been."

Billy Ray had regained consciousness on Wednesday, but the trauma to his head had resulted in permanent brain damage. (Having retained no memory of what had happened to him, he was unable to help investigators.) There was little dignity in his condition; he drooled and soiled himself, and his speech was severely impaired. When he tried to talk, his lips and tongue would not cooperate, and to all but a few family members who grew accustomed to the way he grunted his words, he was unintelligible. He had difficulty swallowing food and walking unassisted, and he often sat in his hospital bed and cried in frustration. After a month, when he still could not feed or dress himself, he was transferred to a nursing home in nearby Texarkana, where he gradually learned to walk again and recovered control of his bodily functions.

And yet, after Corey, Wes, Colt, and Dallas were each arrested and charged that October with aggravated assault (Lacy, who cooperated with investigators, was not charged), they were seen, by some, to be victims as well. "These boys' names are ruined for life," Corey's mother, Martha Howell, later told one reporter. "And [Billy Ray] is better off today than he's ever been in his life. He roamed the streets, the family never knew where he was. Now in the nursing home he's got someone to take care of him."

Sympathy for the four young men only deepened tensions. "She talked as if her son had done us a favor," observed Lue. And the casual attitude about the harm done to Billy Ray was not limited to one defendant's mother; among most whites, the crime seemed to provoke little outrage. "When this happened, the white community was quiet," said the Reverend David Keener, of the Pleasant Hill Missionary Baptist Church, where blacks have worshipped since 1843. "No one stepped forward and said, 'This is wrong.' What had happened was awful enough, but the silence was worse." To blacks, who make up 20 percent of the town, the indifference was only the latest symptom of what many considered to be an Old South mindset that permeated life in Linden, most plainly in a mural that had hung in the town's post office since the late thirties called *The Cotton Pickers*, in which three dark-skinned, barefooted sharecroppers are depicted toiling in the fields. The image and its prominence in one of Linden's most public buildings were telling, some said, since neither native sons Scott Joplin, the ragtime composer, nor T-Bone Walker, who introduced the electric guitar to the blues, had ever been memorialized. "Generations of blacks saw that mural every time they sent a letter or bought a stamp," Benjamin Dennis, the president of the Greater Texarkana NAACP, told me. "And the message they took away from it was that they shouldn't aspire to be anything greater than a cotton picker."

But the criticism from outsiders struck a nerve. Residents did not want to endure more scrutiny or hear assessments of their town's flawed race relations. Most of all, they worried that any stain on its reputation could scuttle chances of economic renewal. Linden, which lacks even a stoplight, is bleak. US 59, which used to be the main thoroughfare through town, was rerouted around Linden in the fifties, and two decades later, a Wal-Mart opened in the nearby town of Atlanta. Now the courthouse square is deserted, even in the middle of the day, and handwritten signs that read "Closed due to illness" and "Back later" hang indefinitely in empty store windows. People must commute to find steady work, and so they punch the clock at the paper mill in Domino, the steel mill outside Lone Star, and the Army depot west of Texarkana. Civic leaders had hoped to bring in visitors by showcasing Linden's rich musical heritage, using the Music City Texas Theater, a restored American Legion hall that had proved successful in booking big-name acts, as an anchor. (The Eagles' Don Henley, who has played sold-out shows at the theater, also grew up in Linden.) But the bad publicity threatened all that, and many locals hoped that if they ignored what had happened, it would simply disappear.

When I visited Linden last fall, few white people would agree to speak to me about the case. Those who did were wary of being quoted, and few of them showed much sympathy for Billy Ray. Anger still ran deep, and not at the defendants; it was Billy Ray, somehow, who had brought this upon Linden. People told me he was "a street person," "a drunk who wandered the streets," "a homeless guy who danced for money," "a known crackhead." Never mentioned was the defendants' own prodigious alcohol consumption. By his own admission, Dallas had drunk ten beers before arriving at the pasture party, and he knocked back eight or nine more once he was there. But he and his friends were "typical teenagers," residents told me, and "good kids." Billy Ray was not even mentally disabled, I was informed by the executive director of Linden's Economic Development Organization, Russell Wright. "He cooked his brain on drugs," he explained. To see things any other way was to see Linden in a very ugly light.

Not until March 2005, a year and a half after the arrests, did the first defendant go to trial, and from the start of the *State of Texas v. Christopher Colt Amox*, it was apparent that justice might be hard to come by. Cass County District Attorney Randal Lee had his assistant district attorney, Tina Richardson—a black woman who was the county's only other prosecutor—try the case. But during the five-day proceeding, Lee did not assist her or take part in the state's prosecution. "I drove fifty-five miles each morning to attend the trial, and I never saw the district attorney walk across the hall," said the NAACP's Dennis, who had previously attended a less-high-profile trial of a black defendant at which Lee had been present every day. "A DA who wants to bring the full judgment of his office down on an individual is going to make sure that jurors see him in the courtroom. It was obvious from the start that the full resources of the DA's office had not been thrown behind this case."

Colt, the defense's only witness, took the stand and testified on his own behalf. "I want everybody to know the truth," the clean-cut young man told the jury, which was made up of ten whites and two blacks. Colt's attorney, Corky Stovall, began by guiding him through a show-and-tell of photos that pictured him smiling beside black teammates and acquaintances and then brought him to the crux of the message that he needed to impart to the jury: He had acted in self-defense. "He was coming toward me," Colt testified, explaining that he had feared Billy Ray and had taken several steps away from him. "I mean, he could have hit me, stabbed me, shot me. I don't know this man from anybody. . . . Once he got to me, I felt like he was going to hit me, so I hit him, one hit in the mouth." Colt denied ever using racial slurs, and he told the jury that he had made bad decisions—like driving Billy Ray into the woods and then washing out the bed of his pickup afterward—because Corey had pressured him to do so. Even the false accounts he had given to investigators had a noble justification. "I was trying to keep my friends out of trouble," he told jurors.

In her cross-examination, Richardson pressed Colt to explain how the well-built former athlete could have felt physically intimidated by a man whom she estimated to weigh just over one hundred pounds—and who, unlike Colt, had had no friends with him to back him up. "Even a small person can shoot somebody or stab somebody," Colt replied.

But Richardson overlooked one of the most powerful pieces of evidence that the state had to discredit his defense, which the FBI had turned up during its investigation: the morning after the assault, when Dallas had showed up for work at the Dairy Queen, he had confided in a friend that Colt and Corey were planning on making up a story to tell police that cast Billy Ray as the aggressor. Dallas, who had turned state's witness, was not questioned about this at trial. He only testified that he had not seen Billy Ray behave aggressively toward Colt and that the assault had been unprovoked.

After several hours of deliberation, jurors acquitted Colt on both felonies—aggravated assault with bodily injury and injury to a disabled person by omission—which had each carried the possibility of a ten-year prison sentence. In doing so, they rejected the idea that Colt had targeted Billy Ray because of his race. They settled instead on a lighter charge, misdemeanor assault. The jury also recommended a suspended sentence: in other words, no jail time. Billy Ray's family wept as the verdict was read.

A similar scene played out when Corey was tried two months later. There were plenty of unflattering facts entered into the record; Wes, who had also turned state's witness, testified that Corey had said of Billy Ray, "Someone needs to whip the shit out of him." But the jury was disinclined to convict him of assault when he had not thrown the actual punch. Corey was found guilty of injury to a disabled person by omission, or essentially failing to render aid. The jury was split along racial lines over the proper punishment, with its one black juror a holdout for jail time. But in the end, once again, the jury recommended a suspended sentence. When I met with the jury foreman, a warehouse manager named John Reed, he explained that some jurors had thought Billy Ray—who had taken the stand to give a few halting answers—had faked his symptoms and had practiced seeming slow and walking poorly. "As far as I'm concerned, everyone's to blame," Reed said. "'Wes Owens shouldn't have carried him out to that party, and Billy Ray should have known better than to go drink beer with a bunch of white boys."

Judge Ralph K. Burgess, citing the graveness of the crimes, set aside the juries' recommendations and gave each of the defendants short jail terms. Corey received a sixty-day sentence, to be served at the Cass County jail, which he had been summarily fired from during the investigation. The other three received thirty-day sentences. But the penalties were little consolation to people like Lue, who had fed and bathed Billy Ray between his stopovers at different nursing homes and who had seen firsthand how his cousin had suffered. "The verdicts sent a message: 'It's okay to treat a black man that way,'" Lue said when I visited him last fall. He showed me a small item he had clipped from the *Cass County Sun*, which he had glued to a piece of loose-leaf paper for safekeeping, about a black man named Burks Mack, who had illegally dumped some tires near Old Dump Road. For his crime, Mack had received six months in the county jail. "The only way I can figure it, a bunch of old tires is worth more than Billy Ray," he said.

Lue echoed the sentiments of many blacks in Linden when he told me that the outcome would have been different had the races of those involved been reversed. "I didn't go to law school, and I'm not a well-educated man," said the Vietnam veteran and retired steelworker. "But I know enough to know that something ain't right. If four black men had taken a mentally retarded white man to a party, made a monkey out of him, called him racial slurs, assaulted him, dumped him by the side of the road, and lied to the police about it, you can bet they would've gone to the penitentiary for a long, long time."

The civil suit, which the Southern Poverty Law Center has filed on Billy Ray's behalf, is slated to go to trial on April 12. Based in Montgomery, Alabama, the nonprofit group takes on high-profile civil rights cases, as it did most famously in 1987, when lawyer Morris Dees won a $7 million verdict that bankrupted the United Klans of America after two of its members in Mobile lynched a young black man named Michael Donald. Billy Ray's suit, which names the four defendants, is seeking unspecified damages to cover the cost of speech and physical therapy as well as long-term care. "This justice system totally failed Billy Ray and his family," Dees told me. "We want to give a jury the chance to correct an injustice in their community by presenting all the facts, many of which were not available to the juries in the criminal cases." When I asked if he was worried about the odds of finding twelve impartial people to impanel, Dees claimed to be unconcerned. "These jurors grew up in a Christian community, and they know what's right from wrong," he said. "We have to present the case so they can see that Billy Ray is a human being who deserves to be treated just like anyone else."

Just as hard as winning a settlement may be extracting any money from the defendants, who have spent the past three years working menial jobs while their friends have gone on to college. Wes intermittently works construction in Alaska; Colt is a truck dispatcher in Mount Pleasant; Dallas works for a heating and air company in Little Rock, Arkansas; and Corey is employed at a company that finds jobs for felons and minorities. They have all left Linden.

Billy Ray currently lives in a nursing home in Texarkana, where I went with Lue to visit him one afternoon last fall. Bouquets of plastic flowers brightened what was otherwise a dreary place. Just beyond the entryway, an Alzheimer's patient wheeled himself down the hall, which smelled of bleach and urine. An obese man in a nursing gown sat next to a beat-up piano, chewing his lower lip and watching *Gunsmoke*. We went to Billy Ray's room, where a small window afforded a glimpse of the sidewalk outside; his roommate dozed while a TV droned in the background. Billy Ray broke into a grin when he saw Lue, and he nodded at me, wordlessly sticking his hand out in greeting. He was even thinner than in the photos I had seen of him. His T-shirt hung loosely from his delicate frame, and his gray sweatpants were secured at his waist with a belt. He wore his hair in braids, and each time he smiled, he revealed a few wildly uneven teeth. Along the side of his shoes' thick white rubber soles his name was written in indelible black ink.

Billy Ray sat quietly with his hands clasped in front of him while Lue asked him a few questions. He had trouble making even simple conversation, and when he did, his words came out as strange, mangled sounds that Lue often had to decipher for me. Still, he was eager to communicate; he showed us his collection of audio tapes, which he kept in a plastic bag, handing over each cassette for us to look at. Afterward he took us on a tour, and he proved to be popular with the nurses. "How you doing, Billy Ray?" said each woman who strode by, and he returned the attention with a shy smile. He did not need a wheelchair any longer, but he still walked stiffly with his shoulders hunched over, moving like a man nearly twice his age. When we passed a woman with snow-white hair, Billy Ray pointed at her and said, "We friends." We followed him outside into the courtyard, where he stopped and stood in the sunlight for a moment and closed his eyes, taking in the warmth of the late fall afternoon.

When we went back inside, we sat down in the lounge to talk. Lue said that it would be all right to ask Billy Ray about the assault, but as soon as I broached the subject, he began folding and refolding the white jacket in his lap.

"Do you remember anything about that night?" I asked him.

"Bonfire," he said, nodding.

"Do you remember anything else?"

He thought for a longtime, "Country Store," he said.

"Do you know how you were hurt?"

"No, ma'am."

"What do you think about what happened?"

Billy Ray furrowed his brow, and Lue and I had to lean forward to hear what he said next. "Wasn't right," he said, shaking his head. "Wasn't right."

Afterword

Twenty-First-Century Texas Race Relations

Bruce A. Glasrud

Texans in the "modern" twenty-first century cannot yet escape the racism in their midst despite the fact that today they have an African American president of the United States. On the other hand, anti-black violence appears lessened. Likely, a majority of the Texas population condemns and finds inexplicable violent, racist, and anti-black actions by individuals in Texas today. As late as the first decade of the previous century, however, one hundred African Americans were lynched and countless others killed via pogroms, race riots, and whitecapping with often little condemnation from the public at large. Although the total number of incidents decreased, outbreaks of racial violence continued through the first decades of the twentieth century. By the beginning of the twenty-first century, incidents of race-hatred still flared on occasion but in more limited parts of the state and more limited numbers overall. However, racism in Texas was not dead.

Three incidents in twenty-first century Texas bear mention. The first concerns a mentally disabled, forty-plus-year-old African American, Billy Ray Johnson, who in 2003 at Linden, Texas, was beaten severely at a party to which he had been driven. There he had been teased relentlessly by four white males prior to being beaten, and his body was later dumped by the side of the road. Brought to trial, ultimately each of the white assailants was judged not guilty by juries in Linden. In fact, the people of Linden blamed the victim, not the four "good" white youths. Fortunately, Johnson survived; later, in a civil trial sponsored by the Southern Poverty Law Center, Billy Ray Johnson received a $9 million settlement from a Cass County jury. He could at least be taken out of a rest home. Information about this case can be found in the *Texas Monthly* article, "The Beating of Billy Ray Johnson," by Pamela Colloff, an article so good that the SPLC requested permission to reprint it and distribute the article to its membership. The article also serves as chapter twelve in this book.[1]

Five years later, in September 2008, a black man, Brandon McClelland, nicknamed "Big Boy" for his substantial size, rode with two white fellow workers to locate some beer. When McClelland later got out of the pickup, he was first hit and run over, then dragged between forty and seventy feet underneath the carriage of the truck. His torn-apart body was discovered along a bloodstained rural road. His mother said pieces of his skull could still be found three days later. This incident took place in Paris, Texas, which for over a century was plagued by brutal examples of anti-black animus (see the article by Brandon Jett, chapter one in this book). The police took a long time to investigate the matter; blacks say too long. At least one report refers to the Paris murder as a "Jasper-style lynching," that is, one similar in nature to the murder of James Byrd in the late twentieth century.[2] The two white men with McClelland were charged, but the prosecutor cited lack of evidence and dropped the charges against the two men. The dragging death was judged an accident. That decision was made despite the evidence of the estranged wife of the driver that the driver—according to what the driver told her—began to bump McClelland with the front of his truck, McClelland fell, the driver drove over his body, and then dragged him. Since criminal charges were not filed, a civil suit brought in October 2013 was settled for monetary damages.[3]

After another five years from the death of McClelland, on November 7, 2013, a twenty-eight-year-old black man, Alfred Wright, a married father of three children, went missing from a Jasper, Texas, grocery market. Eighteen days later, his nearly naked body was located. It had been gruesomely mutilated—his tongue cut out, eyes gouged, teeth missing, one ear gone, and his throat slit. After an autopsy was performed, the Sheriff's Department declared that Wright's death was due to a drug overdose. No investigation was made of the death and no explanation offered for the mutilation of Wright's body. Was this but one more example of white racism and hatred in Jasper?[4] So far, the combined forces of the Texas Rangers, the FBI, and the Department of Justice have provided no additional report, nor reasonable, responsible answers.

These three twenty-first-century incidents, however, are not enough to comprehend the extent of anti-black racism among whites in Texas. As the Texas NAACP's prominent and productive leader, attorney Gary Bledsoe, emphasized in an interview, the Wright case is not an anomaly. Over the past couple of years, sixteen or seventeen, perhaps even more, African Americans have disappeared or been found dead in mysterious circumstances in the region around Jasper. As Bledsoe remarked, "These are blacks who have died under circumstances that suggest that there might be a racial component to these killings."[5] Although the Department of Justice has been asked to investigate, as has the Texas Department of Public Safety, no official action appears to have been taken. What does all of this mean? It appears that even in today's Texas, deep-rooted racial antipathy retains its foothold.

To understand the present we must recognize that present actions are important, but also that our history both explains and influences present activity. This book, *Anti-Black Violence in Twentieth Century Texas*, hopefully holds us to the truth of our past. We must not forget our history, and we must not turn a blind eye to how that history persists and continues to echo in parts of our population. It is important to recognize that *all* race relations—in Texas, in the South, and in the United States—are colored by not only the fact and the history of white-on-black violence, but also by the differential awareness of it. That whites repress that memory and seek to minimize the ongoing threat is all the more necessary to acknowledge in light of the fact that blacks are very aware of the past and often wary of the present. Black parents once again have a story to caution their sons and daughters about where they could/couldn't go, what they could/couldn't wear, what they could/couldn't say. Studying history is also important because it illustrates how people form a community and work together to protect themselves from rampant violence. The disparate "memories" of violence against blacks make up part of the story, the significance of history is real, and this book is one way to bring it into focus.

Notes

1. Pamela Colloff, "The Beating of Billy Ray Johnson," *Texas Monthly*, February 2007; also a special insert reprinted and distributed by the Southern Poverty Law Center.

2. Gretel C. Kovach and Arian Campo-Flores, "Problems in Paris, Texas," *Newsweek*, February 9, 2009, 44–45; Jesse Muhammad, "Jasper-style Lynching in Paris, Texas?" The Final Call, http://finalcall.com/artman/publish/printer_5348.shtml. On earlier Paris anti-black behavior, see the informative and well-written article by Brandon Jett, "Paris is Burning: Lynching and Racial Violence in Lamar County, 1890–1920," *East Texas Historical Journal* 51.2 (2013): 40–64.

3. Muhammad, "Jasper-style Lynching in Paris, Texas?"; "Death of Brandon McClelland," Wikipedia http://en.wikipedia.org; "Attorneys Settle Brandon McClelland Case," http://theparisnews.com/news/article.

4. "A Missing Man Race, and Old Familiar Wounds in Jasper, Texas," www.texasobserver.org/old-wounds; "Alfred Wright, Jasper," www.texasobserver.org/alfred-wright-jasper; "Alfred Wright Murder, Update Part 2," http://rollingout.com/news/alfred-wright-murder.

5. "Unsolved Black Killings Continue in Texas," http://rollingout.com/news/texas-naacp.

Selected Secondary Sources

Bruce A. Glasrud

Adams, Thomas Richard. "The Houston Riot of 1917." Master's thesis, Texas A&M University, 1972.

Ainslie, Ricardo C. *Long Dark Road: Bill King and Murder in Jasper, Texas*. Austin: University of Texas Press, 2004.

Akers, Monte. *Flames after Midnight: Murder, Vengeance, and the Desolation of a Texas Community*. Austin: University of Texas Press, 1999.

Barbeau, Arthur E., and Florette Henri. *The Unknown Soldiers: African-American Troops in World War I*. 1974. New York: Da Capo Press, 1996.

Bernstein, Patricia. *The First Waco Horror: The Lynching of Jesse Washington and the Rise of the NAACP*. College Station: Texas A&M University Press, 2005.

Blakeslee, Nate. "Bust-Town." *Texas Monthly*, November 2002.

———. "The Color of Justice." *The Texas Observer*, June 23, 2000.

———. *Tulia: Race, Cocaine, and Corruption in a Small Texas Town*. New York: Public Affairs, 2005.

Burran, James A. "Violence in an 'Arsenal of Democracy': The Beaumont Race Riot, 1943." *East Texas Historical Journal* 14.1 (1976): 39–51.

———. "The Beaumont Race Riot of 1943." Master's thesis, Texas Tech University, 1973.

———. "Racial Violence in the South during World War II." PhD diss., University of Tennessee, 1977.

Carrigan, William D. *The Making of a Lynching Culture: Violence and Vigilantism in Central Texas, 1836–1916*. Urbana: University of Illinois Press, 2004.

Chapman, David L. "Lynching in Texas." Master's thesis, Texas Tech University, 1973.

Christian, Garna. *Black Soldiers in Jim Crow Texas, 1899–1917*. College Station: Texas A&M University Press, 1993.

Colloff, Pamela. "The Beating of Billy Ray Johnson." *Texas Monthly*, February 2007.

Cox, Mike. "The Sherman Riot." In *Texas Ranger Tales II*. Plano: Republic of Texas Press, 1999, 193–205.

Davies, Nick Davies. *White Lies: Rape, Murder, and Justice Texas Style*. New York: Avon Books, 1991.

"Death of Brandon McClelland." Wikipedia, http://en.wikipedia.org.

Du Bois, W. E. B. "The Riot at Longview, Texas." *The Crisis* 18 (October 1919): 296–298.

Durham, Kenneth R. "The Longview Race Riot of 1919." *East Texas Historical Journal* 18 (1980): 13–24.

———. "The Longview Riot of 1919," *The Handbook of Texas Online*, http://www.tshaonline.org/handbook.

Elias, Sarah Davis. "Grimshaw's Ecological Analysis of the Longview Riot." Master's thesis, Morgan State University, 1974.

———. *Recalling Longview: An Account of the Longview, Texas Riot, July 11, 1919*. Baltimore: C. H. Fairfax Company, 2004.

Estes, Mary Elizabeth. "An Historical Survey of Lynchings in Oklahoma and Texas." Master's thesis, University of Oklahoma, 1942.

Findley, James Lee Jr. "Lynching and the Texas Anti-Lynch Law of 1897." Master's thesis, Baylor University, 1974.

Foley, Neil. *The White Scourge: Mexicans, Blacks, and Poor Whites in Texas Cotton Culture*. Berkeley: University of California Press, 1997.

Fort Worth Star-Telegram, July 30, 31, 1910.

Freidberg, Bernard. "Houston and the TSU Riot." In *Life Styles in the Black Ghetto*, edited by William McCord, John Howard, Bernard Friedberg, and Edwin Harwood. New York: W W Norton, 1969, 36–51.

Ginn, Duane. "Racial Violence in Texas, 1884–1900." Master's thesis, University of Houston, 1974.

Glasrud, Bruce A. "Black Texans, 1900–1930: A History." PhD diss., Texas Tech University, 1969.

———. "Child or Beast? White Texas' View of Blacks, 1900–1910." *East Texas Historical Journal* 15.2 (1977): 38–44.

———. "Enforcing White Supremacy in Texas." *Red River Valley Historical Review* 4.4 (1979): 65–74.

———. "Jim Crow's Emergence in Texas." *American Studies* 15 (1974): 47–60.

Glasrud, Bruce A., and Harold J. Weiss Jr., eds. *Tracking the Texas Rangers: The Twentieth Century*. Denton: University of North Texas Press, 2013.

Gruening, Martha. "Houston: An NAACP Investigation." *The Crisis* 15 (November 1917): 14–19.

Hall, Jacqueline Dowd. *The Revolt against Chivalry: Jessie Daniel Ames and the Women's Campaign Against Lynching*. New York: Columbia University Press, 1979.

Haynes, Robert V. *A Night of Violence: The Houston Riot of 1917*. Baton Rouge: Louisiana State University Press, 1976.

Haynes, Robert V. "The Houston Mutiny and Riot of 1917." *Southwestern Historical Quarterly* 76 (1973): 418–39.

Jensen, F. Kenneth. "The Houston Sit-In Movement of 1960–61." In *Black Dixie: Afro-Texas History and Culture in Houston*, edited by Howard Beeth and Cary D. Wintz. College Station: Texas A&M University Press, 1992, 213–15.

Jett, Brandon. "Paris is Burning: Lynching and Racial Violence in Lamar County, 1890–1920." *East Texas Historical Journal* 51.2 (2013): 40–64.

King, Joyce. *Hate Crime: The Story of a Dragging in Jasper, Texas*. New York: Random House, 2002.

Kovach, Gretel C., and Arian Campo-Flores. "Problems in Paris, Texas," *Newsweek*, February 9, 2009, 44–45.

Krenek, Harry. "Race Riots at Longview and Sherman." In *The Power Vested: The Use of Martial Law and the National Guard in Texas Domestic Crisis, 1919–1932*, 105–37. Austin: Presidial Press, 1980.

Kuhlman, Martin Herman. "The Civil Rights Movement in Texas: Desegregation of Public Accommodations, 1950–1964." PhD diss., Texas Tech University, 1994.

Kumler, Donna J. "'They have gone from Sherman': The Courthouse Riot of 1930 and Its Impact on the Black Professional Class." PhD diss., University of North Texas, 1995.

Leiker, James N. *Racial Borders: Black Soldiers along the Rio Grande*. College Station: Texas A&M University Press, 2002.

Livingston, David W. "The Lynching of Negroes in Texas, 1900–1925." Master's thesis, East Texas State University, 1972.

McElroy, Njoki. "The Ninth Day of May." *Common Bonds: Stories By and About Modern Texas Women*, edited by Suzanne Comer, 40–42. Dallas: Southern Methodist University Press, 1990.

Moye, Annette. "Longview." In "Major Race Riots in the Red Summer of 1919," 22–27. Master's thesis, Texas Southern University, 1971.

Muhammad, Jesse. "Jasper-style Lynching in Paris, Texas?" http://finalcall.com/artman/publish/printer_5348.shtml.

Murphy, Thomas Michael. "History of the Sherman Riot." Master's thesis, Austin College, 1931.

NAACP. *Mobbing of John R. Shillady, Secretary of the National Association for the Advancement of Colored People*. New York: NAACP, October 1919.

Nalty, Bernard C. "A Racial Battleground in Texas." In *Strength for the Fight: A History of Black Americans in the Military*, 87–106, 370–72. New York: The Free Press, 1986.

Nevels, Cynthia Skove. *Lynching to Belong: Claiming Whiteness through Racial Violence*. College Station: Texas A&M University Press, 2007.

Ohler, George. "Background Causes of the Longview Race Riot of July 10, 1919." *Journal of the American Studies Association of Texas* 12 (1981): 46–54.

Olsen, Lawrence. "Black Texans in the 'Red Summer' of 1919: The Longview Race Riot." Master's thesis, Southwest Texas State University, 1974.

Olson, James S. "Beaumont Riot of 1943." *The Handbook of Texas Online,* http://tshaonline.org/handbook.

Olson, James S., and Sharon Phair, "The Anatomy of a Race Riot: Beaumont, Texas, 1943." *Texana* 11 (1973): 64–72.

Park, Phocion Samuel Jr. "The Twenty-Fourth Infantry Regiment and the Houston Riot of 1917." Master's thesis, University of Houston, 1971.

Phillips, Edward Hake. "The Sherman Courthouse Riot of 1930." *East Texas Historical Journal* 25.2 (1987): 12–19.

Pruden, Durward. "A Sociological Study of a Texas Lynching." Master's thesis, Southern Methodist University, 1935.

Raper, Arthur Franklin. "Burning Down the Courthouse: Sherman, Grayson County, Texas." In *The Tragedy of Lynching*, 319–55. Chapel Hill: University of North Carolina Press, 1933.

Ross, John R. "Lynching." The *Handbook of Texas Online*, http://www.tshaonline.org/handbook.

Schuler, Edgar A. "The Houston Race Riot, 1917." *Journal of Negro History* 29 (July 1944): 300–338.

Seals, Donald Jr. "The Wiley-Bishop Student Movement: A Case Study in the 1960 Civil Rights Sit-Ins." *Southwestern Historical Quarterly* 106 (January 2003): 419–40.

Smith, C. Calvin. "The Houston Riot of 1917, Revisited." *Houston Review* 13 (1991): 84–102.

———. "On the Edge: The Houston Riot of 1917." *The Griot* 10 (Spring 1991): 3–12.

Smith, Rogers Melton. "The Waco Lynching of 1916: Perspective and Analysis." Master's thesis, Baylor University, 1971.

SoRelle, James M. "The 'Waco Horror': The Lynching of Jesse Washington." *Southwestern Historical Quarterly* 86.4 (April 1983): 517–37.

———. "Jesse Washington Lynching," *The Handbook of Texas Online*, http://www.tshaonline.org/handbook.

Stuard, Linda Sue Stuard, "Racial Disorder in East Texas: The 1910 Slocum Incident. Unpublished paper, University of Texas-Tyler; copy in the hands of this author.

Swindle, Howard. *Deliberate Indifference: A Story of Racial Injustice and Murder*. New York: Viking Penguin, 1993.

Temple-Raston, Dina. *Death in Texas: A Story of Race, Murder, and a Small Town's Struggle for Redemption*. New York: Henry Holt, 2002.

Thompson, Nolan. "Sherman Riot of 1930," *The Handbook of Texas Online*, http://www.tshaonline.org/handbook.

Tuttle, William M. Jr. "Violence in a Heathen Land: The Longview Race Riot of 1919." *Phylon* 33 (Winter 1972): 324–33.

Utley, Robert M. *Lone Star Lawmen*. New York: Penguin, 2007.

"The Waco Horror," *The Crisis* 3 (July 1916): supplement, 1–8.

Waide, C. D. "When Psychology Failed: An Unbiased Fact-Story of the Houston Race Riot of 1917." *Houston Gargoyle*, May 15, 22, 29, 1928; June 5, 1928.

Wang, Tabitha C. "Beaumont Race Riot, 1943." *Blackpast Online Encyclopedia*, http://www.blackpast.org.

Waskow, Arthur I. *From Race Riot to Sit-in, 1919 and the 1960s*. Garden City, New York: Doubleday, 1966.

Wheeler, Jared. "Prelude to Anarchy: The Longview Race Riot of 1919." *The Texas Ranger Dispatch* 30 (Fall 2009): 4–14.

White, Norris Jr. "Bad Saturday: Revisiting the 1910 Slocum Massacre." Unpublished paper, Stephen F. Austin State University; copy in the hands of this author.

Contributors

MONTE AKERS is an attorney who served as counsel for Dow Chemical, the Texas Municipal League, and in private practice in Austin. In addition to *Flames After Midnight*, Akers also published *Accidental Historian*, and with his spouse participates in historical reenactments.

PATRICIA BERNSTEIN was born in El Paso, raised in Dallas, and works in Houston for her public relations firm, Bernstein & Associates. She published *Having a Baby: Mothers Tell Their Stories* and articles in magazines including *Texas Monthly, The Smithsonian*, and *Cosmopolitan*.

NATE BLAKESLEE is senior editor at *Texas Monthly*, for which he has written numerous investigative stories. He also published in *Texas Observer*, and is author of *Tulia: Race, Cocaine, and Corruption in a Small Texas Town*.

JAMES A. BURRAN earned a PhD in history from the University of Tennessee. Subsequently he taught and became academic vice president at Abraham Baldwin Agricultural College and then president of Dalton State College, from which he retired in 2008. Burran was particularly interested in the study of southern racial violence.

PAMELA COLLOFF is executive editor and a frequent contributor at *Texas Monthly*; an intrepid investigative reporter, Colloff covers stories on criminal justice, politics, women's rights, and racial issues, among others.

W. MARVIN DULANEY is chair of the department and professor of history at the University of Texas at Arlington. Among his publications are *Black Police in America* and, as coeditor, *Essays on the American Civil Rights Movement*.

BERNARD FRIEDBERG is coeditor of *Life Styles in the Black Ghetto*. He also served on the staff of the *New York Times* and as regional director of the Anti-Defamation League in Houston.

BRUCE A. GLASRUD is professor emeritus of history, California State University, East Bay; retired dean, Sul Ross State University; and a resident of San Antonio. A Fellow of the Texas State Historical Association, Glasrud is editor/coeditor of twenty-nine books.

BRANDON JETT is a doctoral student at the University of Florida; he earned his master's degree at Texas State University, San Marcos. His article, "Paris Is Burning," won the C. K. Chamberlain Award for best article.

JOYCE E. KING wrote the acclaimed *Hate Crime* and also *Forgotten Hurricane*, the latter about Rita in southeast Texas. A writer from Dallas, she also writes for *USA Today*, the *Christian Science Monitor*, and *The Dallas Morning News*.

EDWARD HAKE PHILLIPS was professor of history and department chair at Austin College, where he taught for many years. Among his publications are *A Short History of Austin College*, a coedited *Mr. Speaker*, and three coauthored books about Gideon Lincecum.

C. CALVIN SMITH was presidential distinguished professor of heritage studies at Arkansas State University. Especially interested in the Houston Riot of 1917, Smith also published *War and Wartime Changes: The Transformation of Arkansas, 1940–1945* and *Educating the Masses: The Unfolding History of Black School Administrators in Arkansas, 1900–2000*.

HOWARD SWINDLE was born in Texas and later served in Vietnam, which led to a book, *Once a Hero*. In addition to *Deliberate Injustice*, he also published *Trespasses: Portrait of a Serial Rapist* and *America's Condemned: Death Row Inmates in Their Own Words*.

WILLIAM M. TUTTLE, JR. was a well-known history professor at the University of Kansas. Among the late professor's publications were *Race Riot: Chicago in the Red Summer of 1919*, *Daddy's Gone to War*, and *W. E. B. Du Bois*.

Index